Innovation Generation

Innovation Generation

How to Produce Creative and Useful Scientific Ideas

ROBERTA B. NESS

OXFORD
UNIVERSITY PRESS

Oxford University Press, Inc., publishes works that further
Oxford University's objective of excellence
in research, scholarship, and education.

Oxford   New York
Auckland   Cape Town   Dar es Salaam   Hong Kong   Karachi
Kuala Lumpur   Madrid   Melbourne   Mexico City   Nairobi
New Delhi   Shanghai   Taipei   Toronto

With offices in
Argentina   Austria   Brazil   Chile   Czech Republic   France   Greece
Guatemala   Hungary   Italy   Japan   Poland   Portugal   Singapore
South Korea   Switzerland   Thailand   Turkey   Ukraine   Vietnam

Published by Oxford University Press, Inc.
198 Madison Avenue, New York, New York 10016
www.oup.com

Library of Congress Cataloging-in-Publication Data
Ness, Roberta B.
Innovation generation : how to produce creative and useful scientific ideas / Roberta B. Ness.
    p. cm.
Includes bibliographical references and index.
ISBN 978–0–19–989259–4 (hardback)
1. Creative ability in science.   2. Science—Study and teaching.
3. Creative thinking—Study and teaching.   I. Title.
Q172.5.C74N47 2012
501'.9—dc23   2011034698

9 8 7 6 5 4 3 2 1

Printed in the United States of America
on acid-free paper

ACKNOWLEDGMENTS

My most heartfelt thanks to Michael Goodman and Sara Ness, who gathered data, tracked down ideas, added great thoughts, and commented on drafts. These two young people are the best of the next generation of creative thinkers. The InGen Group provided wonderful research help and brainstorms for which I am truly grateful: Jack Smith, Nancy Turner, John D'Amore, Rhiannon Dodge, Angie Lloyd, Alana Harrison, and Christopher Neil. Thanks also to Tracie Chase for her, as always, flawless technical assistance.

My parents, of course, have my everlasting thanks for 18 years of forming me into the person I am. I thank my children, Joel and Sara, who shaped me as much or more during a subsequent 18-plus years.

Finally, thanks to my husband David, who has, for decades, been the grease to my imaginings. As always, he showed great patience and fortitude through the writing of this book. His comments sometimes got me over a hump, and his love and support kept me climbing up this seemingly endless mountain.

CONTENTS

1   Don't Read this Book 1

The Big Picture: Understanding and Overcoming Barriers to Innovation

2   It All Depends on How You Look at It 11

3   Overcoming Frames 20

4   Say It Like you Mean It 30

5   Overcoming Metaphors 36

6   Check This Out! 42

7   Becoming a Keener Observer 53

8   How Biased Are You? 62

9   Overcoming Bias 71

10 The Brain and Creativity: The Seat of Inspiration 75

11 The Brain and Creativity: Getting Out in Front 81

Asking and Answering a Scientific Question Through Innovation

12 The Joy of Science 93

13 Asking the Right Question 98

14 How Is a Marriage Like a Matchbox? 107

15 Flip it! 117

16 A Man Walked into a Bar 131

17 The Power of Group Intelligence 144

18 Getting the Most from a Group 156

19 Incubation 162

20 Testing Your Ideas 168

21 That Right Idea 180

22 The Stodginess of Science 191

23 Overcoming the Stodginess of Science 197

24 Innovation Incubators 208

References 217

Answers to Exercises 235

Index 253

Innovation Generation

Don't Read this Book

"Come to the edge. We might fall. Come to the edge. It's too high! Come to the edge. And they came. And he pushed... And they flew."

—*Christopher Logue*

The symptoms come on suddenly. Your eye sockets ache and your temperature races the mercury up the thermometer. You are overcome by a sense of lethargy so profound you cannot raise your head from the bed. Others with the sickness have no choice but to go to work, but you cannot even imagine undertaking such a heroic effort. In a few days or a week you may be fine, but you may instead be one of the unlucky ones—the disease may club you down with great speed and force. Tiny purplish spots begin to erupt over your face, chest, and abdomen, where capillaries can no longer hold their contents. You vomit blood. You cough blood. Suffocation advances as your own bodily fluids flood your lungs. Within hours or days, you have lost all hope.

Such was pandemic influenza. In 2009, the world held its collective breath as the same strain that had killed between 50 and 100 million people in 1918 reemerged. One-third of all of humanity were brought low by the 1918 flu. Young adults in the prime of their lives were destroyed in such vast numbers that graves had to be dug by bulldozers. Imagine a disease that in modern terms would equate to illness among 2.2 billion people and death among 220 million—a death toll equal to two-thirds of the entire U.S. population.

■

Nothing could be done to stop influenza's advance in the spring of 2009. After sickening 60% of the town of Veracruz, Mexico, it began to sweep through the U.S., taking its first victims in Texas and California. To prevent further spread, the European Union took the dramatic step of warning travelers to avoid all non-urgent trips to Mexico and the United States. But it was too late. The next day influenza was reported in Israel, New Zealand, and Spain.

A century and a half earlier, two innovative geniuses, Robert Koch and Louis Pasteur, revolutionized science by discovering that specific diseases are caused by single "germs". With the inspired creation of a vaccine for rabies, Pasteur gave mankind a fighting chance against infectious diseases. Ever since, the first best hope for containing a viral epidemic like H1N1 has been to develop a vaccine. But although the entire genome of the 1918 flu was published in 2005, the archaic manufacturing process for any new vaccine (weakening the virus, then growing it in hens eggs) has not changed since the time of your father and your grandfather.

H1N1 was free to run rampant around the globe for 39 weeks in 2009 awaiting a vaccine. Fortunately the scourge was more benevolent than anyone had dared to hope; although 200 countries were affected, fewer than 12,000 people died. But will we be so lucky next time?

For the world to be safe from the next influenza outbreak requires innovation. Imagine you could scan the new strain's genome in a day, reassemble an attenuated viral genome base pair by base pair in a week, and grow billions of clones in a month. Science is working on inventive solutions but will these be ready before the next pandemic hits?

■

Innovation, defined as creativity with a purpose, is widely considered to be the engine of scientific progress. Innovation feathers the nest of human well-being and prosperity. A miraculous 30 years of life expectancy has been gained by the average American since 1900. If you lived in 1900, you could expect to live, on average, to age 47 years. In 2011, most Americans are blasting past age 77 years. A single kind of wonder has prolonged lives and fueled technical inventions such as the Internet, cell phones; cochlear implants; the Space Station; DNA sequencing; laser surgery; and on and on. That marvel is innovation.

■

So much has been accomplished in the last century that science should be able to sit back and relish its successes. Yet new dangers loom. And these will not be fixed by old solutions. Indeed, there is a growing concern that the threats to human health and success are building faster than is the capacity to creatively address them.

Many modern-day perils have eluded science. After 40 years and a $105-billion dollar investment in "The War on Cancer," cancer mortality rates among adults remain only modestly lower. Not a single highly effective treatment is available for Alzheimer's disease, which swallows 5.3 million minds and costs $172 billion dollars each year in the United States. One-third of all Americans are obese, and its disabling consequence, diabetes, has grown to affect a whopping 16% of adults. Earth's fragile ecosystems are fracturing with water scarcity and global warming. Could it be that your children will live in a world where the ravages of diabetes cause average Americans to live ever shorter lives? Where economies collapse under the burden of caring for elderly disabled by dementia? Where a paucity of potable water and global warming will spark wars over food and water? Could all of this come true for lack of imagination?

■

In August 2010, *Newsweek* declared that America is facing a creativity crisis. For the last two decades, American children have been slipping in the originality of their thinking. Whereas IQ tests have been rising every year for the past 20 years, scores on standardized tests of creativity have been falling.

Science, too, seems to be faltering. Recent commentaries in *Business Week* and *National Review* have decried an innovation slow-down.

Tyler Cowen's influential book *The Great Stagnation* (2010) although it applauded advances in information technology, agonized about sluggishness in innovation in many other technical and science sectors. David Brooks in an essay entitled, *Innovation Stagnation is Slowing U.S. Progress*, describes a female time traveler from 1970 who in 2011 does not find hoped-for, "Space colonies on Mars, flying cars, superfast nuclear powered airplanes and artificial organs." Brooks' time traveler expects to find the same pace of progress that was experienced by a person born in 1900 who arrived on earth in an era of horse-drawn buggies and died watching men walk on the moon. She is disappointed.

Major deficits in America's scientific enterprise with respect to the "Principal ingredients of scientific innovation and competitiveness—knowledge capital, human capital, and a creative ecosystem," were uncovered by two blue ribbon Committees of the National Academies of Science in 2007 and 2010. When the first report generated little attention, a second upped the volume. Entitled *Rising Above the Gathering Storm Revisited: Rapidly Approaching Category V,* it sounded the alarm that America is losing its international dominance in science. *Science* magazine validated the concern. American research productivity, according to a 2010 article, was surpassed by the European Union in 1995 and by Asian-Pacific countries in 2008. Solutions proposed by *The Gathering Storm* to strengthen American scientific innovation included more funding for America's scientific universities and more rigor in secondary school science education.

This book proposes another approach: harnessing and enlarging your own intrinsic capacity to invent.

■

Are you are as creative as you want to be? If you are, then don't read this book.

If you aren't, then think back to when you were 3 years old. If you were like other 3-year-olds, you asked an average of 100 questions a day. Your inventiveness knew no bounds. You took out your crayons and colored grass purple and hair green. You fantasized that by zooming a can of string beans around the kitchen you were well on your way to the moon. In short, you were a budding scientific innovator.

Sir Ken Robinson, Chairman of the 1998 national commission on creativity, education, and the economy for the United Kingdom quotes a study of 1600 children who were tested for divergent (creative) thinking. Ninety-eight percent of 3–5-year olds attained scores within the highest range, 32% of 8–10-year olds achieved such scores, as did 10% of 13–15-year olds. If you notice a pattern, you will guess that when 25-year olds took the test, the proportion with high creativity scores was not impressive; indeed it was only 2%. Robinson claims our industrial style of public education extracts the creativity out of us. Whatever the cause, I believe that ingenuity may be buried with age, but it is not gone. It can be rekindled.

Whether you are young or old, you can be taught to be more imaginative. Yet, America's schools rarely teach creative thinking skills. In fact, all my attempts to find an innovative thinking curriculum in science education have come to naught. When asked, "Why?," professors in the sciences have responded that creativity is entirely a matter of temperament—you have it or you don't. Yet this is simply not true.

Decades of scientific research demonstrate that well-designed creativity training programs improve scores on standardized creativity tests. Two sizable meta-analyses have recently summarized dozens of evaluations of these programs: 40 studies were assessed by Clapham and colleagues (2003) and 70 studies by Scott, Leritz, and Mumford (2004). Among college students, business professionals, and engineers, formal creativity training increased scores on tests of creative thinking. In particular, trained individuals thought more flexibly (nonlinear patterns), fluently (number of ideas), and originally. Particularly for programs that contain the elements incorporated in this book, professionals adopted more positive attitudes toward idea generation in problem solving. More impressively, newly trained innovators went back on the job and generated more and higher-quality ideas.

Creativity training programs impressively improved novel thinking independent of age, gender, IQ, and professional or academic setting. Training translated into improvements in problem solving, performance, and attitudes/behaviors. In short, the benefits of training are broad and comprehensive.

Creativity test scores, in turn, predict novel outputs decades later. In a study remarkable for its duration, Torrance and colleagues (1993) followed 400 Minnesota children of high intelligence, measuring their creative outputs over 50 years. Childhood creativity test scores were 300% more powerful than IQ scores in predicting the number of inventions, creative writings, and other creative outputs. Thus, improving creativity test scores through training may launch you on a lifelong course of inventive accomplishments.

The fact is that creativity programs are effective for anyone at any age. Evidence-based training can enhance novel thinking.

■

The question is not *Can* innovation be taught? but *How* do you become a more novel thinker? The training program in innovative scientific thinking described in this book was first offered at the University of Texas in 2010 to about 20 graduate students in the health sciences. Elements of the program were derived from successful, existing models, but the content and many of the concepts are entirely new, in accordance with data showing that disciplinary specificity improves training impact. This program is designed explicitly to enhance innovative thinking in science. The graduate students who completed the course improved their creativity test scores by 297%. The class improved thinking flexibility, fluency, and originality by 212%, 345%, and 381%, respectively—all highly significant. A second cohort, instructed in the method in 2011 had a similar response. The most important comment that students made about the course was, "It put the fun back into science."

■

This book does three things. First, it sets forth a novel explanation for why uniquely original thought is unnatural and difficult. To think "outside of the box" means to cast aside habitual maps for navigating the everyday world. Barriers at every level from basic brain function to complex social function must be overcome.

Second, this book teaches you how to surmount creativity barriers. You will learn to expand your ability to generate reams of original ideas using a set of tools. These include analogy, expanding questions, pulling questions apart, reversing thinking, and working in multidisciplinary groups, to name a few. Scientist role models will speak to you of their path to innovation: Jane Goodall, whose work with chimpanzees reconceptualized the definition of humanity; Herb Needleman, whose research resulted in the removal of lead from gasoline; and Ignaz Semmelweis, whose discovery of infection control saved millions of lives.

Finally, the book recombines your newly acquired skills in innovative thinking with the normal process of scientific thinking. In so doing, it will ensure that your new tools are more than playthings. They must become useful compliments to the rigorous process used by scientists to achieve ever better understandings of reality.

■

If I blindfolded you and told you to make yourself at home in a furnished room, then some of you would immediately march around and bump into things. Some would slowly inch around with hands outstretched. Some would freeze. The only ones that would never adapt would be the last group. The others, even the most hesitant of explorers, would learn how to avoid the obstacles and over time would become confident navigators. Practice makes perfect, and the same is true with creative thinking.

Almost certainly, some people are more prone to creativity than others. But like any talent, learning to think originally is 1% inspiration and 99% perspiration. Ericsson (2010) demonstrated this quite clearly. Violin students at the Music Academy of West Berlin were divided into three groups based on their professors' assessments: superstars (expected to become top performers), very good, and future music teachers. The single characteristic that distinguished the groups was former hours of practice

(10,000 hours by age 20 years for superstars, 8,000 hours for very good performers, and 4,000 hours for future teachers). Without exception, repetition was the most powerful predictor of who would become a virtuosi. Like any talent, the more you practice, the better you'll get. To change your pattern of thinking, you must go beyond your comfort zone and allow your mind to stretch. I urge you to ponder deeply about the concepts presented in this book. Try all of the exercises. And imagine!

EXERCISES

Try these few exercises to get a sense of your baseline level of creativity. Time yourself and spend on each a maximum of 5 minutes. You will find answers in the back of the book. Don't worry if you don't do too well. You will get better as you go along.

1. Connect the dots. Use a single line: do not take your pencil off the paper.

●　　●　　●

●　　●　　●

●　　●　　●

2. How do you correct this equation without adding any new numbers or other marks to it?

$$8 + 8 = 91$$

3. In 5 minutes, name all of the things you can think of associated with a table.

4. In 5 minutes, name all the uses you can think of for a needle.

The Big Picture: Understanding and Overcoming Barriers to Innovation

It All Depends on
How You Look at It

"Problems cannot be solved by thinking within the framework in which
the problems were created."

—Albert Einstein

I
nnovative thinking is not normal—it is messy and erratic. It is scrib-
bling outside the lines, marching without a map. Habitual thinking, in
contrast is, "neat" and "defined", allowing you to experience the world
in a way that is efficient and predictable. Normal thinking involves using
tried-and-true expectations to process new information and make inferences. Linguists call these expectations or assumptions *cognitive frames*.
Frames, as it turns out, are far more powerful than you might imagine.

■

Frames are everywhere and affect much of what you observe and infer.
Consider your frames when you go to a restaurant. There you expect to
order a meal, to have food provided, and to pay for these services. These
elements describe almost all restaurant experiences all over the world.
But what if the events did not quite happen that way?

Sitting at a lovely neighborhood bistro, you order pasta. The waitress,
a young brunette with an infectious smile, brings a steaming plate of lin-
guini. She gently moves your fork aside and sets down the dish. Then

she takes one step back. You are thinking how impressed you are with the service, but not with the food. The sauce on your noodles is barely enough to be detectable. When the waitress asks if there is anything else you need, you thus politely ask for a bit of extra marinara. Her reply is, "Go to the kitchen and get it yourself."

Such an out-of-expectation response would stop you in your tracks. You wonder, "Did I misunderstand?"; "Did I insult her?"; or "Is she crazy?" Your emotions swing between embarrassment and anger. Why such confusion? Because the waitress just took your frame and violated it.

Frames are ubiquitous and compelling. The restaurant frame is that you are served—not that you must scavenge for your own food. When standing in a line, you join in behind the last person, consider it rude to cut in, and get agitated if each person is not serviced in turn. In a classroom, you consider it unacceptable for the teacher to simply not appear or to spend the whole class period reminiscing about his summer vacation.

When your assumptions are fulfilled, you are able to react swiftly and effortlessly. A breach of your expectations forces you to stop, figure out what went wrong, and ponder what to do next. Frames are the grease that allows you to speed through life. A frame break is an unanticipated and unwelcome disruption.

Think through a day and recall all of your many expectations and assumptions. If only a small fraction of your frames were breached, imagine how unsettling that would be.

Science too, has frames, sets of tightly held expectations termed *paradigms*. The germ theory (transmissible diseases resulting from viruses and bacteria), evolutionary theory (change in the genetic pool through natural selection), and the scientific method (data collection informing theory) are all paradigms. These frames allow scientists to rapidly progress in their mission to better understand nature. If science needed to validate with each experiment the presence of gravity or of atoms or of each chemical structure, envisage how much more slowly it would advance. Established first principles allow scientists to interpret rigorous, reproducible experiments with ease and thereby efficiently improve prediction for how the world works.

Scientific progress has not only established its own expectations but also America's. Advances in public health, for example, have led you to assume that your household tap provides clean water—you would be dismayed if out came a liquid that was brownish-orange. You assume that the food you eat is safe—certainly not that it will give you a case of bloody diarrhea.

■

Frames have several characteristics that impact innovation. First, frames are not permanent—they can change over time and with context. This turns out to be good for innovation because creativity (as you will later see) benefits from frame shifts. In a restaurant, it is clearly aberrant for a waitress to say, "Go to the kitchen and get it yourself." However, in other situations, this statement would be expectable. A little brother asks a big brother to fetch more pasta sauce. At best, the big brother replies, "Go to the kitchen and get it yourself." Worse, he gives the little one a shove to reinforce that it is not okay to ask. In a cooking class, a student nags the teacher to bring more sauce. At best, he gets a negative response, or worse, a lower grade. So your reaction to "Go to the kitchen and get it yourself" all depends on context.

Let's say you are a very frequent flier. You are on a plane bound for a usual destination. Headphones on, listening to a lazy Schubert waltz, you are happily focused on practicing a scientific talk. You barely notice those couple of bumps the plane takes as it descends through the clouds. Even when you take a pretty deep drop, you smirk at the other wide-eyed passengers, knowing that in Houston, in April, the thermals always make for a bumpy landing.

Now let's consider other contexts and see what happens to your frame, your expectations. What if you were a journalist embedded with the 13th Marine Expeditionary Unit flying on a dangerous reconnaissance mission in Afghanistan? What if you were on a single-engine Cessna 172 wandering into an unexpected rainstorm? How about if you were Orville Wright on one of his first attempts at manned air flight? Pretty different expectations, eh? Those circumstances change your reaction to the plane taking an unexpected dip. But would you worry that the laws of physics might change during your flight? Likely not.

Some frames that guide your experience are relatively fixed. Your sense of security about the laws of physics remains constant even while place and time affect your level of anxiety about the risk of flying. Similarly, in an undeveloped country, your assumption about the chemistry of water does not change even while your expectations about the purity of what will come out of the hotel tap do.

Imagine your expectations if you were a scientist working before Robert Koch and Louis Pasteur formalized the germ theory in the 1860's and 70's. Microscopy had been available since 1670 when Anton Van Leeuwenhoek visualized cells within plants and animals. After the discovery by Siebold in 1865 that bacteria are unicellular, scientists like you were regularly recognizing microbes within diseased human tissues. But what did the presence of such bacteria mean? Today, of course, scientists know that microorganisms in those tissues are pathogenic. Yet as a pre-germ theory scientist you had no context for such an interpretation. Instead, you were steeped in the idea that bacteria spontaneously generate. The line of reasoning was that if bacteria simply mysteriously arose in fetid meat, the same agents could spontaneously (and meaninglessly) arise in human organs.

Only after Pasteur and Koch established that specific diseases are caused by specific bacteria did you and other scientists have a context for understanding what you saw under your microscope. Before that revolutionary innovation, disease seemed to appear out of nowhere and thus could never be prevented. Afterwards, you understood the cause of infectious diseases and Joseph Lister spearheaded antisepsis.

■

A second characteristic of frames is that breaking them arouses strong emotions. This turns out to be bad for innovation because frames are thereby all the more hard-wired. Take that flight with the 13th Marine

Expeditionary Unit. A plane dropping in Houston in spring is expected. A plane dropping in Afghanistan is not. When this happens, you don't "alter your assessment." In fact, you don't think at all. You hold your breath, break into a sweat, and dig your fingernails into the flesh of your fists. You are terrified. Even before you hear that "Pop," "Pop" around you, your assumption is the plane has dropped because it has taken enemy fire.

When frames are broken, such as in, "Go to the kitchen and get it yourself," you experience confusion, embarrassment, and/or anger. When your plane descends unexpectedly in Afghanistan, you panic. Your reaction upon experiencing a frame break is immediate and visceral.

If I said, "I have a great new paradigm for the science of city planning. Let's eliminate all traffic signs and signals from inner city streets and intersections." Would you react by stopping and thinking about all the pluses and minuses? No. You would think to yourself, "This is madness. Get this dangerous woman locked up."

But seven European cities have, in fact, removed all their inner city traffic signals.

According to Hans Monderman, the Dutch inventor of this idea, "The greater the number of prescriptions, the more people's sense of personal responsibility dwindles." In the town of Drachten, where the experiment is being tried out on a large scale, traffic planner Koop Kerkstra reports that the only two rules remaining are "Yield to the right," and "Get in someone's way and you'll be towed." The absence of traffic lights and signs means that drivers must proceed slowly and carefully rather than relying on external cues. This focuses their attention very acutely on other cars as well as bicyclists, moped riders, and pedestrians. Driving becomes an activity that is not for the faint of heart. This clears out traffic and may make roads safer. Remarkable, isn't it? There are all sorts of logical reasons to remove traffic signs and signals from inner city streets—and you had such an immediate negative reaction.

The point is that cognitive frames are not just logic. They are a mixture of logic and passion. Their force in shaping the way we perceive and respond to our world is in their ability to elicit both reason and emotion.

In both daily life and in science, a common reaction to a frame or para-digm break is rejection.

■

A final characteristic of frames, and their most anti-innovative, is that frames are constraining. This constraint is useful in that it provides efficiency and predictably in the customary process of thought. Huge volumes of sensory input and complex social interactions are handled via frames with efficiency and effectiveness. Using frames, you quickly size up situations and prepare to react. But frames also limit the range of your thoughts. You assume that the waitress is crazy; you don't imagine that you are on the TV show "Hidden Camera." You assume that orange-brown water is tainted; you don't envision that the color represents a new indicator for chlorination. Rather than juggling in your mind multiple possibilities, you jump to a single interpretation. Frames limit novel ideas, and this has consequences.

■

Frames in science, that is paradigms, can also be constricting. Paradigms necessarily narrow the range of hypotheses that scientists propose and the experiments they undertake. Like any other frame, paradigms can be constraining, emotionally laden, and entrenched but not immutable.

Before Jane Goodall devoted the second half of the twentieth century to studying chimpanzees in Gombe National Park, scientists thought of *Pan troglodytes* as unthinking, unpredictable animals. Chimps startled by teams of researchers barging into their habitats reacted with threat displays. Scientists labeled chimps as chronically aggressive, lower beasts. Despite the fact that Darwin's evolutionary theory had, a century earlier, directly linked humans to primates, the deeply held paradigm was that behavior among humans and primates was entirely distinct.

What differentiated Jane Goodall from her colleagues was, in part, that she was untrained. Without a baptism in the prejudice of human superiority, her hypotheses were agnostic about the meaning of chimpanzee behavior. She did not approach the chimps in a posture of domination. Instead, she hid. At first, the nearby chimp troupe, aware of her presence, exhibited sometimes cautious, sometimes menacing behaviors. But Goodall did not immediately interpret this as proof that chimps are chronically aggressive, and she continued to watch until the animals went back to their normal habits. Then Goodall watched some more. Within a year, a discovery emerged that was none other than revolutionary. Chimps take branches, strip them of leaves, and use them to extract termites from termite nests. In other words, Goodall reported that chimpanzees, like humans, make tools.

Many learned experts proclaimed that this could not be. Tool-making, they asserted, is one of the sentinel behaviors that makes humans unique.

Undeterred, Goodall returned to the Gombe. In 1986, she published the massive tome: *The Chimpanzees of the Gombee: Patterns of Behavior.* In it, she again revealed a series of bombshells. Chimpanzees interact using highly complex social conventions that, passed down through generations, can only be defined as culture. They engage in cannibalism, persistent male battering of females, and adolescent-led intercommunity raiding, some motivated by revenge. Chimpanzees grieve and protect other family members. All of these chimp behaviors blurred the distinction between primates and humans.

Although Goodall was initially discredited for her lack of training and unusual methods, her findings were eventually accepted. Goodall's work, considered narrowly, changed the experimental method for studying animals. More holistically, it shattered conventional beliefs that human behavior is uniquely superior. Before this paradigm shift, calling someone a chimpanzee would have been a profound insult. After the shift, such name calling would at most extract a smile.

Goodall encountered a limiting, entrenched, emotionally laden scientific paradigm. Using novel methods that were untarnished by *a priori* assumptions, she shed pre-existing hypotheses. She frame-shifted. She innovated.

EXERCISES

1. To get a sense of how powerful frames are, take a look at these images. You will likely have an immediate association. Can you think of anything else they may be?

2. There is something odd about this map of the United States. What might the reasoning be for the reframing?

Source: The York Group (http://www.theyorkgroup.com/)

3. Consider the following mismatches between expectations and occurrence:

- Walk into a classroom: What might happen that we would find really strange but, in another context, would be completely in keeping with your predictions?
- At a scientific conference on bio-engineering, a speaker steps behind the podium and does something really jarring that would be expected in another context. What might it be?

4. Design an experiment that might arise from each of the following divergent frames regarding the policy of military vaccination. First frame: mass vaccination is necessary to protect against possible bioterrorism. Second frame: mass vaccination is an involuntary intrusion foisted on a captive population.

3

Overcoming Frames

"The only interesting answers are those which destroy the questions."

—*Susan Sontag*

Recognizing that you think within habitual patterns may open pathways to self-discovery. Your natural response to the disruption of expectations explains why you react with irritation to someone in the library singing opera. It similarly explains why a soprano in the midst of an opera who suddenly breaks into Rap elicits your shock and dismay. Would a 16 year-old driving a bus cause you to consider prematurely exiting? Would a colleague who launches into a 20-minute dissertation about his children during an important business meeting make you want to muzzle him? Now you understand. These are frame-breaks.

But alone these insights do not lead to innovation. To open your mind to new imaginings requires knowing how to jump outside of frames. Normal scientific practice is deeply embedded in necessary assumptions and expectations. But large-scale progress can require upsetting existing theories that lend stability to the scientific world view. Albert Einstein understood this intrinsically when he said, "No problem can be solved from the same level of consciousness that created it."

How are frames changed? Where do you even start?

■

If you happen to find yourself strolling near the University of Pittsburgh on some brisk autumn afternoon, you may pass a squat, balding man with his shirt not fully tucked beneath his belt and a coffee stain on his tie. You might wonder if he is the man from the neighborhood deli counter. Actually, for 30 years, he was Chairman of the University's renowned Department of Epidemiology. Lewis Kuller, Long Island-born, Johns Hopkins-trained physician and public health expert is, in his mid-70s, still one of the nation's leading cardiovascular researchers. He is also fabulously imaginative. To explain the distinctive way Kuller sees the world, think of yourself looking through a high-magnification telescope that creates an exceptional image of a sliver of the night sky. Kuller sees the image too, but he also sees the rest of the universe.

Kuller has been in the thick of many things we now take for granted: establishing blood pressure and cholesterol as a risk factor for heart disease and stroke; demonstrating the risks associated with post-menopausal hormone therapy; bringing new diagnostics to coronary heart disease. Together, these breakthroughs have prolonged your life by years.

He spoke at a recent conference about novel solutions to the obesity epidemic. For decades, medical experts have begged obese people to diet and exercise. It is an idea that works—but only temporarily since virtually everyone who loses weight this way gains most of it back. At the conference, experts explored a different approach using the kind of policy interventions that have been successful in combating tobacco. One of the most promising, advocated by Kelly Brownell at Yale University, is taxation of sugared beverages. Sugared beverages have no nutritional value and contribute 10–15% of the calories consumed by children and adolescents. Taxing cigarettes was one of the most powerful policy tools for reducing smoking; might a tax on sugared beverages lower child and adolescent consumption and thus put a dent in obesity?

Two weeks later, Kuller took me aside at another meeting and said, "You know, I was thinking about taxation to get kids to stop drinking soda. And I realized that there is another problem. Water." I gazed at him quizzically. "No one drinks just plain water anymore," he continued.

"We think it's all full of pollutants and bacteria. But really water out of your tap is amazingly pure and safe. What we really need is a public health campaign to convince people to drink water." Think of it: Water is wonderful—free, safe, eco-friendly. Yet few others are considering water as a solution to reducing excessive consumption of sugared soda or as a partial solution to the obesity epidemic.

How did Kuller get such an original idea? You might say he expanded the problem from, "How do we get kids to stop drinking high calorie beverages?" to "How do we create a dietary environment that supports health?" Or you might say he flipped the question from, "What's negative about drinking sugared beverages?" to "What's positive about the liquid to which we have the greatest access?" Either way, Kuller's spark of genius was to reframe.

■

Brainteasers are mental games that are solved by jumping out of frames. The trick is to think outside the parameters given or to set aside framed assumptions.

Try this: "Gary and Nancy are lying dead on the floor. Around them is a puddle of water and some shards of broken glass. What were the circumstances of their death?" Likely you instantly imagine yourself as some TV detective like Kojak, puzzling over the case. You see yourself standing behind the yellow "Caution" tape on a disserted side street in Lower East Side, Manhattan staring at two blood-spattered bodies. Who could have broken the glass, how, and why? What could it mean—a puddle of water?

Now imagine those classic yellow outlines that police draw around dead bodies. As you gaze at them, they begin shifting into a shape that is something entirely different: fish.

The easiest explanation to the brainteaser is that Gary and Nancy are fish who suffocated when their fishbowl broke. Our standard frames suggest that names imply humanity. Take away the frame, and you solve the puzzle.

Here are some other brainteasers, except now see if you can figure out the answers yourself. If you give up, fear not, as the solutions can be found at the back of the book.

- A visitor to a mental asylum asked the director how they decide to hospitalize a patient.

  "We fill a bathtub with water," said the director, "then we offer a teaspoon, a teacup, and a bucket to the patient and ask them to empty the bathtub." "I see," said the visitor. "A normal person would choose the bucket. The bigger the implement, the faster they can empty the water." What was the director's response?

- A duke and his party were hunting in the forest when they came across a tree painted with a target. Right in the middle of the target was an arrow. Later they passed another such target and then another. "Who did this?" cried the duke. "I must find this amazing archer."

  Shortly thereafter, the party came upon a small boy carrying a bow and arrow. The duke asked, "Are you the one who shot all those bullseyes? You didn't just do them standing right next to the trees, did you?"

  "No, my Lord. I shot them from a hundred paces. I swear it!" "That is remarkable," said the duke. "I admit you as one of my men-in-arms. But you must tell me how you came to be such an outstanding shot." What did the boy say?

- Tom and his wife went out to dinner and a show. They had been eating and enjoying the show when Tom started losing voluntary control over most of his body. His heart began to race, and his blood pressure skyrocketed. His arms, legs, and his chest tensed up. His stomach muscles and diaphragm began to spasm. Yet nobody came to his aid. Why not?

- When a rich man's son was kidnapped, the ransom note instructed him to bring a multimillion-dollar diamond to a phone booth in the middle of a public park. Plain-clothes police officers waited nearby, intending to apprehend the criminal before his escape. The rich man arrived at the phone booth and followed instructions, but the police were powerless to prevent the diamond from being whisked away. How did the villain get away?

■

Reframing has had profound effects on science and prosperity. Einstein's special theory of relativity is best known for providing a theoretical basis for $E = mc^2$. It is not the work for which he received the 1921 Nobel Prize (given for discovery of the photoelectric effect). Nevertheless special relativity turned physics on its head, positing that distance and time shrink at the limit of the speed of light; suggesting a new dimension of space-time; and predicting that space is curved, among other almost unimaginable constructs. Such notions have brought us the physics behind global positioning systems (GPS) and black holes.

Similarly, a notion that was once novel: that toxicants can become widespread in the environment and have pervasive influences on health has rid the society of many ubiquitous pollutants.

■

By the time Herbert Needleman, as a pediatric resident, took care of his first case of childhood lead poisoning in the late 1950s, lead toxicity had been known for millennia. Lead at high doses was known to cause coma and death, like overdosing on alcohol or aspirin. In an important medical breakthrough, medications that bind lead, called chelating agents, were discovered to successfully treat lead intoxication and avoid fatality. But even better was to simply avoid lead ingestion. This, the thinking went, could be done through appropriate personal precautions.

The child Herb Needleman cared for was in a coma when she arrived on his pediatric unit. After 3 days of intravenous treatment with a chelating agent, the child began to cry and then smile. Needleman's clinical frame was joyfully validated; he had saved the child's life. The scene that came next was not what he expected. "I told the mother that her daughter would be all right but that she could not return home. Her house was dangerous and a second exposure would leave her brain damaged. The mother looked at me in anger and asked, 'Where can I live? Any house I can afford is just as bad as this one.'" Needleman then says of himself, "My understanding of lead poisoning was, at that moment, abruptly altered. I suddenly understood that it was not enough to make a diagnosis and give a drug: the disease was a product of the living situation of poor people in the city."

Starting in the early 1970s, Needleman conducted a series of ingenious studies to show just how common were the effects of lead among the poor of Boston. Because lead concentrates in bone, and bone is found in teeth, he collected more than 2000 shed teeth from inner city and suburban children. City children had a fivefold higher level of lead than did their more affluent brethren. He then showed that children with higher lead levels had subtly lower IQ scores. Even worse, mothers with high blood lead levels bathed their fetuses in the toxin during pregnancy, and those children were fated to have lower IQs through the age of 10 years. In fact, two-thirds of poor children in Boston had evidence of clinically unrecognized toxicity from lead.

Needleman's findings led him to believe that lead was a widespread environmental pollutant in inner cities. There was no way to take precautions. If you lived in the wrong neighborhood, as millions of children did, then you were likely suffering its effects.

When Needleman's vocal advocacy for removing lead from paint and gasoline began to pay off, he believes his policy stance made him a target of the lead paint industry. Charged with scientific misconduct, Needleman battled for half a decade to regain his reputation. Only after hundreds of thousands of dollars in legal fees and years of lost productivity was he vindicated. He went right back to work.

In the 1990s, Needleman showed that not only was IQ affected by lead but so was behavior. He has shown that children exposed to lead have a greater propensity to commit violent crimes as young adults. Ironically, this finding harkens back to a historical belief about the fall of the Roman

Empire. Acidic liquids, such as wine, leached lead out of the paint that coated Roman drinking vessels. The historians believe that heavy wine consumption may have thus caused the entire ruling class to become erratic and aggressive. Nero's fiddling while Rome burned may have been a psychiatric symptom from his own lead intoxication.

Needleman believes that fluctuations in environmental lead partially explain the rise (1970s–1990s) and fall (1990s to present) of homicide rates in major American cities. Just imagine, as he does, that the unexplained and sizeable decline in homicide rates in the United States over the past 15 to 20 years has been the result of the removal of lead from paint and gasoline.

Needleman, now heralded as a much-honored hero, switched the paradigm within medicine and society. He moved science from a clinical mindset to a population frame: from treating poisoned patients one at a time to eliminating low-dose lead from inner city residences by the thousands. Today he is working on a second frame shift to explain the baffling decline in homicide rates in the United States: from a criminal justice frame (the triumph of community policing) to one of environmental toxicity. The implications of Needleman's reframing were profound. Before the shift, medicine sought to develop individualized clinical protocols. After the shift, America enacted policies to eliminate lead from paint and gasoline, and average IQ scores among American children have been rising since.

■

Let's consider a systematic, stepwise approach for making frame-shifts. Identifying deeply fixed frames is hard and finding alternatives is harder. A defined algorithm can help extricate hidden concepts.

Step 1: Develop an awareness of the current frame.
Step 2: Consider consequences of the current frame.
Step 3: Devise an alternate frame.

Step 4: Consider consequences of the alternative frame, both positive and negative.

Example 1: Attitudes toward the end of life.

1. Frame—Life is sacred. Death, as viewed by the medical establishment, is a failure.
2. Consequences—Society's approach to end-of-life care is that the defenders must win. Living as long as possible is a noble duty by patients and families, and giving up is giving in. Thus, every moment of life is precious and must be maintained, independent of quality.
3. Alternative frame—Death is inevitable. With modern technology, life can often be extended but sometimes the cost of that extension is enormous and the quality of the additional life is low. If death is inevitable in the relatively short term, then autonomy and dignity may trump length of life.
4. Consequences of alternative—The emphasis on autonomy and dignity reframe the question of life extension as, "Are days or months of life worth being burned, poisoned, and skewered versus the alternative of dying more quickly but with quiet and grace?" On the other hand, do any of us have the right to interfere with a dying person's desire to prolong their life?

Example 2: Education.

1. Frame—The purpose of higher education is to teach content. To be prepared for life, students must have mastered large quantities of information.
2. Consequences—Students are stuffed with facts and figures, much of which they will forget. (For a piercing satire that brings this point home, see the *YouTube* video where Father Guido Sarducci from *Saturday Night Live* promotes his idea for the Five-Minute

University. He argues that in 5 minutes and for $20 he can provide everything the average college graduate remembers 5 years after graduation. So, for example, the Spanish class consists entirely of teaching students, "Como esta usted?" and the theology class answers the question, "Where is God?" with the answer, "God is everywhere—because he likes you.").

3. Alternative frame—Context should be as important as content. Higher education should focus on the attainment of skills that enhance critical and creative thinking. The reframed emphasis on context in higher education relies on an assumption that content has either already been taught in the K-12 setting and/or that high-quality content is readily available via the Internet. Universities should provide tools for how content can be appreciated, used, and extended. Medical schools, for example should focus not only on facts to make diagnoses but on how facts translate into probabilities in decision-making. Such a contextual approach would allow students to not only learn which diagnostic tests to choose but to further calculate how much additional information would be gained from ordering a given test.

4. Consequences of alternative—Students would be better able to think critically and creatively. Because content is the backbone of learning, educators would need to take care in balancing context and content.

■

Reframing consists of identifying the current frame and its consequences. If those consequences are all positive and helpful, then there is no need to reframe. But if the consequences are mixed, then you are on solid ground proposing an alternative frame. The alternative frame need not be correct. It may not necessarily even be useful. It only needs to get you to think differently.

EXERCISES

1. Continue to work on identifying frames and alternatives using the four-step approach for the following concepts:
   Step 1: Identify the current frame.
   Step 2: Define consequences of current frame.
   Step 3: Devise an alternate frame.
   Step 4: Define consequences of alternative frame.
   • Time
   • Labor
   • Social group
   • Discovery
   • Ideas
   • Theories
   • Unknown

2. Try to find solutions to these problems that force you to think outside the parameters given or to set aside assumptions. See whether you can solve these brain teasers. Can you identify the assumptions that make it hard to solve them?
   • Water lilies double in number every day. It takes 60 days for lilies to cover a pond. On what day is half the pond covered?
   • A boy goes to visit his mother, who is on the top floor of a 20-story building. This is before the days of cell phones. He kisses her goodbye and takes the elevator to the lobby, but before he gets off, he knows his mother is dead. How?
   • A man is found hanging from the ceiling by a rope in an empty, locked room. The only thing in the room (except the man) is a puddle of water on the floor. How did he hang?
   • What always runs but never walk s; often murmurs but never talks; has a bed but never sleeps; and has a mouth but never eats?
3. Think of different ways to frame an initiative to tax sugared beverages so that even the supermarkets will see it as desirable.

4

Say It Like You Mean It

"The metaphor is probably the most fertile power possessed by men."

—Ortega Y. Gassett

Frames are deeply tied to language. They form the meaning behind your utterances. In turn, language strengthens your frames. The bi-directionality between frames and linguistics (called the Sapir-Whorf hypothesis) means that speech and frames are constantly reinforcing each other. What you say reveals what you mean; your expectations are fortified by patterns of speech.

The fact that what you say expresses what you believe seems fairly obvious. "Bigger is better." Your frame provides the meaning. This may mean *spend* big now/get big car now in Western society versus *save* big now/get small car now in certain Eastern cultures. Same phrase—different frames—different meaning.

■

A less obvious insight is that language reinforces frames. How does that happen? Recent experiments have shown that English speakers tend to attribute cause. The English statement is: "John broke the glass." But in Spanish and Japanese, the expression would be "The glass broke itself" (in Spanish, "Se quebró el vaso"). This turn of phrase actually appears to determine native speakers' expectations. Caitlin Fausey at Stanford University in 2010 published some intriguing studies on how speakers of

English, Spanish, and Japanese reacted to videos of people breaking eggs, popping balloons, and spilling drinks, either purposefully or accidentally. When later asked who had the accidents, the Spanish and Japanese speakers were less able than the English speakers to remember (although they readily remembered who committed purposeful acts). That is, speakers of languages that avoided attribution were less likely to assume that someone was to blame.

Similar observations have been made linking language to frames around time and space. Speakers of languages in which direction is not "right or left" but instead "north, south, east, or west" have better spatial orientation. If I ask you to close your eyes and point to the north, you, like most other westerners, would be hard pressed to get the direction correct. But any 9-year-old Australian aborigine would find such a task laughably simple. People speaking Kuuk Thaayorre greet each other not with "Hello" but with "Where are you going?" And the answer to this greeting might be, "A long way to the north-northwest." So if you speak Kuuk Thaayorre, when you say "Hello," you are relating your expectation that life is a compass. Your every greeting is reinforcing your direction-intensive frame.

■

The linguistic element that conveys your frames is the metaphor. Metaphors equate one concept (typically more abstract) to another (typically more concrete). "Bigger (concrete) is better (abstract)" is a metaphor. Metaphors are the essence of the potent mental pictures that both reflect and shape your thinking. As representations of frames, metaphors influence the way you think. Indeed a well known metaphor describes much of what we have been talking about: creative thought outside of habitual frames. It is "thinking outside the box."

Metaphors are almost as ubiquitous as frames so, not surprisingly there are many types, a few of which are described here. Structural metaphors are a general category that describes abstractions more concretely. An example is: "Time is money". "Time is money," conveys the frame that time is a limited resource and a valuable commodity. The inference is that time used other than purposefully is wasted. Like any frame, "Time is money" is contextual. Not all societies accept the assumption of time as a kind of produce.

Orientational metaphors relate a spatial dimension to a more abstract concept. Metaphorically, up is good (e.g., " I feel up" and "Moving up in the world") and down is bad (e.g., "I feel down" and "I've been taken down a notch"). Up and down metaphors, representing good and bad frames, have real consequences. Taller people are of higher socio-economic status and more sexually desirable. Living on a hill is a sign of status.

Ontological metaphors portray experiences as objects or substances. This makes experiences easier to quantify and categorize. "I've got a mountain of work to do," quantifies the work as a lot because we associate mountains with being tall or large. "I can feel the magnetism between us" portrays love as a physical force.

■

Metaphors are everywhere, and their influence is pervasive. The following are all cooking metaphors. All represent frames and all heighten the phrase's level of vibrancy. For example, "He was *burned* by her refusal." Rejection is painful. But, you could cool down (another metaphor) the phrase by simply saying, "He felt rebuffed." Moreover, the frame is cooking: hot, sizzling, steamy—is your temperature rising?

- She knew she was going to be *toast* after her boss read her review. *Toast refers to a burned and thus bad outcome.*
- The worried parent *grilled* the child who returned home long after curfew. *Tough questions apply heat to the recipient.*
- He knew his team was *cooked* when the other team members all turned out to be twice their size. *Cooked implies being defeated or finished.*
- He was *burned* by her refusal. *Rejection causes damage similar to meat cooked.*
- The plan was *half-baked. Not finishing the planning process is like cooking.*

- The riots began to *simmer* down. *Intensity of an action is like that of heat.*
- The mother's-in-law intrusion made the newlywed *boiling* mad. *An overflow of emotion is like that of water.*
- He has an *appetite* for destruction. *When you have an appetitie, you have a hankering for something.*
- The know-it-all's classmates *roasted* him for his mistake on the group project. *To deliberately put someone in an uncomfortable situation is a roast.*
- I'm in a *pickle*. *Pickles are prepared in a vinegar mix.*
- The three of them together is really a *recipe* for disaster. *A recipe brings different elements together that can lead to an undesirable outcome.*
- It took the audience a while to fully *digest* the importance of the point the speaker just made. *Digestion is to put energy into internalizing something.*
- That kiss *stirred* up all kinds of emotions. *Stirring brings up things to a more noticeable location.*

■

Metaphors have the same characteristics as frames. First, as you just saw, they are omnipresent. Second, metaphors are laden with emotion. George Lakoff, author of *Metaphors We Live By* (2003), describes metaphors as bringing together objective information (the real things we encounter) with imagination (the way we constructing meaning). Metaphors convey what Lakoff calls "imaginative rationality." Consider the terms "illegal aliens" and "economic refugees." They both describe non-nationals moving to our country while eliciting very different visual imagery. But both illegal aliens and economic refugees produce a stronger emotional kick than, say, "Non-nationals moving to our country." Thus, metaphors, like frames, grab at your heart strings and leave a lasting impression.

■

Third, metaphors are entrenched. Like frames, metaphors limit your thought patterns. If you believe Douglas Hofstadter, author of the Pulitzer Prize winning novel *Goedel Escher Bach* (1979), metaphors and the frames they represent organize your very memories. Why is it that we remember things in chunks: a written fact linked to its location on the page; a recalled experience when we revisit a place? According to a theory posed by Hofstadter in a Stanford lecture in 2001, it is because metaphors organize memories. Such a cognitive design around framed/metaphorical chunks explains two curiosities: why babies do not remember events and why each year seems to pass more quickly as we get older. His answers are that the young child has not yet learned to chunk. Babies see distinct events and cannot combine these into readily stored, related sets of concepts. "It is as if babies were looking at life through a randomly drifting keyhole, and at each moment could make out only the most local aspects of scenes before them. It would be hopeless to try to figure out how a whole *room* is organized, for instance, given just a keyhole view," said Hofstadter. He uses the same idea to explain why life seems to accelerate with age: As people get older, they store information into larger packets and fewer chunks. Thus experiences seem sparser with each passing year. Surely if frames/metaphors are the file folders for memories, it goes without saying that the representation and organization of those file folders would restrict your patterns of thinking.

■

Metaphors, although entrenched, are not immutable. They can change and they can alter underlying frames. Indeed, the creation of a metaphor can so define a new concept that it can literally bring it into being. Back in the 1800s you would not have felt "spaced out" because such a feeling with its exact connotations had no label and did not in its present sense exist. Similarly you could not have had the experience of "blasting off," "coming up for air," and surely not "being wired." Newly created metaphors can actually bring a concept into being. Your experience of the world is nuanced by the available metaphors.

A single word can also be defined by more than one metaphor, reflecting a complexity of shifting frames. Ideas can be plants, as in, "His ideas have finally come to *fruition.*" Ideas can be food: "All this paper includes is *half-baked* ideas and *warmed-over* theories." Fashion can be a metaphor for ideas: "That idea *went out of style* years ago."

■

In so far as metaphors and their frames systematize your memories and add an emotional valence, metaphors really matter. Metaphors can influence questions of profound import. Is a military attack against another nation a rape, a threat to our security, or the defense of a population against terrorism?

Metaphors can change meaning, and metaphors themselves can change. Fortunately for creativity, that means that by way of metaphors you can voluntarily alter frames. One of your best tools to identify a frame or paradigm and then shift out of it is your friendly neighborhood metaphor.

EXERCISES

1. Consider the metaphors "Child-bearing hips" or "I like a woman with a little meat on her bones" and the metaphor "We've got a big fat problem." What do they mean? How might you react to them if you are in the United States? In India? At the time of a food crisis?

2. Make a metaphor: List as many metaphorical phrases or clichés as possible using the following words: death, time, compliance with rules, discovery, overeating, lack of exercise.

5

Overcoming Metaphors

"Stone which does not regenerate is the only thing in nature that constantly dies."

—*Francis Ponge*

Frames are so central to your thinking and functioning that they are like powerful drugs. In Alcoholics Anonymous, the first step to recovery is admitting that one cannot control one's addiction or compulsion. Controlling frames is not entirely feasible either. It is too much to expect that you will have no visceral reaction when someone next cuts you off on the freeway. A more attainable goal in regulating your reaction to frames is recognition. Once recognized, you can work to construct alternative frames. Metaphors are a practical means for recognizing frames.

■

Why do so few Americans have *advanced directives*, otherwise known as living wills? In a population study of people of age 50 years on average conducted in Sioux Falls, South Dakota, only 30% of respondents said they had a living will. Another survey conducted among patients with terminal illnesses found that only half had written directives (e.g., resuscitation, living on a respirator, force-feeding). Without these instructions, doctors must assume that patients want everything done. This explodes societal costs at the end of life. About one quarter of all Medicare dollars are spent on patients in their last year of life, the majority in the last sixty days. Some of these expenditures are unnecessary or even unwanted. Organ donation also suffers from the lack of advance directives because the best time for patients to agree to give a gift of life to others is while they still are able to decide.

The usual framing of death is that it is frightening and mysterious. "*I'm scared to death. Dead zone. The void. The grim reaper. Time's bony hand grasping the soul. The eternal abyss.*" Death implies awe, fear, and guilt. Not surprisingly, patients and their families acting within this frame have a terrible time discussing death.

Reframing the problem entails envisioning an alternative frame. Again this can be accomplished through metaphor. Benjamin Franklin once said, "*Nothing can be said to be certain except death and taxes.*" Could this aphorism represent an alternative frame? "Death and taxes" is a metaphor that removes the awe. It links death to something that is less feared than disliked. Advance directives become something that is grudgingly tolerated; something downright bureaucratic. The old frame represented fear/guilt, whereas the new one represents distasteful obligation.

Could such an alternative framing help patients decide how they want to die? Consider a procedure wherein every year, when you submit your taxes, you are required to also submit a tax-like "Advance Directives" form? The form would consist of check-off choices just like a tax form but with each check-off box representing an end-of-life preference. Almost surely you would think about the options. Likely you would discuss the matter with loved ones.

Death as fearsome—death as a bureaucratic necessity—the frame is mutable. The initial frame restricts solution finding. The alternative expands the range of possible solutions. Reframing through revising metaphors can be a powerful tool for innovation.

■

Another ubiquitous metaphor is the one we use to communicate how science and medicine relate to disease. War. "*The war on cancer…fighting diabetes…battling infectious disease…eliminating a scourge.*" The implication when fighting a war is that there will be a winner and a loser. In the war on disease, humans believe we have no choice other than to be absolutely victorious. Success is judged by the degree to which disease has been eradicated.

But is it always judicious to rid the population of every last bit of disease? Consider the controversy over mammographic screening to detect breast cancer in women ages 40 to 49 years. Fierce debate has arisen and re-risen around this question. On the one hand, can we allow even a single woman to die from a preventable cancer? On the other, is it acceptable to engage in a program among younger women in which a far greater number of non-cancer abnormalities will be detected than cancers? In a risk assessment conducted by the prestigious national panel, the U.S. Preventative Services Task Force in 2009, the estimated number of women needing to be screened to detect one breast cancer among 40–49 year old women was 1900. While less than 1 per thousand screened women will have a cancer detected, about 1 in 10 will have a false positive test. The cost—both psychological and monetary—of the large burden of needless invasive procedures required to detect every possible cancer among young women is thus great. If it were clearly best to eliminate all disease no matter the cost, then there would be no dispute. The dispute suggests that the war metaphor is not ironclad.

On an individual level, "*cancer as war*" also has flaws. Cancer patients forge ahead with aggressive treatment, often without seriously question-ing its harms. Chemotherapy is a poison not only to the cancer cells but to normal host tissues. Radiation burns away tumor but also damages adjacent tissue. In the case of uniformly fatal tumors, is it better to con-tinue at all costs to extend life even if it is at the expense of quality of life? Some would say "No," and instead elect for non-curative palliative care. If our relationship to cancer were truly an out-and-out war, then we would not stop to consider collateral damage. We would poison and burn until victory or death.

The "*cancer as war*" metaphor makes us less likely to think about cost (to the population or the individual) and more likely to seek conquest. Consider an alternative metaphor: "*Cancer as neighbor.*" If you are like most people, then you react to this idea with outrage. You think, "I'm not about to walk around with some cancer eating me while I invite it to have more dinner." But consider Robert Frost's notion that we don't have to be hospitable to neighbors, only to live beside them. *"Good fences make good neighbors,"* he wrote. *"Cancer as neighbor"* is a metaphor that denotes a frame shift: *"Coexistence with cancer."* Limited tumors rarely kill us-metastases do.

What if our basic research approach to cancer moved from a focus on elimination to a focus on containment? Rather than striving to destroy every single cancer cell, this alternative strategy focuses on strengthening our body's immune defenses so as to limit a tumor's spread and metastases. A branch of cancer science is exploring harnessing immunological mechanisms so as to limit metastatic growth without harming the rest of our bodies. Who knows if this new avenue of research will be productive, but it is certainly worth a try.

■

Let's see how metaphors can help you to innovate. Going back to the systematic, stepwise approach to frame-shifts, this time your task will be to identify the frames with the help of metaphors. Bringing metaphors into the approach, the steps are now these:

Step 1: Develop an awareness of the current frame in part using metaphors.
Step 2: Consider consequences of the current frame.
Step 3: Devise an alternate frame with the help of metaphors.
Step 4: Consider consequences of the alternative frame, both positive and negative.

Example 1: *Life.*

1. Frame—gambling game. Metaphors: *I'll take my chances. The odds are against me. That's the luck of the draw. Where was he when the chips were down? He's a real loser.*

2. Consequences—The approach to future health (among some) is one of risk-taking. For example: the gambling metaphor might lead to intermittent or no barrier contraception use, smoking, drunkenness, unsafe speed driving.
3. Alternative frame—take no risks. Metaphors: *Life is all we have. Life is sacred.*
4. Consequences—This alternative frame with its associated metaphors suggests that protection trumps risk-taking. Prevention becomes paramount. On the other hand, screening can go too far (no experts, for example, recommend mammographic screening for average risk populations under age 40 years). Another concern is how much can we legislate?

Example 2: *Discovery.*

1. Frame—causation is viewed as the emergence from a source, similar to birthing a physical object (a baby) from a container (the mother). Metaphors: *Edward Teller is the father of the hydrogen bomb. He conceived a brilliant theory. Universities are incubators for new ideas. His experiment grew from a fertile imagination.*
2. Consequences—Implications of the emergence frame are that ideas must be nurtured and defended just like children. Thus scientists should continue along a line of reasoning and defend that reasoning even when it does not fully explain all observations.
3. Alternative frame—ideas should be spawned and left to fend for themselves. Metaphors: *Toss out a new proposal and see if it sticks. Go out with your idea and spread the gospel. The only way to prove something is to repeat it.*
4. Consequences—This alternative suggests that the object is to generate novel approaches/concepts/theories but to let others try to defend or refute them. In this way, the assessment of new ideas will be unbiased. Flaws in established ideas will become evident more quickly and new theories will arise more readily. On the other hand, if the scientist who spawned an idea does not defend it, perhaps no one else will.

EXERCISES

1. Identify the metaphors for the frame and alternative frame exercises you completed from Chapter 3: *Overcoming Frames.*

- Time
- Labor
- Social group
- Discovery
- Ideas
- Theories
- Unknown

6

Check This Out!

"When a finger points to the moon the imbecile looks at the finger."

—Chinese proverb

"We cannot create observers by saying "observe," but by giving them the power and the means for this observation and these means are procured through education of the senses."

—Maria Montessori

How observant are you? It turns out that no matter how hard you try, you cannot pay attention to the hundreds of sensory cues that come at you every minute of every day. Attention is limited. Indeed, it is selective. And that selectivity is shaped by your frames. Not only what you say (a la metaphors) but what you see reveals and reinforces your frames.

Try this simple exercise. Draw the face of your cell phone; place every number and every letter where it should be (don't peek now). This should be pretty doable right? You use your cell phone dozens of times a day. Yet very few people can accurately place every number, letter, and symbol in its correct position. Embarrassing though it may seem, you (and I) are not very observant. So, you think, "I am a little distracted—is that so bad?" The answer is, yes—if you are trying to innovate. Normal observation is anti-innovative. To innovate, you must learn to become a profoundly acute observer.

■

Imagine you are imprisoned and in solitary confinement for 10 years. Your whole world is confined to the inside of a 6' x 9' gray cement-walled cell. A good day is when you get to pace around a featureless exercise area.

Then one day you are released. What would you feel as you exit the prison and walk into the brilliant sunlight? How intensely would you experience the smell of tree buds; taste of a gentle rain; sensation of warmth from sand underfoot as you peel off socks and shoes to run onto a beach? Would it be different than the way you experienced these things before you knew you were going to prison?

Sights, sounds, tastes, and sensations, when first experienced, seem surprising and wonderful. Imagine: that initial bite of a chocolate brownie; a baby's first steps on wet grass; the wail of an oboe breaking a silence; your lover, adorned in evening attire, descending the stairs. But with repetition, these experiences are no longer so extraordinary. With familiarity, sensory stimuli become mundane. As you walk through your daily routines (driving to work, hiking to classes, chatting in the lunchroom), you rarely see, really observe, what is around you. Henry Thoreau and Ralph Waldo Emerson, nineteenth century transcendentalists, believed that familiarity would numb your thinking and blind your perceptions.

Their belief has since been confirmed by studies in the microscopic roundworm, *Caenorhabditis Elegans*. Because *C. Elegans* is so small (having just 302 neurons), scientists can study in precise detail the course taken by its nerve signals. From this they have discovered that when the same sensory input is repeated over and over again, it causes fewer and fewer neurons to fire. Repeated familiar stimuli result in a neurologic process called habituation—that is, not paying attention.

The barrage of familiar sensory input that you are exposed to every minute is too much for your brain to process. Your eyes alone have a visual arc of 120 degrees, with about 200 pixels per degree, yielding an ever-shifting 500-megapixel picture (better than your conventional camera). To continually attend and react to all of that information would take enormous brain energy. Evolutionarily, it is more efficient to select what you pay attention to. Familiarity may not always breed contempt, but it surely breeds complacency.

If you remain skeptical about your own limited scope of observation, then try another exercise in drawing from memory. Take some common space—say, a conference room, classroom, or café. Try to capture every little thing in that room, where all the furniture is, what the colors are, the kind of carpet on the floor and the kind of tiling on the ceiling, the lighting, the materials that make up the tables and chairs, pictures on the wall, things on tables—everything. When you go back into the room, compare the precision of your drawing to what you see. If you recorded half of everything that was there, then you are doing well.

■

Given an assault of information and your limited ability to process it, how do you know what to pay attention to? Once again, the answer is frames. Frames direct what you see, hear, smell, feel, and taste. You selectively attend to what your frames tell you are important. But think about what that means—it means that the details outside the frame are missed. What a self-fulfilling prophecy! Your frames direct what you observe, and those observations reassure you of the correctness of your frames. How could you ever hope to see details that would lead to alternative frames? How perilous is it to see only the expected?

■

It happened in the South Bronx in February 1999. In one of the tightly packed nineteenth century brick townhouses that sheltered the working poor and harbored an active drug trade lived a Guinean immigrant named Amadou Diallo. Just before midnight, Diallo found himself standing on the stoop of his building, taking in the chilly night air after a long day's work. Four officers from the Street Crimes Unit of the New York City Police Department, patrolling the neighborhood, noticed him. Their unmarked Ford Taurus slowed. As Malcolm Gladwell tells the story in his book, *Blink: The Power of Thinking Without Thinking* (2007), one of the plain clothes officers, Sean Carroll, later claimed that the Guinean fit the description of a serial rapist who had been active in the area.

The car approached as Diallo was just glancing around, leaning back, and glancing around again. It stopped directly in front of the stoop. Diallo did not move; a fact that Carroll later said, "amazed" him. "I'm like, alright, definitely something is going on here." The officers piled out, held up their badges, and called out, "Police—can we have a word?" Rather than responding (perhaps because he did not speak English well or because all he noticed was a group of enormous White men striding toward him), Diallo turned to flee. With one hand he pulled the doorknob and with the other, he dug into his pocket.

Carroll yelled, "Gun! He's got a gun!" In the next few seconds, all was action. The officers opened fire, each emptying whole clips (16 shots per clip) into the man. When the ear-shattering uproar was over and the officers approached the bullet-ridden body, they found Diallo's right hand splayed out. In it was not a gun, but a wallet.

The police-precipitated shooting death of a poor, Black man is catastrophic on an uncountable number of levels. An innocent man was robbed of life's joyful pulsations; four others were laden with his bloody legacy. When police officer Carol realized what had happened, he slumped down on a nearby stoop and cried. Clearly, he had committed the ultimate, irrevocable error. But had you or I been one of those officers, we probably would have acted the same way.

The elements that influenced how Carroll and the others saw Diallo were: a drug-infested neighborhood; a Black man "just standing there," and a dark and empty street after midnight. When Diallo reached into his pocket to hand these men, whom he presumed to be robbers, his wallet, these policemen "saw" him reaching for a gun. Their frame was so set (i.e., drugs and guns in a bad neighborhood), they did not notice something that under other circumstances would have been blatantly obvious: Diallo was not threatening; he was terrified.

■

You see what you expect to see on the basis of your framing of a situation. With sensory information, as with linguistic information, frames are the sets of expectations that allow you to move from new information to inferences. So your visual system works in particular ways such that you "see" and interpret certain things and do not "see" others. For example, the visual system processes information in framed chunks.

To illustrate this, read the following paragraph:

"Aoccdrnig to rscheearch at an Elingsh uinervtisy, it deosn't mttaer in waht oredr the ltteers in a wrod are, olny taht the frist and lsat ltteres are at the rghit pcleas. The rset can be a toatl mses and you can sitll raed it wouthit a porbelm. Tihs is bcuseae we do not raed ervey lteter by ilstef, but the wrod as a wlohe."

Surprisingly easy, right? Humans are so good at fill-in-the-blanks that to read, we need only have the first letter and last letter of the word and a bit of semantic context. The rest you can discern because you don't actually read each letter, you read the word as an expected chunk.

Here is another example. Let's say I show you a set of five cards: the Ace of Spades, the 3 of Diamonds, the Jack of Clubs, the 6 of Hearts, and the 10 of Spades. Then I pause as you wonder what my point is. "But," I say, "Look again." Suddenly you realize that the 6 of Hearts is black and not red. You simply didn't notice it because you expected red and likely "saw" red. Don't feel bad, more than half of the people who see the hand don't realize the switch. Your frame, and thus the way you see visual chunks, is that clubs and spades are black and diamonds and hearts are red. So you see hearts as red rather than processing these pieces of information as discrete sensory inputs. You see what you expect to see.

Finally, imagine the following scene. A male actor holding a map approaches a pedestrian and asks for directions. Kindly, the pedestrian begins to explain how to get to the location. Halfway through the pedestrian's explanation a large sign is carried in between the actor and pedestrian, after which the two people finish their discussion. But look again—when the sign temporarily obscures the actor, another actor takes his place. Surely the pedestrian notices. But no, even if the replacement actor is much older or of a different race, the switch is not noticed. The phenomenon is called "change blindness." "Change blindness" experiments show that substitutions of one person for another are not recognized by about three-fourths of people. One of the few reasonable explanations for this odd lack of detection is that a change of actor is simply something that the pedestrian does not expect.

■

Your visual system is hierarchical in its priorities. This, too, is a frame—one in which you assume that certain objects or events are more important than others. Consider how you notice movement. You see moving objects instantly. Presumably this is a useful evolutionary adaptation that allowed our prehistoric ancestors living in sub-Saharan Africa to readily notice a lion jumping out of the bush.

If a moving object is placed within your visual field, it can be hard to appreciate aspects of the scene that remain constant. Consider a speeding car or a tree falling or a microscopic view of motile sperm. Eye-catching as these moving visuals are, they focus your attention while the background fades out. To notice other details, you have to exercise a special level of awareness.

Assessing distance carries its own hierarchy of assumptions. We expect closer objects to be more important. Closer objects, as compared to more distant ones, appear larger and more sharply defined. These strategies allow you to make sense of complicated situations, but they can also be misleading, sometimes fatally. In high visibility, you tend to underestimate the distance between yourself and an object. In low visibility, where contours are blurred, you tend to overestimate distances. Too much overestimation on a dark and rainy highway and you might end up smashing into the car in front of you.

■

Science is empiric: observations are the backbone of scientific reasoning and advancement. Observations feed hypotheses. New hypotheses lead to shifts in paradigms. Thus in science, there is nothing more fundamental to progress than careful scrutiny. Want to win a Nobel Prize? Be prepared to observe.

Robin Warren was a clinical pathologist in the sleepy town of Perth, Australia, where life's slow pace and professional isolation typically led physicians to comfort and obscurity. On his 42nd birthday, in 1979, he noticed a detail that had been previously overlooked.

Perhaps it was his need to overcome the epilepsy that barred him from obtaining a drivers license and made it surprising that he persisted through medical training. Perhaps it was his consuming curiosity. Warren did not limit himself to habitual frames. Using a clinically standard silver stain for the examination of stomach tissue, he noticed that within the gastric crypts resided small curved anomalies. Later he and his colleague, Barry Marshall would discover that these were bacteria. Studying them further, he realized that the bacteria resided in fully half of patients who had been biopsied for peptic ulcer disease. Any other pathologist could have visualized the bacteria at the time (and in retrospect, they had been seen but not pursued by an earlier German team), but all the textbooks said that the stomach, because of its acidic environment, was sterile. Stress and acid were considered to be causes of gastritis. In fact, acid *must* be the cause because peptic ulcers could often be treated, at least temporarily, with antacids. Warren's own wife told him that the finding of bacteria residing in the stomach was impossible.

But Warren turned out to be right. With his colleague Barry Marshall, Warren won the 2005 Nobel Prize in physiology for their discovery of the bacterium *Heliobacter pylori* and its role in gastritis and peptic ulcer disease. Marshall, a recently trained medical registrar, joined Warren in 1981 to replicate the startling observation and expand the range of studies. Marshall was able to culture *H. pylori* from gastritis tissue, a key step in proposing the hypothesis that the pathogens caused peptic ulcers. Skepticism on the part of the scientific community was rampant. Marshall and Warren's early papers were rejected. Marshall was 1 of only 3 (out of 67) applicants to a Belgian meeting whose abstract was not invited for presentation. After unsuccessfully trying for several years to infect pigs so as to show that the bacteria not only resided in the stomach but caused the ulcers, Marshall ultimately drank a petri dish full of *H. pylori*. He developed symptoms of gastritis. Assuming that the scientific community would not believe his own report, Marshall allowed himself to be subjected to endoscopy, the invasive procedure of plunging a tube down the esophagus to directly see the tissue. Marshall's endoscopy clearly demonstrated the classic signs of peptic ulcer disease.

Today it is known that 80% to 90% of peptic ulcers are caused by *H. pylori* and antibiotics are a backbone of treatment. Anyone could have seen it, but only Warren and Marshall were willing to trust their eyes rather than their expectations.

■

In August, 1928, Alexander Fleming also discovered something that others had seen but not appreciated. After several years of studying staphylococcus bacteria, he returned from vacation to a stack of petri dishes that he had carefully inoculated and left to grow. To his chagrin, he found one dish contaminated by mold. Around the mold growth was a clear green ring in which the staph bacteria had dissolved. Fleming later freely admitted that his observation was not new. Other scientists had encountered fungus ruining their experiments in the same way—and had tossed them out. The difference was that Fleming did not discard the dish. He became fascinated by it. What did it mean that a fungus had completely destroyed the bacteria around it? How could such bacterial killing have occurred?

What Fleming did next marked him for fame. He redirected his research and spent the next years trying to figure out what might have caused the mold's effect. Because he identified the mold as being of the *Penicillium* sp, he called its extract *penicillin*.

Although Fleming did not know how to grow penicillin in quantity, chemists Howard Florey and Ernst Chain later did, and they licensed their process for isolating mass amounts of the new antibiotic to the pharmaceutical industry. By D-Day, industry had produced enough penicillin to provide Allied troops a way to treat infected wounds. Penicillin became the first mass-produced antibiotic, saving the lives of millions and changing the face of medicine.

Fleming not only saw—he thought about the implications of what he saw. He discarded the tunnel vision wherein his contributions were all about understanding the staphylococcus bacteria and instead veered off to investigate fungus. His frame told him that his contaminated experiment had failed, but his eyes told him that he was seeing something fascinating and important. Truly observing may require overcoming visual tendencies and frames. Almost always it requires paying closer attention to oddities than we otherwise might.

■

Observing anomalies is such a central step in the process of scientific insight that there are far too many examples to try to catalog them all. We sometimes consider anomalies to be "happy accidents" or serendipity. Scientists who are prepared to notice and make something of unexpected observations sometimes turn these into great discoveries. Fleming benefitted from serendipity; so did Raytheon scientist Percy LeBaron Spencer who discovered the utility of microwaves. During World War II, while working on the development of a radar system to assist the Allies in the detection of Nazi warplanes, Spencer stood in front of an operating magnetron. Later, he realized that the candy bar he had hidden in his pocket had melted. The magnetron, he later realized from further experimentation, had melted the candy bar. Such was the discovery of the heating power of microwaves. The insight that microwaves cause heat ultimately led to the invention of one of the most useful appliances in the modern kitchen.

A melted candy bar, a moldy petri dish, little bugs in stomach biopsies—what do they represent? Failures turned into transformational discoveries. Observing something that others missed. Jumping outside of pre-existing frames and paradigms. As Louis Pasteur said, "Chance favors the prepared mind."

EXERCISES

1. As you are taking a usual route to work, school, or home, try to become more aware of your environment. Your mind is ever-wandering from the present time and/or location but try to bring your focus back to the now. Observe details of your surroundings (especially relatively permanent ones, such as trees or buildings) with real attentiveness. It is a bit harder than it sounds, and it takes a little time to master, but you will be amazed by the beauty surrounding you.

2. See things from different perspectives. Rather than sitting at your usual desk, stand at a professor's lectern and look out at the room (not during the class, of course). Avoid sitting in the same seat of a classroom or taking the same route to work. Look at a familiar scene from ground level (that is actually get your eye to the ground) and get mano-a-mano (really close up) to check out things like tree bark, a fence, a flower.

3. Try bird watching or photography and see if your powers of observation are enhanced.

(continued)

CONTINUED

4. Find the differences between pictures.

Picture taken from Smart-Kit (www.smart-kit.com) online puzzle playground. Used with permission.

7

Becoming a Keener Observer

"Thinking is more interesting than knowing, but less interesting than looking."

—Goethe

"A few observations and much reasoning lead to error; many observations and a little reasoning lead to truth."

—Alexis Carrel

Hopefully you are now convinced of the import of keen observation. Knowing that your attention is filtered through preconceptions is useful. But training yourself to overcome habituation and frames is even better.

Detectives are taught to discard assumptions and to notice tiny clues that may mean the difference between solving a crime and leaving a cold file. In an unusual step to hone investigators' observational acuity, the New York Police Department (NYPD) takes field trips to the Frick Art Museum. Given just a few minutes to view a complex painting, officers are asked to analyze the "who, what, where and why" of the piece, much like trying to analyze a crime scene. They learn to view the art systematically. They learn to take in every detail. In so doing, they overcome the common prejudice to look at only what is visually attractive or "important." In other words, they learn through art to overcome their frames.

Three tools can be helpful in becoming a keen observer: *(1)* take up art; *(2)* be an anthropologist—get out and observe; *(3)* notice when things seem not quite right, in other words, things that bug you.

Leonardo da Vinci, one of the greatest representational artists of all time, said, "Things in the mind which have not passed through sense are vain and can produce no truth which is not condemned." His remarkably accurate drawings made him not only a better artist but one of the greatest scientific observers of all time. Obtaining consent from a 100-year-old man and from the ecclesiastical sanctioning office (no small task), he was one of the first artists to dissect a human body. Leonardo-the-artist learned so much from the act of drawing the cadaver that Leonardo-the-scientist developed great insight into various anatomical structures. For example, the branching pattern of the vessels and bronchi demonstrated to him that blood and airflow slow as they pass deeper and deeper into the body, because he knew that velocity is proportional to a channel's cross-section. Similarly, his careful observations of human anatomy provided him with a model for his design of the world's first robot.

Drawing enhances observational skills, but only if practiced correctly. Normally, we draw by recording some of what we observe and filling in the rest. When we see an eye, rather than drawing it exactly as it is, we look down at the paper and draw the almond shape that represents an eye's outline. We see a mouth and draw a horizontal line under the nose, two mountain-like shapes above that for the top lips, and a curve underneath for bottom lips. That is drawing, but it is not observing. To learn to better observe, you must practice drawing what you actually visualize. Once you are able to see every part of an image, you will start to recognize things about it that you have never noticed before.

Drawing upside-down. An old trick that proves that really anyone can draw is to turn a picture upside-down. Take the photograph below, turn it upside-down, then reproduce on paper what you see. Betty Edwards, in her book, *Drawing on the Right Side of the Brain* (1999), recommends that rather than drawing the outline and then filling in the innards, you move down the page, drawing adjacent lines and shapes. Most importantly, draw not what you think is there but exactly what you see. This exercise should be repeated with other pictures at least once, if not twice.

Contour drawing. Another way to discipline your eyes is to draw without looking at your paper. You can, again, use the chair, or you can work from a human model or a still life. Tape your paper to the desk or to an easel. Fix your eyes on one spot (e.g., the top of a model's head), and start your pencil at the top of the page. As your eyes track slowly down the side of the face, move your pencil to reproduce the outline, in unison with your eyes. Never let your eye and your hand become uncoordinated. And for goodness sakes, never look down again until you have completed the whole outline. Of course, this is like asking a heroin addict to stop shooting up. The temptation will be unbelievable. Resist!

Rather than thinking of parts of the face in linguistic terms ("I am drawing the nose; I am drawing the mouth"), try to consider these only as shapes to be replicated. You get better as you do this over and over; you should repeat contour drawing at least twice more. Drawing your own hands and feet as models also works well.

Drawing negative shapes. To further practice truly observing what you see, draw the contour of a chair. However, rather than focusing on the outline, focus on the negative shapes that those lines describe. Start with the upper right corner and outline the negative shape. In other words, outline the shape where the chair is not. Then move down, then across to the lower left corner, and finally up to the upper left portion to finish.

■

Once you have refined your skills at seeing what is actually there, you are ready to go out and become an anthropologist—someone who is forever noticing the myriad of details that make up the world.

Real world observation is the means by which IDEO, one of the most influential design firms in the world, detects every detail of the form and function of products they seek to improve. In 2000, *ABC Nightline* with Ted Koppel came to IDEO with a proposition. The firm would take on the challenge of redesigning something iconic using only imagination and perception. IDEO is famous for products such as the Apple Mouse and the Palm handheld as well as the design of medical devices and even the 25-foot mechanical whale in the movie *Free Willy*. On a show entitled *The Deep Dive*, Koppel defied IDEO to "Take something old and familiar, like, say the shopping cart, and completely overhaul it in just five days." One can only imagine what Tom Kelley, the firm's general manager, must have thought, but what he did was to take the plunge.

Monday morning, cameras rolled and IDEO jumped in. In his book, *The Art of Innovation*, Kelley describes what happened next: "We split into groups to immerse ourselves in the state of grocery shopping…we were practicing a form of instant anthropology. We were getting out of the office, corning to the experts, and observing the natives in their habitat." IDEO team members, camped out at the grocery store, saw parents struggle with small children; professional shoppers using their carts as base stations while running the aisle "cartless;" and shopping cart traffic jams. Team members ran down to the bike store to figure out how bikes glide. Others checked out electronic gadgets that might augment the cart. Yet others inspected car seats to explore possible designs for accommodating infants.

Regrouping, the team focused on the themes of efficiency and safety. A wall full of drawings came out of two brainstorming sessions. From these, team leaders extracted the best designs for building quickie prototypes. Over the next 2 days, subgroups split out to dash to the hardware store and find parts. Others emptied out their LEGO® buckets to build models. The best features were combined. The design shop did not call it a day until 3:00 A.M.

By early morning on day five, a thing of beauty stood in the shop: an open, curvaceous frame on futuristic casters—no basket, only hooks on the sides of the frame to hang plastic bags and an open base to nest six removable hand-baskets. The notion of cart as airplane, moving with the shopper everywhere, had become cart as space station, with the shopper darting away and back. The analogy between an airplane and a space station even better captures the old cart's familiarity versus the new cart's design sophistication. Welcome to the process of innovative design.

■

The key to IDEO's success was that team members got out of the comfort of their offices and watched shopping carts in action. They checked out the actions of borrowed design elements, such as from the bike shop and the hardware store. They built prototypes with LEGOs®. In each case, they didn't just imagine carts or draw them. They built them. They played with them. They crashed them into the walls and turned them in steep 360° turns. They learned how existing carts worked and how newly designed carts might work through observation.

IDEO describes five steps to product innovation:

- UNDERSTAND the market, client, technology, and constraints.
- OBSERVE real people in real-life situations.
- VISUALIZE new-to-the-world concepts and the customers who will use them; if possible use computer-based renderings, simulations, prototypes.

- EVALUATE AND REFINE the prototypes through quick iteration.
- IMPLEMENT the new concept.

■

IDEO team members watch the interactions between clients and products—particularly while the product is in use. They figure you can't expect people to tell you what you need to know. But through watching and asking questions, you will find out what is essential. What do customers like and what do they hate? What works well and what makes them crazy? No question is dumb or naïve.

Compare this to the approach in academic science. Do research biologists go out and watch how doctors employ biological concepts? Do academic chemists experience chemistry at work in the petrochemical industry? Do epidemiologists hang out with afflicted patients before spending years studying a disease? Sometimes, but not often enough.

■

Another key IDEO concept is: Pay attention to the things or situations that bug you. Become aware of what doesn't work and repair it.

Consider all the attributes of products you use that are just not "right." How about the software programs you use regularly? Are there things you want to do and can't? Does the program sometimes seem to have a mind of its own? How about your cell phone or PDA? Your DVD player? You regularly accept design flaws and work around them. But product innovation is all about recognizing and fixing the flaws so users are more satisfied.

Recently, I got into a friend's new car and he described, with great delight, all of the nifty design features. One blew me away: the side mirrors lit up when a car moved alongside into the blind spot. When I learned to drive, I was warned to never fully trust my side mirrors. Always glance out the window before moving over, I was told. Now, this design improvement relieves drivers from having to take their eyes off the road to switch lanes. The passenger mirror has always been a flawed design that created the need for a dangerous work-around. Some brilliant engineer noticed it and fixed it.

■

Try this exercise: Observe can-openers in use. Check out an electric one; a manual one. Watch what happens when each of these are used by a young person; by an old person. See how each works on different size cans. Consider what can be opened and what cannot. Try a can-opener straight out of the packaging. Compare that to one that has been around for many years. With all of this, consider all the design flaws; then imagine others, such as when the electricity goes off. Finally, using all of your observations about what aspects of can-openers work best and what work least, try to design a better one.

■

In science, design bugs (e.g., in equipment) can limit progress, but flaws or anomalies in frames and paradigms are more impactful. The more entrenched the paradigm, the less likely anomalies are to be noticed. The more certain you are of the "truth" of a frame or paradigm, the more likely you are to explain away observations that do not conform.

In the years leading up to 1999, when I wrote an article entitled "Possible Role of Ovarian Epithelial Inflammation in Ovarian Cancer," I was frustrated that science understood so little about what caused this terrible disease. An ovarian cancer diagnosis is all too often a death sentence. With more than 25,000 women dying every year, the urgency to prevent the disease is great. One longstanding hypothesis about why ovarian cancer occurs is that it is fueled by gonadotropins—hormones from the pituitary such as luteinizing hormone (LH) and follicle-stimulating hormone (FSH). The hypothesis predicted that higher gonadotropin levels raise risk and lower levels reduce risk. What bothered me, however, was a new finding that fertility drugs such as clomiphene (otherwise known as Clomid) increased the risk of ovarian cancer. Gonadotropins are suppressed by fertility drugs. If the gonadotropin hypothesis was correct, then these medications should lower ovarian cancer risk. Yet they do the opposite.

Another prominent hypothesis, that the more a woman ovulates the greater her risk of ovarian cancer, explained many aspects of the disease but also had a flaw. It did not explain observations that I and others had made that talc use increases ovarian cancer risk and tubal ligation protects women. Indeed, the talc and tubal ligation findings could not easily be explained by any pre-existing hypothesis.

What linked both talc and tubal ligation to ovarian cancer, I wondered? Inflammation is a known trigger for mutagenesis. What if ovarian cancer is accelerated by things that inflame the ovaries? Talc has a structure somewhat like asbestos and asbestos causes cancer through triggering inflammation. Tubal ligation disrupts the passageway that leads to the ovaries, disallowing inflammants from travelling up from the vagina into the uterus and then to the ovaries. Ovulation also increases pelvic inflammation because every ovulation bathes the ovaries in inflammatory mediators. Thus, the inflammation hypothesis explained all of these observations.

A good deal of basic biology now supports the inflammation hypothesis. To prove that inflammation really promotes ovarian cancer will take much more work, but the idea opens a new research avenue. The inflammation hypothesis arose because the existing hypotheses had insoluble anomalies. By recognizing these and trying to find a solution, a new idea emerged.

■

Keener observation can be enhanced in three ways: *(1)* overcoming your natural tendency to observe selectively; *(2)* taking the time and making the effort to get out and observe; and *(3)* questioning the flaws in a designs and in paradigms. You can enhance your observational keenness by learning to hone your senses. You can become an anthropologist by leaving the office and just doing it. You can learn to question flaws in designs and paradigms by asking, "What does not work?" "How can that be fixed?"

All of us are challenged by the number of things in our lives that we must keep track of. I can imagine myself saying, "I am overwhelmed. I am able to live with the flaws—I know how to work around them." But the little flaws may cover up bigger problems. The anomalies in a scientific paradigm may underscore that the paradigm is fundamentally flawed and taking science in the wrong direction. If you become aware that something is wrong and needs to be fixed and yet you don't try to figure it out, then who will?

EXERCISES

1. Open your eyes. "Nobody sees a flower really; it is so small. We haven't time, and to see takes time—like to have a friend takes time." Georgia O'Keeffe, famed painter, reminds us to take a step back and look at something in a fresh and open way. Observe the following tools during use and find the design flaws:
   a. a screwdriver
   b. a vacuum cleaner

2. Using observations on use and function, design a better:
   a. screwdriver
   b. vacuum cleaner

3. Pick up an object from somewhere in the room and challenge each of your expectations about it. It is white: well, is it really white? Or is it a little off-color? It is stained: well, is it meant to be stained? What do the stains add to its appearance? Is it a shoe: well, if you didn't know what a shoe was, what would you think this is?

8

How Biased Are You?

"Who the hell wants to hear actors talk?"

—*HM Warner, Warner Bros, 1927*

Just as observing involves processing sensory information, thinking involves processing decisions. Thinking rationally is presumed to consist of making a series of decisions rationally. Such has been the assumption of philosophers, economists, and scientists of every ilk since the eighteenth century. The mathematician Daniel Bernoulli, in the 1730s, proposed an "expected utility theory" in which betting behavior was represented by a person's mental calculation and personal preferences toward risks and benefits. The message: Man can be counted on to weigh decisions in a way that is sensible and consistent.

But decision making turns out to be more complex than Bernoulli imagined—indeed it is often inconsistent and even convoluted. The problem is that, as with sensory inputs, decision-making inputs are too vast for humans to fully process. Thus you make decisions by taking shortcuts. Those shortcuts help you to make quick judgments about complicated situations. But they can also lead you astray. In fact, human decisions are so often not rational that this irrationality has a name: cognitive bias. Defined as systematic mental errors, cognitive biases lead you to inaccurately assess situations involving numbers, social encounters, and memories.

What often tangles decision-making and creates cognitive biases are (once again) your frames. Frames can lead you to make one choice in one situation and another choice in another situation—but when taken together, the two choices are erratic or even irrational. The frames that generate biases generally direct you toward the familiar and away from the novel. That is, cognitive biases tend to reinforce the tendency to be anti-innovative.

■

How compelling is familiar context? An experiment conducted by Dan Ariely (author of *Predictably Irrational: The Hidden Forces that Shape Our Decisions* [2008]) with students at MIT has shown it is compelling enough to make us decide things capriciously. Ariely offered a pretend subscription to the magazine *The Economist* via the Internet for $59; in print for $125; and through Internet and print for $125 (prices taken from the magazine's actual website). Sixteen percent of students chose the Internet-only subscription, 0% chose the print-only subscription, and 84% chose the combination offer. What a great deal to get the print version for free, eh? But when the combination offer was removed, 68% chose the Internet-only option, and 32% chose the print-only offer. Think about what this means. Students did not really want the print version, but when it was added in as a freebie, it changed the comparisons and thus students tended to choose the more expensive print-plus-Internet option. Students paid more for print-plus-Internet, althrough the print was something they did not want. Similarly, we regularly pay more for virtually the same item at an chic, expensive store than at a cheap, no frills store. How rational is that?

Contextual bias operates through the frame of surrounding comparisons. That is, you assume that a price should be based on surrounding prices. You stick with what seems safe (a freebie, even if you don't want it), or you rely on comparisons that are familiar. In evaluating price, events, social situations, and medical/scientific decisions, you reassure yourself within a frame and it ends up leading you awry.

A social correlate of contextual bias is your desire or tendency to be like your friends and neighbors. *In* their latest book, *The Spirit Level: Why*

More Equal Societies Almost Always Do Better (2009), Richard Wilkinson and Kate Pickett detail how economic inequality increases anxiety, whereas economic equality produces societies that are, on average, happier. Said another way, even happiness is relative.

So is weight. Here again, "normal" is a matter of context. A ground-breaking analysis in 2007 showed that social networks spread obesity. Published in the *New England Journal of Medicine*, Christakis and Fowler studied 12,067 participants living in the small town of Framingham, Massachussetts. Between 1971 and 2003, people became heavier. But that weight was not distributed evenly in the community—it occurred in clusters. A person's risk of becoming obese increased by 57% if a friend became obese, by 40% if a sibling became obese, and by 37% if a spouse became obese. Even friends living at a geographic distance developed obesity together. Same-sex friendships had a larger effect than opposite-sex ones. This was not a matter of shared environment since neighbors did not affect each other's tendency to put on extra pounds. Instead, social contacts and context seemed to cause the adverse effect. On a happier note, Christakis and Fowler noted that networks can also spread healthy behaviors. Smoking, alcohol, and weight loss interventions that provide peer support are more successful than programs that do not. When making decisions, people seem to evaluate actions based on how much they deviate from normal expectations.

Context bias affects the decision-making of all humans including scientists and physicians. The use of various medical and surgical procedures is highly variable from one part of the country to another. Remarkably if you live in Beaumont, Texas, your likelihood of having carotid surgery is nine times higher than if you live in Honolulu, Hawaii. And that is after taking into consideration your age, race, health status, and so forth. The explanation given for this phenomenon is "provider enthusiasm." That is, similarly trained physicians and local practice style determine how a patient is treated. Sound like contextual bias? Sound like decision making within a familiar frame? It should. If you think there are absolute "rights" and "wrongs" in medicine, then you should know that an expert's assessment of correctness is relative to social context.

From how much you will pay for a magazine subscription to how much you weigh to the likelihood of being advised to have surgery, contextual bias influences decision making. What is safe and familiar is valued and chosen. No wonder that innovation, which is risky and unfamiliar, is difficult to decide to pursue.

■

How much would you pay for a bottle of 1998 Cotes du Rhone wine? Thirty dollars? One hundred? Ariely (2008) conducted another experiment involving this question to demonstrate another bias called the anchoring effect. Although many students estimated values higher than the true one (because we tend to overestimate unknowns), the students' prices all clustered around a similar value. Ariely then asked each student to write down the last two digits of his/her social security number and adjust from that until the student felt they had estimated the right price for the Cotes du Rhone. The guesses of students with lower-value social security numbers were, on average, significantly below the guesses of students with higher value numbers. What was going on? Social Security numbers have nothing to do with the actual price of wine!

The anchoring effect is a form of contextual bias wherein rather than imitating what others are doing, you choose based on an initial number, decision, or event. The frame here is, again, the familiar. The anchor is the expected—what you already know or have chosen. If you buy a home in one city and move to another where house prices are higher, then you tend to spend around the same amount of money on a house in the new city as you did in the old, even if it means settling for less comfort than you intended. The same goes for switching from a higher priced market to a lower one; you end up with a mansion that you really don't want.

The anchor within anchoring bias becomes valued over other possibilities, even obviously superior ones. When you vote for a political candidate for the first time, you become anchored to that decision and will probably continue to support him or her unless the candidate is indicted— and maybe even then. Or a doctor who successfully prescribes a particular medicine may be reluctant to use any other subsequently, despite the possibility that a better or less expensive alternative may be available. Anchoring is really a subset of contextual bias wherein the context is a first, accustomed number or event. Anchoring, like context, biases you toward a frame that is established and away from the unusual.

■

Your mind is reluctant to give up first impressions. It may be the example posed by somebody around you (contextual bias) or the first number you see on a price tag (anchoring effect), or it may just be an unwillingness to change an impression. This type of bias is called *perseverance bias*. If I convince you that I am a mass murderer, you might regard me with horror, loathing, and fear. You may be dialing the police when, say, 5 minutes later, I begin laughing and tell you, "I'm joking!" You would think that I have a very weird sense of humor, but you would likely also continue to wonder if the murder story is true. You might never see me the same way again. Perseverance bias occurs when, even after information has been proved to be utterly falsified, people hold on to their original beliefs.

Perseverance bias has a detrimental impact on the pace of progress in science. Once an idea is embedded in the professional psyche, it is difficult to remove or replace. The lag between the time that research supports a medical intervention and when that intervention becomes part of routine clinical care is often one or two decades. Yes—you read that correctly— not years but decades. Change is hard. Even physicians and scientists, who pride themselves on functioning on the basis of data and being "on the cutting edge," find it difficult to accept novelty.

■

It is 7:51 A.M. on a cold January Friday by the doors of a metro station in Washington, D.C. A tall, dark-haired man has just set up his violin in the corner. His case is open in front of him to accept whatever donations the scurrying crowd chooses to give. Just another musically challenged street musician trying to stay warm and keep his stomach filled through the generosity of strangers? No, this is Joshua Bell—one of the world's most famous violinists.

A few days earlier, Bell played at Boston's Symphony Hall to a sold-out audience who paid $100 for merely good seats and much more for a close-up view. Now, positioned near the entryway in a long-sleeved T-shirt and jeans while more than 1000 people rush past him to work, he is barely noticed. Commuters either pay no attention or they pass quickly by, pitching a quarter into his violin case without stopping.

Six Bach pieces and 45 minutes later, Bell's total take amounts to just $32. How is that possible? Out of his usual context, people do not expect to hear a world class musician. After all, how believable is it that a virtuoso would be playing a Stradivarius in a subway corner? Even if you thought you recognized this scruffy street musician as an undercover, famous Joshua Bell, it could not possibly be him.

Expectation bias describes how your decisions are influenced by what you are used to seeing in a particular situation. The frame is your expectations. Frames, of course, are pure expectations. Expectation bias occurs when your frames lead you to filter inputs in a way that leads you astray.

In science, too, what you expect is often what you get. If you expect a particular outcome from an experiment but you do not get it or you get results that are equivocal, does expectation bias influence your interpretation? Considerable research shows that null results—that is, results that do not positively support a hypothesis—are less often published than confirmatory results. When you decide whether the observations fit the hypothesis, is it you who are deciding or is it your expectation bias?

Consider the scientific intervention, the placebo. Placebos have a remarkable ability to produce expected results. They have been shown to reduce the symptoms from any range of ailments, including those that require surgery. In World War II, salt water was used in place of painkillers to offset pain while preventing shock. Recent studies have proven placebos to be as effective as the two top prescription drugs in treating irritable bowel syndrome, and placebos can provide 75% of the relief offered by the six leading antidepressants. Brain surgery is just as effective as placebo surgery (drilling holes in the skull without actually operating) for Parkinson's disease. The success of "patent medications" throughout history (radium-infused water as a means to experience "Perpetual Sunshine" anyone?) has rested on the efficacy of placebos.

The color of a pill, the price, the geographic location in which it is tested, and who administers it all can affect that medication's usefulness in treatment. The fact is that sugar pill or no, the expectation that you have been prescribed a curative will often coax you into thinking that you feel better.

■

Prior to President Nixon's trips to Moscow and Peking in 1972, a group of 119 people were given a list of 15 possible events that might occur during the historic occasion and asked to evaluate the probability that each event might take place. After the trip took place, at several points over the next few months, the subjects were again asked to reconstruct their predictions. A full 84% of the subjects recalled that their predictions had been stronger than they had originally been if events actually happened and weaker than they had originally been if events did not happen. In other words, if President Nixon had cleared up an international dispute with China, the subjects were likely to "remember" that they had predicted the reconciliation in their original guess, even if they hadn't. This effect became more pronounced as time passed. In hindsight, the event was obvious.

Your sense of reality is constructed around memories. In hindsight, you are clairvoyant. *Hindsight bias* is the belief that you remember more accurately than you really you do. More recent expectations alter more distant reality. Think of this as a framing in time. The more vibrant the frame caused by proximity in time, the more powerful the frame's effect on your mental reality.

Indeed, the mere suggestion that something may have existed is enough to cause its inclusion in your mental recreation of the event. Details learned after an event can overturn recalled reality. It's a scary thought—you may

not actually know what you think you know. Memory is so highly mal-
leable. Your spouse's flawed recollection of where you went on your first
date may represent other restaurants in his or her memory. Or perhaps
in yours!

Hindsight bias has become a contentious intrusion into psychiatry
and the law, because if memories are so open to suggestion, then how
can anyone know which recalled events really happened? How fair is it
for a defendant to be convicted on the basis of eyewitness testimony?
How can parents know the truth of their child remembering a sexual
assault?

Hindsight may cause a scientist to be "sure" of having had an idea
in the past when in fact that idea was later conveyed to them from
an outside source. An observation consistent with a current point of
view may be recalled as having been seen but not recorded when in
fact it was not actually observed. Such things are likely unusual since
precise and accurate laboratory notebooks are a central tenant of good
science. But bias in science does exist and it is often the antithesis of
innovation.

■

Your mind is not a computer, nor is it infallible. You give unwarranted
weight to memories that are consistent with more recent events and
expectations. You frame your thinking around context and so are
swayed by the people around you (contextual bias), the first number
we see on a price tag (anchoring effect), a first impression (perseverance bias), or assumptions about reality (expectation bias). You make
inferences on the basis of information but your inferences are not
always rational. Even as frames constrain your thinking, cognitive
biases distort your decision-making. The decisions you consider to be
so well thought-out and rational are strongly encumbered by the safe
and familiar. Without our ever having any inclination toward conven-
tionality, cognitive biases direct your decisions away from ingenuity
and novelty.

EXERCISES

1. Can contextual bias be used to advantage to benefit science and society?

    a. What biases can you use to promote competitive weight loss such as in the fabulously popular television show, *The Biggest Loser?*

    b. How might public health experts describe the quantity of excess radiation involved in a screening mammogram or a CT scan?

2. Consider a recent purchase you made at a swanky shop. Go online and research the cost of that item to see if the anchor of the other prices in the shop fooled you into assuming that prices reflect value.

3. The anchoring effect is particularly powerful when the anchor is something free. We tend to be willing to pay more for a service, for example, when it comes with a freebie. As a doctor, what could you do to get a patient to become enamored of a particular medicine? How could you get them to remain compliant with a medication over time?

4. The use of placebos in medical research can be controversial. However, when used correctly (i.e., with harmless ingredients), placebos can actually help patients. Invent a medical treatment that capitalizes on the beneficial effects of a placebo.

5. Rate your level of contentment with two objects in your home, one whose purchase was on a whim and one that was highly studied. Then write about the process of choosing the studied object—lessons learned, stresses. Rate your contentment with each thing again.

9

Overcoming Bias

"This 'telephone' has too many shortcomings to be accepted as a means of communication. The device is inherently of no value to us."

—*Western Union, the telegraph company, 1876*

If only overcoming cognitive biases were as easy as reading about them! Edward de Bono, in his book *Lateral Thinking* (1990), argues that your mind tends to perpetuate a given thought system and to resist change and novelty. Psychologists have tried to teach people to recognize and defeat their biases, with little success.

You may not be able to overcome cognitive biases by simply being aware of them, but you may be able to overcome them by systematically considering alternatives. Consider a step-wise approach somewhat like the one you used for identifying and overcoming frames. Once you have identified the bias:

Step 1: Define the decision and the information relevant to it.
Step 2. Identify the frame that underlies the bias.
Step 3: Remove or devise an alternative to the frame.
Step 4: Consider consequences of the alternative frame.

Example 1: Contextual Bias

1. Decision—Which cell phone do I buy? The three options I am considering (all using my current provider) are: *(a)* $129 Droid

with Internet access and e-mail plus multiple applications; *(b)* $59 cell with Internet and e-mail; and *(c)* free, cheap replacement with phone only. Relevant to this, I already have an iPod with Internet and applications (apps) but a keyboard that I have trouble using to type e-mail messages. I am struggling financially and taking out student loans so anything I buy contributes to my lifelong debt payments.

2. Frame—Context affects your choice
3. Remove the frame—What decision would I make if the Droid was not in the mix? I need e-mail, so although the freebee sounds great, I choose the $59. What if the free replacement were not in the mix? I already have the iPod and don't want to spend so much on the phone, so I still choose the $59.
4. Consequences—Passing on the free phone causes some regret, but I really need the e-mail capability. Passing on having everything in one Smartphone (rather than having to switch between cell and iPod) may be a little less convenient but it is worth it in order to feel that I have enough funds left over to go out on a date this week.

Example 2: Anchoring Effect

1. Decision—How does one successfully market electric cars? A major roadblock to selling electric cars is their higher sales price. Customers are used to paying $25,000 to $35,000 for a car. The price of a comparable battery-powered car may be $35,000 to $45,000 because of the large expense of the battery. Although many customers want to "go green" so as to limit America's oil dependence, they are only willing to do so if the price is right.
2. Frame—Consumers are likely to pay only as much as their anchor—that is, what they have paid for a car in the past.
3. Remove the frame—Understanding the anchoring effect of initial cost, the Israeli company Better Place (CEO Shai Agassi), one of the largest start-up technology companies in the world, has

devised a plan whereby the cost of the battery is defrayed over the life of the car. You pay $25,000 in advance for the car. A monthly fee covers the cost of replacing the spent battery with a recharged battery. The fee is really an installment plan tied to the number of miles per month you drive. The monthly fee is approximately equivalent to the monthly cost of gas.

4. Consequences—Better Place is obligated to make a sizeable investment to be able to stock car batteries, which will ultimately be paid for by monthly fees. This requires them to raise substantial capital, which has been a struggle but one they have overcome. To be fair, this does not solve another huge problem in marketing electric cars, which is the creation of a grid of battery replacement stations that are geographically convenient, like gas stations. Nonetheless, this novel way to "un-anchor" the cost of the car will jump-start market acceptance. Demand will eventually produce the market pressure needed to fund the building of recharging stations.

Example 3: Hindsight Bias

1. Decision—As a health practitioner, how should you advise women about drinking coffee during early pregnancy? All your patients are concerned about a new scientific result that is blanketing the airwaves. According to this new study, consuming 2 cups or more of coffee per day increases the risk for miscarriage.

2. Frame—Hindsight bias makes you more likely to recall studies consistent with the new finding.

3. Remove the frame—Given the ease of modern access to information, don't rely on your memory. Although no up-to-date systematic review (such as a Cochrane review) is available, a Medline search reveals a dozen previous studies addressing coffee consumption and miscarriage. You find a systematic review that underscores a major methodological flaw with all

research on this question: nausea early in pregnancy is a sign of a healthy fetus but also causes women to stop drinking coffee. This physiologic reality means that continued coffee consumption in pregnancy may not cause miscarriage but instead may be a pre-existing sign that the pregnancy is on its way to miscarrying.

4. Consequences—Your literature review leaves you more baffled than before, but it leads you to conclude that the new research certainly does not "prove" the harmfulness of coffee drinking during pregnancy. Your advice to your patients continues to be, "All things in moderation."

EXERCISES

Try some of these on your own.

1. Perseverance bias

   1. Decision—Should you advise your patients to continue to take Hormone Therapy (HT) after the publication of the results of the *Women's Health Initiative* study (2002), which showed that HT increases the risks of cardiovascular disease and stroke? After all, your patients love taking HT, and you have nothing much else to offer them to relieve their hot flashes.

   • Frame—
   • Remove Frame—
   • Consequences—

2. Context bias

   • Decision—Should you ride a motorcycle, drive a car, or bike the 4 miles to work? Consider pros and cons, including cost, safety, and environmental impact.

   • Frame—
   • Remove the frame—
   • Consequences—

10

The Brain and Creativity:
The Seat of Inspiration

What is the anatomy of innovation? The next two chapters review the latest research on where and how creativity is processed in the brain. I will propose that on an average day your cognitive activity is not terribly conducive to enriching out-of-the-box thoughts. However, on a good day you can access neurologic pathways that enhance innovation. Understanding the anatomy of creative thinking may help you to harness those pathways to inspiration.

■

The "seat of creativity" has been widely believed to reside on the right side of the brain. If you think this statement is odd (that the two halves of the brain are mirror images), then meet J.W. Neurosurgery split J.W.'s brain. In a last-ditch effort to relieve terrible, intractable seizures, doctors severed his corpus callosum, the thin bundle of nerves that connects the brain's two sides. The success of the operation made J.W. seizure-free and otherwise apparently normal. So at age 47 years, he agreed to give back to science. He became a guinea pig for Michael Gazzaniga, a white-haired, intense-appearing psychologist who, since the 1960s has been studying how the brain integrates cognitive functions.

The work of Dr. Gazzaniga and others has shown that in split-brain patients, the two halves of the brain work independently. In the laboratory one day in 2005, J.W. found himself working on simple math problems, a mundane exercise—with the exception that he only got to use half his cerebral cortex. With information entering only one side of his visual field and thus only one side of his brain, he pressed a key if the math answer that popped onto a computer screen was correct and another key if the solution was incorrect. When the problem entered his right visual field, he selected the correct answer about 90% of the time. Because what is seen in the right visual field goes to the left brain and what is seen in the right field goes to the left brain, the experiment showed that J.W.'s left brain was good at math. However, his right brain performance was markedly different. The right side identified the correct answer only half of the time—a rate no greater than chance.

Since Roger Sperry of the California Institute of Technology started conducting similar experiments on cats and monkeys in the 1960s, scientists like Sperry and Gazzaniga have consistently replicated these findings. Sperry received the Nobel Prize in 1981 for his discovery that humans have not one brain but two.

■

Joe, another split-brain patient being tested in Gazzaniga's laboratory, was shown a picture of an orange. With his right visual field (left brain), he readily named it. But, remarkably, the word was completely unknown to his right brain. His right brain could draw it but simply could not conjure the name. In contrast, Joe's right brain (which works through the left hand), could easily solve a block puzzle. Not so his left brain (right hand). When Joe was told to use only his right hand to solve the puzzle, his left hand kept trying to sneak up to the blocks atop the table to try to show the right hand what to do. It turns out that each side of the brain is good at some tasks and not so good at others. Below are some things better done by each side.

RIGHT BRAIN:
- Interpreting complex, whole patterns
- Recognizing and appreciating music and the visual arts
- Producing dreams during REM sleep

- Processing novel situations
- Abstract thinking, including interpretation of metaphors

LEFT BRAIN:

- Analytic and linear processes
- Recognizing and identifying language (grammar and vocabulary)
- Understanding and processing mathematical concepts
- Processing routine or well-rehearsed situations

■

You are now wondering why all this discussion—surely the right brain, with its holistic, abstract capabilities is, indeed, the locus of creativity. Several prominent creativity training programs have worked on this assumption. Because the hemisphere that is better at performing a task can be trained to take over, the goal of these programs is to develop right-brain dominance. But the answer to "Where is the seat of creativity?" is not so simple.

In 2010, Mihov and colleagues conducted a meta-analysis on studies examining hemisphere dominance during creative activities. Eighty-eight studies had assessed this question. No dominance by either hemisphere was noted in 26 studies; right-brain dominance was shown in 48; and left-brain dominance was the result found in 14.

How can we understand such disparate results? First, different methods were used by each study for measuring brain function. A simplistic and unfortunately imprecise approach, using indirect psychological tests to intuit brain activity was used by most studies. Only a handful used more direct and accurate measurements such as sophisticated magnetic resonance imaging (MRI) of cerebral blood flow. A summary of these is shown is the Table. Blood flow is a way to assess structural activity because the hardest working parts of your brain get the most blood flow just as when exercising your muscles get more blood delivery.

In one illustrative example, Carlsson and colleagues (2000) published a cerebral blood flow experiment in which 2 groups of 12 men each were first given a creativity test and on that basis designated as either high or low creative. Measurements were taken during a resting state and again while subjects worked on a task requiring the generation of numerous, novel ideas (imaging all possible uses for a brick). The high creative group exhibited increases in blood flow to both frontal lobes. The low creative group had an increase only in the left frontal lobe. So far, this seems to support the idea of a right-brain creativity locus, right? Wrong. The observation common to both groups is that they used the left side. Use of both right and left together characterized the high creative group, but neither group used the right side alone. Similarly, the use of both sides of the brain characterized creativity tasks in other blood flow studies.

Studies of Brain Activity during Creative Tasks Using Functional Tests

First Author (year)	Cohort	Test	Task	Regions Activated	Side
Bechtereva (2001)	16 young men	rCBF*	Creative correlates of unrelated words	Prefrontal Occipital	L>R L and R
Bechtereva (2004)	25 young men	rCBF	Creative story generation from given words	Prefrontal Parieto-temporal	L and R L
Carlsson (2000)	12 High-creatives and 12 low-creatives	rCBF	As many uses as possible for an object	Prefrontal	L and R (high creatives) L (low creatives)
Chavez-Eakle (2007)	High-creatives and low-creatives	rCBF	Unusual uses for common objects	Frontal Cerebellum Temporal	L and R R L
Howard-Jones (2005)	8 men and women	fMRI**	Creative story generation	Frontal	R>L
Seger C (2000)	7 men and women	fMRI	Generate unusual verb-noun relations	Frontal Cerebellum	L and R L and R

*rCBF = regional cerebral blood flow; **fMRI = functional magnetic resonance imaging.

Now the story gets even trickier. The "uses for a brick" task involves the use of language: a left-brain function. What if the task were a visual pattern problem? It turns out the result would have been different. The tasks used in various studies included: verbal fluency, creative imagery, creative story creation, creative drawing, and so on. Different tasks themselves use different brain regions and sides, independent of whether they are tasks requiring creativity. No surprise that different studies came to different conclusions.

Fortunately, this chaos is not just confusing, it is revealing. The different results suggest that creativity is not just one thing. Storytelling, drawing, insight, idea generation—they are all different functions. Each uses different parts of the brain. So, innovation is domain-specific, meaning that artists, musicians, writers, and scientists are all coming from somewhat different angles in achieving creative output. Teaching how to innovate in science is not the same as teaching how to be creative in art or music.

So where is the "seat of creativity?" The right-side myth is almost surely wrong. But the question is also probably wrong: There is likely not a single "seat," and creativity is not a single thing.

■

Remember that the creative group in Carlsson's experiment used both sides of the brain. The advantage held by creative people is their ability to exploit their full, broad-ranging cognitive potential. Alone, each hemisphere is relatively poor at solving complex and difficult mental tasks. Although simple tasks can readily be processed in one hemisphere, complex tasks require the power of the full brain. Right and left hemispheres must cooperate. The right side of the brain cannot interpret novel information without the left first examining evident facts and solutions. Creativity is not just right-sided pattern recognition. It also requires left-brain functions of word associations (for language problems) or quantitative analysis (for math problems) as well as the left sided function of judging the appropriateness of solutions.

The most common hypothesis among scientists studying creativity today is that unique thinking comes from mental integration. Consider all the parts of your brain needed to generate alternative frames. You must interpret individual words; access memories; decode the meaning of metaphors; envision inferences; and imagine new metaphorical patterns. Escaping from cognitive biases likely takes all of this plus perhaps more. Learning to think "out-of the-box" is the equivalent of training yourself to mentally integrate.

Innovative training grows your ability to assimilate brain functions. The more you do it, the better you get. Tone up those cognitive muscles! Exercise them together! Sound like physical exercise? It is. Every new technique you learn and put into use more fully develops your mind's abundant potential.

11

The Brain and Creativity: Getting Out in Front

Creativity may be less a matter of right versus left than a matter of front versus back. Although there is no "seat of creativity," there is almost surely a "conductor of creativity." It is the prefrontal cortex. This region of the brain, representing the front half of the front (frontal cortex) section of the brain, is the center of cognitive integration.

No more vivid description of the workings of the prefrontal cortex can be found than in the famous story of Phineas Gage. Gage was a hardy, well-respected railroad construction foreman. Working in Cavendish, Vermont, one day in 1848, the 25-year-old Gage set about doing what he did every day—blasting holes in masses of solid rock. He added blasting powder, a fuse, and sand to the hole. He then tamped down the charge with a large iron rod.

The accident probably occurred because Gage was distracted and forgot to add the sand. When he lit the fuse, the powder exploded prematurely, sending the 13-pound rod with its ¼-inch point through his left eye and out the top of his head. The thrust of the rod was so great that when it landed, it was 80 feet away.

Amazingly, Gage spoke and walked only minutes afterward. To passersby who came to gawk, he explained the nature of the accident, even as brain tissue leaked from the wound. Within 2 months, Gage was able to travel by horse cart back to a doting family who restored him to health. One eye was missing and the left side of his face was paralyzed. Yet, Gage recovered full mobility and later returned to working as a long-distance stage coach driver.

But Gage was not normal. A physician named Harlow who had first seen Gage within hours of the accident explained two decades later the marked change in the man. He described Gage before the accident as a "great favorite" of the men on his gang and the "most efficient and capable foreman" in his company's employ. After the accident, his friends and colleagues said he was "no longer Gage." Harlow writes:

> The equilibrium or balance, so to speak, between his intellectual faculties and animal propensities, seems to have been destroyed. He is fitful, irreverent, indulging at times in the grossest profanity (which was not previously his custom), manifesting but little deference for his fellows, impatient of restraint or advice when it conflicts with his desires, at times tenaciously obstinate, yet capricious and vacillating, devising many plans of future operations, which are no sooner arranged than they are abandoned in turn for others appearing more feasible. A child in his intellectual capacity and manifestations, he has the animal passions of a strong man.

■

The damage from the impaling rod had destroyed the better part of Gage's left frontal lobe. Gage became the kind of human oddity that populates medical texts—the first patient to suffer what has since been called "the frontal lobe syndrome." The syndrome includes difficulty taking initiative, inability to undertake tasks in sequence, and inappropriate social behaviors. Surprisingly, however, patients with frontal lobe lesions retain their other mental capabilities.

In his book, *Descartes' Error,* Antonio Damasio (1994) describes the case of a patient named Elliot who, to remove a brain tumor (meningioma), required removal of a large portion of his right and left prefrontal cortex. He seemed unable to perform complex mental processes or decision tasks. After the operation, Elliott was much like Gage. He could not get ready for work without prompting. Once there, he could not organize tasks and seemed unwilling to switch between tasks. Decision making was beyond him. Elliott lost his job. He took to collecting things at home, spending hours and days trying to decide how to sort objects that were, unfortunately, junk.

In Damasio's laboratory, Elliott was of superior IQ. His memory, language, visual perception, arithmetic, and block construction skills were excellent. Normal also were tests of personality and social functioning. How could Elliott appear to be so normal in the laboratory and yet be so debilitated in real life?

■

Elliott was not able to make real-life social decisions and to feel emotion. The operation seemed to have amputated these critical life skills. Things that would have previously bothered Elliott simply didn't anymore. In fact, when hurt, he felt the pain in a distracted kind of way, as though the systems that trigger emotion remained, but they caused no suffering. Was there a connection between the lack of emotion and the hindered decision making, Damasio wondered?

To probe this, Damasio's team conducted a revealing experiment using a lie detector. Emotional arousal (as indicated by skin's electrical conductance) is the thing that makes a lie detector squeal. What controls emotional arousal is the autonomic nervous system. Popularly known as controller of "fight or flight," the autonomic nervous system elicits responses in the viscera (organs) such as a quickening of the pulse, elevation of blood pressure, dilation of pupils, and redirection of blood flow from internal organs to muscles. That is, the system allows us to react to threat. Its control center in primitive parts of the brain such as the amygdala connects by neuronal projections to the various organs, including the skin. A "visceral" reaction thus literally means an emotional response that quickens the heart, gives you a stomachache, and makes your skin crawl.

Elliott's response to skin conductance testing was normal. But Damasio wondered what his autonomic function would look like during a decision-making task. The experiment went like this: four decks of cards (A, B, C, and D) were set out, and Elliott was told to turn over as many cards as he wanted from whatever deck he wanted until the interviewer told him to stop. A "loan" of $2000 in real-looking play money was given to Elliott and he was told to try to earn as much money as possible. Unknown to Elliott, the rules of the game were that at the "Stop," if the last card was from decks A or B, then he would be paid $100; if from C or D, then the payout was $50. But randomly, instead of a payout, a tax as high as $1250 would be leveraged on decks A or B, whereas the maximum tax on decks C or D was $100. Normal players generally start the game by turning over cards from the decks randomly. Early in their play, they prefer A and B, but with more experience, they will tend toward the safer C and D decks. This was not Elliott's strategy. Early on, he favored decks A and B. But he stuck with decks A and B. Despite getting hit with huge taxes that wiped out his store of cash and required him to garner loans, he continued to make risky decisions and to lose.

The insight as to why Elliott persisted in making seemingly irrational decisions came from the lie detector. In normal players, a gain or loss during the game triggered a skin conductance response—that is, it made their skin crawl. Particularly as they deliberated after having made a dangerous pick, a normal player's skin conductance climbed. Could it be that their viscera participated in the decision? In the 1890s Pavlov conducted classic experiments in which dogs (which, through their autonomic system, salivate to meat) were conditioned to salivate to a bell that had been linked to the offering of meat. Here, players' autonomic nervous systems raised their skin conductance to an anticipated punishment. But Elliott was different. Elliot made illogical decisions while his autonomic system slept.

■

To explain this, Damasio posited a theory that he called the "Somatic Marker Hypothesis." He argued that (as you have seen) all humans take decisional shortcuts. If you took the time to carefully value all possible actions and all possible outcomes from each action, you, like Elliott, would never decide anything. Damasio hypothesized that to get on with your life you rely on your gut. When you imagine that a particular decision may have a bad outcome, your autonomic nervous system sends a warning. "Eliminate that decision," it says. Each appraisal that a decision is risky triggers a visceral reaction and the removal of that decision. Within no time, you find yourself with a nicely narrowed set of options.

The Somatic Marker Hypothesis does not suggest that scientists are like Pavlov's dogs. In fact, scientific decisions almost certainly are not entirely from your gut. More correctly, visceral reactions assist decision making through weighting. Some decisions are simply less stomach-wrenching than others.

Where is this little gnome in your brain triggering visceral reactions and translating them into the thought that, "This decision is risky"? It is sitting in that seat of executive functioning, the prefrontal cortex. Assessing the perilousness of decisions is a prefrontal job. In the pre-frontal cortex, working memory and directed attention mix with a variety of other inputs to allow for the most complex kinds of thought. With all its sophistication, the prefrontal cortex is the most modern part of the brain acquired during evolution and the last portion of the brain to develop during childhood. It holds the prize within the cortex for having the most reciprocal neuronal connections. The prefrontal sub-region of the dorsolateral area receives extensive information from brain centers controlling the senses of touch, sight, and hearing. The orbitofrontal sub-region has connections with all elements of the primitive brain, including the director of the autonomic nervous system, the amygdala.

When the prefrontal cortex and the amygdala get activated together is when you have to make choices that set off your worst decision-making stomachaches. Try deciding which gift to get your significant other, which city to move to, or which car to buy. Despite all the discussions, the consideration, the lists of pros and cons, you often just aren't sure. That's when your prefrontal cortex and autonomic nervous system both get going—when the outcomes from a decision are risky and unknown.

This is just what would be predicted by Damasio's Somatic Marker Hypothesis.

The prefrontal cortex does one more thing: It organizes working memory into chunks. Neuroscientists call this relational complexity. You know these chunks as frames, represented by metaphors. Thus, the prefrontal cortex likely processes frames.

■

Let us now (finally) return to the question of innovation. There is good evidence that the frontal lobe facilitates creative thought. One of the most consistent findings among studies that have measured blood flow in the brain during idea generation is the involvement of the frontal lobes. In the Table in Chapter 10 describing studies of cerebral functionality during creativity tasks, note that in all of these studies, the frontal lobe is involved. So creativity should be easy, as the prefrontal cortex is so sophisticated at thinking. But finding unusually inventive solutions, particularly out-of-frame solutions, is far from easy. Why?

I suggest that the frontal lobe is ambivalent about creativity: it both assists and hinders. Recall that frames define and limit how you interpret new information and they arouse strong emotions. Out-of-frame ideas trigger the frontal cortex to issue a danger signal, warning you to take that thought right out of contention. Imagine that you get some wild spark of an idea, such as "cancer as neighbor." Your prefrontal cortex has to decide what to do. The idea clearly defies normal patterns of thinking. Others will surely reject the idea. Pursuing it will make you look foolish, eat up your time, and ultimately result in failure. Your autonomic nervous system goes on the defensive. Your stomach feels queasy, your blood pressure rises, and your palms sweat. Before you even "give it a second thought," the notion is labeled as "crazy" and booted from your decision-making queue.

Let's call this the "Innovation-Frame Hypothesis."

Two questions must be answered affirmatively for the Innovation-Frame Hypothesis to make sense. First, does frame-shifting generate a visceral rejection reaction? The response to alternative frames like "cancer as neighbor" or "cities should eliminate road signs and signals" is not one of amusement but of outright hostility. In both cases you think, "That's downright dangerous!" My guess is that you don't even think through the consequences long enough to judge these ideas as harebrained. Your reaction is at a gut level.

In his book *The Structure of Scientific Revolutions*, Thomas Kuhn (1962) argues that frame shifts are generally considered by other scientists to be somewhere between oddities and threats. Kuhn describes "normal science" as the activity in which almost all scientists spend their efforts reinforcing preexisting paradigms. When confronted with a competing paradigm, the initial reaction is to oppose it. Jane Goodall, Herb Needleman, Warren and Marshall, and many other scientists proposing paradigm shifts experienced such rejection. Out-of-frame insights, when first proposed, are almost universally rejected.

■

The second question is: Is decision-making a key process in innovation? Creative thinking entails the generation of ingenious ideas. But it also involves the decision to pursue an unaccepted and possibly unacceptable idea. Without the will to invest in the experiments that will prove or disprove an idea, there is no innovation. By definition, a person must make the decision to pursue an idea with great persistence. One example of an innovator who followed-up his pivotal hypothesis against great odds is Joseph Goldberger.

Goldberger, a shy Pennsylvania practitioner turned Public Health Service officer, had spent a career battling infectious epidemics. He was fighting an outbreak of diphtheria in Detroit in 1914 when the U.S. Surgeon General to the southern United States dispatched him to investigate a mysterious outbreak. In the southern United States at the time, the suffering from a disease called pellagra was affecting hundreds of thousands. Like a biblical plague, patients broke out in boils, suffered intractable diarrhea, became irritable and intolerant to light, got dizzy with the slightest movement, and eventually died.

Goldberger assumed (as did all other scientists of the day) that pellagra was a germ. But in the orphanages and mental hospitals where he worked, he noticed something that simply broke all the rules of contagions—the patients became ill but the staff did not. Why would an infection attack one group of people and ignore another? What might cause such an unusual pattern of disease? Over time, it occurred to him. Patients in confinement ate only the unappealing slop that was most economical to serve to the masses. Staff went home to hot nutritious meals. Goldberger provided fresh vegetables, milk, and meat to children in two orphanages and to inmates in the Georgia State Asylum. The results were dramatic: those fed Goldberger's diet recovered from their pellagra and new cases stopped occurring. When he published these findings, critics called his work "half-baked" and accused him of fraud. But Goldberger only redoubled his efforts to prove the dietary hypothesis and disprove an infectious one.

In April 1916, he and his assistant injected pellagra blood into each other and swallowed capsules containing scabs from pellagra rashes. Had it been an infection, they both would have gotten it, but neither did. Still, staunch opponents remained, and Goldberger became vilified in the South when he proposed that the only way to feed the poor was to impose land reform. Nonetheless, he persisted in calling for nutritional reforms. At age 55 years he died prematurely of cancer, having never found the specific nutrient that caused pellagra. A decade later, a lack of niacin (Vitamin B6, found in the fresh meat that Goldberger provided to patients) was found to be the cause of this devastating disease, and its precursor, tryptophan, is now used to fortify cereals. Pellagra is virtually unknown in modern America.

Goldberger went beyond his idea. He was driven by the idea. He took surprising personal risks. He had no compunction about challenging authority. Goldberger's are the classic characteristics of innovators. Innovators pursue an insight to the bitter end because they decide that the quest is imperative.

During the 1990s, the creative research world was abuzz with a theory that proposed that freeing oneself from logical and constricting thoughts was the source of creativity. Martindale and colleagues (1999) posited that creative cognition is the result of a brain state characterized by low levels of frontal lobe activation. They prescribed diffused attention and free-flowing ideas. One stage in the creative process is called *incubation*, defined as laying the issue aside until a new insight arises. Many scientists now believe that giving the mind a break to work through an innovation is part of the creative process, although likely not all of it.

The Innovation-Frame Hypothesis suggests that there are several stages in innovative thinking. One of these may involve freeing the frontal lobe from frame-laden constraints. Perhaps diffused attention such as through meditation may be useful (*see* Chapter 19, *Incubation*). I believe that other stages may involve recognition of the power of frames and a concerted approach to jumping out of frames. Yet another stage, I believe is the tenacious pursuit of often risky ideas.

In general, the Innovation-Frame Hypothesis posits that the prefrontal cortex acts as a kind of Dr. Jekyll and Mr. Hyde. It conducts the orchestra of neural connections needed for creativity. But it also blocks the creativity process by truncating concentration on risky ideas. Of course, the Innovation-Frame Hypothesis is only a theory. Rigorous testing must be conducted to prove it. But on the basis of the indirect evidence presented here, it is a novel idea worth pursuing.

■

The last decade of brain research has provided exciting observations about how you think creatively. We now know that different creativity tasks activate different brain centers. We also know that the more complex the mental task, the greater the need to integrate a multitude of brain regions. Finally, although its function is still debatable, creativity almost certainly involves activity within the frontal lobe..

More is unknown than is known about the neuroscience of creativity. Is the Innovation-Frame Hypothesis true? Does teaching innovative thinking help you to recruit more brain regions, as you might suspect it would? Is neurologic activity different during different phases of the creative process? Does this change with training? Does training help to overcome the gut-rejection of novel ideas? These are only some of the questions in a field still in its infancy. Learning these and other answers as the neuroscience of creativity matures should provide insights that will allow you to better reach your innovative potential.

Asking and Answering a Scientific Question Through Innovation

12

The Joy of Science

"I know one freedom and that is the freedom of the mind."

—*Antoine de Saint-Exupery*

I fear that by now you have the misimpression that original thought is some grueling climb up an insurmountable mountain. Oh what a half-truth that is! Although generating and pursuing bold new solutions takes remarkable persistence, what keeps people coming back for more is sheer joy. Imaginative thinking is freedom. It encompasses something unbelievably rare and magical—that moment when you are the only person on Earth who has envisioned something so remarkable or strange or unexpected that it may change the world.

If it were not pleasurable to innovate, why would so many of the world's greatest scientists work until they are almost in the grave? Lew Kuller is in his late 70s and Herb Needleman recently turned 80 years old. Both were recently still working. Jeremy Morris, discoverer that physical activity prevents heart disease, wrote his opus magnum at 99 years of age, just 3 months before his death. Katherine Detre, who early advanced the science of clinical trials, was awarded the largest individual National Institutes of Health grant ever at the age of 70 years. The list goes on, seemingly without end. In fact, few scientific geniuses ever fully retire.

■

One of the most celebrated examples of a man whose delight for science matched his lust for life is Richard Feynman, winner of the Nobel Prize in physics in 1965. Feynman's work explained quantum electrodynamics, the theory that describes all interactions involving light and charged particles (i.e., photons and electrons). Feynman revolutionized the field by explaining these interactions as occurring not one-at-a-time but as an infinite number of possible interactions. By integrating (adding up) the probabilities for every possible path a photon could take, he calculated the path it does take. Suffice it to say that when tested, Feynman's idea showed tremendous accuracy. His genius, like Einstein's, was to devise thought experiments—that is, to think about what happens under various experimental conditions, not by taking it to the laboratory but by imagining it in his head.

But quantum electrodynamics is not what defined Feynman. He was defined by his escapades dissecting radios, picking locks, playing bongos in a samba band, beating the odds at Vegas, beach bumming in Rio de Janiero, and shocking the world with a single glass of ice water. Feynman became an icon in science, but he was no myopic workaholic. From the cover of his best selling autobiographical collection of essays, he beams a Cheshire cat smile that epitomizes the title of the book, *The Pleasure of Finding Things Out*.

From an early age, Feynman was fascinated by how things work. While in high school, he developed a knack for fixing radios. He started out building his own crystal set and quickly became the family healer for all things electronic. His reputation spread, and soon he had become the expert repair man for friends and neighbors. One day a stranger asked him to fix a radio that emitted a terrible noise. Feynman glanced at the set and then began to pace. After several minutes, the owner of the radio became agitated and asked what the kid was doing. Feynman replied, "I'm thinking." Soon thereafter, Feynman swapped the order of the two tubes within the radio—and voilà, the device worked perfectly. Thereafter, the radio owner became Feynman's biggest referral source, telling all his friends, "He fixes radios by *thinking!*"

Creativity is hard to pursue when you have to work on something that isn't all that interesting to you. Confronted with this at times while working at Los Alamos on the atomic bomb project during World War II, Feynman distracted himself from the routine by learning how to pick all of the facility's locks and crack all of its safes. In doing so, he underscored the vulnerabilities of the top security facility.

At only one point in his career did Feynman find himself stumped for ideas, and it was when he felt the greatest pressure to produce "serious" research. Feynman solved the problem by becoming less of the boy genius and more of the buffoon. Rather than continuing to strain to address the equations he should have been solving, he questioned the physics of a plate thrown in the air in a cafeteria and worked out the math in his free time. Eight years later, his struggle to solve that curiosity led him to the Nobel Prize.

There are countless other examples of Feynman's passion for learning and understanding. On a year-long visiting professorship in Brazil, he lectured in the mornings and learned how to play bongos in a samba band on the beach in the afternoon. He trained with a professional gambler to beat the odds at Vegas. He studied painting with a philosopher and sold paintings to Pasadena's best department store.

Feynman's most public contribution to science occurred in the aftermath of the tragic explosion of the Space Shuttle Challenger in January 1986, which killed six professional astronauts and a school teacher. Becoming the only scientist on the Roger Commission, tasked with identifying the root cause of the disaster, to actually go out and investigate, he noticed that the O-rings, which hold together the joints of the booster rockets so as to prevent the escape of hot gas, showed scorching. NASA engineers had assumed that because the erosion was only one-third of the way through the O-rings, they had a "safety factor of three." Feynman turned this contention on its head. This would be like saying that it would be acceptable for a bridge to crack one third way through, he contended. Any crack, in his mind, was a failure of design. In one of the most dramatic moments in science, he embarrassed NASA as the TV cameras rolled by immersing an O-ring into a glass of icy water. It cracked. Feynman found the culprit that caused the Challenger disaster, but more fundamentally he exposed a flaw in the thinking of the scientific establishment.

■

Feynman's joy of learning encompassed, but did not stop at, science. He would try anything for sheer mental enjoyment. Success or failure made little difference to him—it was all a game of exploration. Feynman epitomized many of the characteristics of creative scientists. From a large body of research, these can be summarized by saying that many of the field's greatest geniuses are:

- Internally motivated (self-directed, driven, energetic)
- Tolerant of ambiguity, curious, and open-minded
- Self-confident and willing to take risks
- Happy to challenge authority
- Perseverant and able to delay gratification
- Experienced and knowledgeable often in several areas
- Willing to fail

Innovators are naturally curious so they readily observe anomalies and generate hypotheses. But, perhaps more importantly, when they see an anomaly, they make the decision to challenge the pre-existing frame. In fact, highly innovative people appear to make these decisions with what seems to be unusually little anxiety. A reporter once asked Thomas Edison how it felt to have gone through 1,000 experiments before he invented the carbon filament in the light bulb. Edison replied, "I have not failed, not once. I've discovered one thousand ways that don't work." Edison's curiosity never waivered. His internal motivation, willingness to take risks, and (most importantly) self-confidence gave him an unshakable belief in his ultimate success.

■

Israel has emerged, in the past generation, as one of the most innovative countries on Earth. Despite living under the constant threat of political instability and war, Israel currently has the world's highest density of high-tech start-up companies: 1 for every 1,844 Israeli men, women, and children. In 2008, per capita venture capital investments in Israel were

2.5 times higher than in the United States and 80 times higher than in China. A clue as to why this is so comes from the following joke:

> Coming upon an American, a Russian, a Chinese, and an Israeli, a reporter asks: "Excuse me…what's your opinion of the meat shortage?" The American says, "What's a shortage?" The Russian says, "What's meat?" The Chinese says, "What's an opinion?" And the Israeli says, "What's excuse me?"

Known for being audacious, pushy, and unintimidated, Israelis buffer their fear of failure through a cultural norm that they call "constructive failure." In the Israeli military (2–3 years of service is mandatory for all citizens), there is a tendency to treat all performance—successful and unsuccessful—as value-neutral. As long as the risks taken are not reckless, failure in the military and in business is accepted.

■

Innovative thinking generally combines curiosity with a desire for intellectual adventure. It is not a job, it is a passion. Imaginative scientists do not grind away at their work like Jacob Marley, chained to his desk in the bleak winter of a *Christmas Carol*. They delight in the glow of discovery. They revel in the wonder of new ideas. They take risks because that's part of the fun. They pursue innovation for the sheer joy of it.

EXERCISES

Unleash the curious cat within, and ask as many "why" questions as you can think of. Adopt the viewpoint that dumb questions lead to new perspectives. What do you wonder about? What does it seem silly to even ask about? Remember the end of the saying (which no one ever seems to quote): "Curiosity killed the cat, but satisfaction brought him back."

13

Asking the Right Question

"One of the most creative qualities a research scientist can have is the ability to ask the right questions."

—*David Gross, 2004 Nobel Laureate in Physics*

Half the battle to finding an ingenious and creative solution is to ask the right question.

A few weeks after KS Joseph started work at the Canadian Centre for Disease Control, an epidemic of low-birth-weight babies in Ontario exploded into the news. Infants born too small are a major cause of infant mortality. It is a tragedy when any baby dies. But when deaths among babies mount, it generally indicates some dysfunction in the health-care system. The United States spends almost twice what Canada does on each of its citizens, yet the American infant mortality rate is well higher than Canada's (7.2 deaths/1000 births in the United States vs. 5.2 in Canada). When the Canadian news media learned of the spike in low-birth-weight babies, it went into spasms about the sudden erosion in health care quality. Think of it: Ontario might be slipping down the slope of its profligate neighbor to the south.

The case was referred to Joseph, who was told to answer this question: Why is pregnancy care in Canada suddenly slipping? Urgent examination of prenatal care waiting times, the quality of prenatal care, and delivery room procedures could and should have been the focus of Joseph's investigation. Instead Joseph decided to ignore the question of why pregnancy care in Canada was slipping. Despite the need to respond quickly to such a politically charged emergency, he sat back and asked: Is there a problem?

Joseph's approach to finding an answer lay in a simple exercise. The birth weight of every baby born in Ontario was graphed to assess the shape of its normal distribution. If the normal distribution was shifted downward in total, then it could mean one thing; if he saw a bulge in the lower birth weights, then it would mean another. But he saw neither. The curve itself was not normal. At several birth weight points on the Ontario plot, there were unexpected spikes. Joseph knew that delivery rooms tend to record birth weights in rounded numbers, but the upticks weren't even whole numbers. They fell oddly on numbers such as 5.1 pounds, 6.1 pounds, 7.1 pounds. Moreover, how could rounding errors explain an epidemic of low birth weight?

Statistics Canada is the department that gathers and records birth weight reports from around the provinces. Like in many bureaucracies, the Department of Vital Statistics and Joseph's department rarely interacted. But a powerful need to understand what was going on took Joseph across town to a meeting at their offices. After formalities, he peppered his Vital Statistics colleagues with questions. "How is birth weight recorded? Who enters them into the database?" The strangeness of the conversation grew with each answer. Overburdened by budget cuts and reductions in personnel, the staff of Statistics Canada revealed that they had kept up with the masses of incoming data in the only way they could think. They had simply stopped recording as many digits. So, 5 pounds 11 ounces had become 5 pounds 1 ounce. Contrived reductions in weight became an epidemic of low birth weight with infant losses as great as 13 ounces for a weight rounded from 14 ounces to 1. It didn't take long for babies put on this new "database diet" to create an illusory disaster. The right question really was: Is this epidemic real?

■

Asking the right question is the first step in a series of steps that move you along a route toward developing a new innovation. You can remember these steps by way of this attractive acronym: **PIG In MuD**.

- **P**hrase a question based on interest, observation, and knowledge
- **I**dentify the frames and find alternatives (discussed in Chapters 2–5)
- **G**enerate all possible solutions
- **I**ncubate
- **M**eld your single best idea back into the process of normal science (validate that your innovation works or is true)
- **D**isseminate your innovative finding

■

The motivation to create is born from a question about which you are really curious or, even better, really passionate. You are looking for a question that evokes curiosity, can be tackled, and will benefit science and society.

Questions are the characters in memorable dramas. Like good characters, good questions are innately compelling. Yet it is only through getting to know them that they truly come alive. Questions start from an interest that is broad and compelling. How do we cure cancer; how do we stop global warming; what makes up mass in the universe? The starting point represents a broad area of curiosity. But how do you know that the general area is worthwhile? No one wants to spend a lot of time working on an interest that is irrelevant or, worse, frivolous. How do you know what is consequential? Consider these three characteristics:

- *Plausible:* Your area of interest should not already have a clearly established solution. A paradigm, theory, or observation with no clear anomalies or reason to initiate change might not be worth your time.
- *Actionable:* Technology should exist and society should be organized in such a way that a solution is within the realm of possibility. Actionable does not necessarily mean "readily achievable." The solution may not be immediately available because it has no clear market, or because the technology may be only partially developed. Actionable simply means that your feet are still on this planet.

- *Useful:* Hopefully, your area of interest has scientific or societal significance. A constructive impact on science or economic development makes a question particularly worth your investment.

Jules Verne, a nineteenth century French writer of science fiction, is the second-most translated author in history (Agatha Christy outdid him a couple decades later). His delightful works include *A Journey to the Centre of the Earth* (1864), *From the Earth to the Moon* (1865), and *Twenty Thousand Leagues Under the Sea* (1869–1870). Inventive ideas filled the pages of his books. Why is Verne considered a writer of science fiction rather than a scientific innovator? Motivated by curiosity and asking questions that were enormously useful, his interests seem to fit the above criteria. But not fully. Verne's pursuits were not actionable. The ideas they spawned were simply not supportable by any technology available within his century. Of course, some of his flights of fantasy (particularly manned space flight and deep sea exploration) became reality well after Verne's death. But he never enjoyed that knowledge. Addressing your interests will be the most fulfilling if your questions can be addressed during your lifetime.

■

To posit a question that is plausible, actionable, and useful, you must know what has been shown by previous research, where technology stands, and the problems and needs of society. These require facts. A single mind working alone rarely grows innovation in the sciences that are empiric (based on the collection of data). Instead, science develops out of years of collective knowledge. Mathematicians and physicists generally achieve star power in their late 20s and early 30s. In one study, botanists and geologists did not achieve their greatest accomplishments until, on average, the ripe old age of 52 years. Experience and learning are needed to mature the thinking of empirical scientists. Just as you have begun to practice keener observation, so knowledge must be gained from amassing and understanding the observations of others.

Few things in life are more mind-expanding than reading. In the office of Lewis Kuller, the famed cardiovascular researcher and innovator, stacks of papers, books, and journals cover every available table and chair. Meeting with him presents quite a quandary—the meek simply stand rather than trying to figure out if it is okay to move a stack. The aggressive hand him the debris covering a chair and make themselves comfortable. If you flip through any of the scores of journals lying around the office, you find that Kuller has underlined many passages, showing that he has read each paper in each and every publication. Fascinating articles arrive regularly to the inboxes of his friends on topics far afield from Kuller's own interests. I recently received one, for example, about the genetics of birth weight—mind you, his area of science is heart disease. Suffice it to say, Kuller's pattern of reading is wide-ranging.

Reading regularly and broadly will expand your exposure to questions and solutions. Feel free to delve deeper when you find topics of interest. But never swap depth for breadth. Broad-based knowledge exposure will almost surely get you thinking about new questions, new answers, and new possibilities.

■

Here are some important plausible, actionable, and useful questions posed by scientific giants of the past (some you will encounter later in the book):

- Why do some women admitted to a single obstetrical hospital in the mid-1800s die of puerperal fever shortly after childbirth whereas others do not? (Semmelweis)
- Does hormone therapy (HT) use among post-menopausal women in the United States in the 1990s reduce the risk of coronary heart disease and stroke? (Women's Health Initiative investigators)
- How does a king living in the third century, B.C., know that a crown said to be made of pure gold is really made of pure gold? (Archimedes)

- How can modern American teenagers be prevented from becoming regular cigarette smokers? (Gladwell—not yet answered)
- What behaviors are observed among chimpanzees living in natural conditions in Gombe National Park in the late twentieth century? (Goodall)
- What causes patients of mental asylums and orphanages at the turn of the twentieth century to die of pellagra? (Goldberger)

Observations or previous research motivated each of these questions. Each was unanswered. Each was of great interest and immense use to science and humanity, and each seemed possible to answer in its time.

But these questions no longer represent general areas of interest. They have become like fully developed characters—truly alive. The way you have gotten to "know" each question is by incorporating in each a, "Who," "What," "When," "Where," and sometimes "Why." Sound like detective work? It should. When you get to know a character or a question, you are conducting an inquiry. Every detail is an object of curiosity, and once you describe the person or the question they become real and meaningful. A general area of interest sparks a question but facts define it.

Notice that although they are specific, these famous scientific questions are remarkably free from frames. When frames creep into the posing of a question, the answer will likely not deviate from the habitual. Frame-free questions maximize the generation of ideas. Goldberger derived his frame-free question directly from what he saw rather than from his expectations. The Who: inmates; the What: pellagra; the When: at the turn of the twentieth century; and the Where: mental asylums and orphanages. He did not accept the standard question, "Which infectious disease causes pellagra?" Instead, he posed the question as "What causes… " or rephrased, "Why do the specific individuals that seem to be at the greatest risk die of this specific disease?" Without a frame, he was free to observe that inmates contracted pellagra but staff at the same institutions did not—the sentinel clue that led him to discover that pellagra is a nutritional deficiency.

■

What was the question in the mind of Ignaz Semmelweis, who came
to the Vienna General Hospital in 1846 to be a lowly junior assistant
to the famed obstetrical Professor Kline and left having discovered
how to make childbirth safer for millions of women? "Why," the new
attending asked, "do some women in labor admitted to one ward die
of puerperal fever shortly after childbirth, and women in other wards
do not?"

Puerperal fever, now known to be infection by bacteria such as
Staphylococcus aureus struck down women in the nineteenth century,
seemingly at random. A healthy mother after a normal delivery would
develop a fever and genital inflammation, and within hours she would
have progressed to sepsis, coma, and death. The frame held by physicians at
the time was that all disease was generated by a balance of humors unique
to each person. But the women being admitted to the Vienna General
Hospital believed that disease somehow emanated from some aspect of
the hospital. Their pleas to be admitted to the ward of the hospital they
considered safer were ignored. Semmelweis listened. To his chagrin, he
found that indeed, deaths were far higher in the First division, where residents delivered babies (12%), than in the Second division, where mid-
wives performed deliveries (4%). What caused the disparity between the
two divisions? Meticulous data collection revealed that the only difference
was the staffing, but the reason that different staffing led to different outcomes remained a mystery.

The breakthrough came tragically. Semmelweis's friend, Jacob
Kolletschka, was accidentally poked with a scalpel during a puerperal
fever autopsy, became febrile, and died. His symptoms and pathology
on autopsy mirrored those of the dying women. It was the clue that
Semmelweis needed in order to realize that puerperal fever was being
passed from ill women to healthy women through "cadaverous particles"
sticking to the hands of residents who, as part of their modern obstetrical
training, regularly performed autopsies. Death was accompanying doctors' best intentions to understand the nature of disease. By enforcing a
policy of strict hand-washing, Semmelweis slashed the maternal mortality rate to 1.3%.

Unfortunately, the story did not end happily. Doctors did not accept the chlorine solution Semmelweis made them use, which reddened and chaffed their hands. They refused to wash their hands. Others, reading Semmelweis's work from England, declared that he had found nothing new, although they did not understand the implications of his revolutionary discovery. When his term at the hospital expired, Semmelweis was not reappointed. He moved to Pest (modern Budapest), where he worked as an unpaid obstetrician at the small St. Rochus hospital. There, he again virtually eliminated puerperal fever. Still, his method and the theory behind it were not accepted and not widely adopted. Eventually, his mind broke and he died prematurely in an insane asylum. It took another 100 years for the practice of hand-washing to be generally adopted, but today it is the mainstay of infection control that makes childbirth and other medical procedures safe.

Semmelweis's question contained a "Who": women shortly after childbirth. It contained a "What": death from puerperal fever. The "When" was in the mid-1800s, and the "Where" was a single obstetrical hospital. From this very specific question, he explored many possibilities with respect to "Why." Each of the "Who, What, When, and Where" questions came directly from Semmelweis's observations. Each was actionable. He did not let preconceptions influence his question, which if he had allowed the current frame to interfere, would have become, "Which humors cause the death of this woman and which humors cause the death of that woman?" Rather, he asked the frame-free and transformational question: "Why do some women die while others do not?"

Sometimes the ingenious answers are right in front of us if we are only able to ask the right questions. If we assemble the basic pieces of the question from observation and information rather than from preconception, then we are on our way to innovation. Plausible, actionable, and useful questions can reveal insights transformational to science and humanity. Questions specified in terms of "Who", "What", "When", and "Where" can produce enlightening answers. Questions phrased too narrowly on the one hand or too fantastically or broadly on the other, run the risk of generating answers that take us nowhere. In the farcical novel *The Hitchhiker's Guide to the Galaxy*, the ultimate computer Deep Thought is asked, "What is the meaning of Life, the Universe, and Everything?" After eons of pondering, the ultimate computer finds the universal answer, but it is far from illuminating and satisfying. It is the number 42.

EXERCISES

1. For each of the classic questions posed above, identify a Who, What, When, Where, and (if relevant) Why? Explain why each is plausible, actionable, and useful.

2. From the newspaper, find a science story and identify what question the scientists were trying to sort out. Carefully pose the question in the way it likely was posed to come up with a solution. Now again pose the question in other ways that would not have led to the solution.

3. Identify the Who, What, When, and Where of a current scientific or medicinal problem in the world. Then think of a couple of different ways to ask a frame-free Why (if the cause is not known), or How (if the cause is known) about the problem. Consider in particular differences between one event or situation and the norm. (For example: "Why do American children get fat?" "How can we best deal with an oil spill in the Gulf of Mexico?"—each question has a particular place and target and is free from preconceptions such as that obesity is a disease rather than a consequence of lifestyle or that oil must be removed). Gather empirical information and observations on your question, and come up with three possible plausible, actionable, and useful solutions to each.

14

How Is a Marriage Like a Matchbox?

"…analogy is the very blue that fills the whole sky of cognition—analogy is everything, or very nearly so, in my view."

—*Douglas R. Hofstadter*

Think of innovation as the opening of the American West. If every frontiersman and homesteader had gone by a single route, little of the fertile landmass between the Mississippi and the West Coast would have been discovered and exploited. Each new set of explorers opened up a route for others to traverse. Louis and Clark headed up the Missouri and then west to Oregon. The Mormons trekked to Utah. The Argonauts opened the southern Santa Fe Trail. With only one trail, prospects would have been limited, but with many, land and opportunity were in abundance.

So it is with innovation. Innovation tools, starting with analogy, increase alternatives and open new avenues. Using a range of tools you can explore a wide terrain of ideas. As you make your way toward your destination, I urge you to delight in every wild notion and flight of fantasy. These may take you afar from your original trail and if so you may decide that the new course has its own merits, or you may decide that you are better off returning to the original route. Either way, you will have enjoyed the adventure.

Analogy and a series of other techniques that you will be learning in the next chapters are tools for generating new ideas. They are the **G** (Generate all possible solutions) step of the **PIG In MuD** innovation process. The **G** for generative step is all about growing the innovation space.

■

Analogy is one of the tools most commonly used for scientific discovery. Hiero, king of Syracuse, contracted to have an artisan make him a magnificent crown using a precisely weighed amount of gold, so the story goes. Exquisitely crafted, the crown was a thing of beauty that delighted the monarch. But shortly thereafter, the king received a troubling tip that the artisan had cheated him. The gold, it was alleged, was contaminated with silver.

Archimedes, known for his brilliance in mathematics and physics, was summoned. "Is the accusation true?" the king asked. "I do not know how one could tell," Archimedes replied, "Let me consider the problem," and he went to sit in the bath to think. Sinking into the water, he noticed that the more of his body he immersed, the more water ran out of the tub. A light went off in his head. Could this be the solution? It needed to be tested. He took equal weight blocks of gold and silver and submerged them into a tub of water. The amount of water that ran out of the tub (lost) for silver was greater than the amount of water lost for gold. That is, the bulkiness of silver exceeded that of gold. Now Archimedes turned back to the crown. If the accusation was true, more water would run out than should for the weight of gold—and that is just what happened. The artisan was arrested. Archimedes was rewarded. And the world got an innovative law of physics: Archimedes' law, which says that a submerged object will displace an amount of water equal to its volume. A body has volume like gold has volume. Archimedes was thinking in an analogy.

■

Unlike metaphor, which is a linguistic concept in which two things are equated, analogy compares things but does not imply that they are the same.

Analogy extends the concept of metaphor in three ways. First, in an analogy, because the things being compared are only similar (not the same), they are also clearly different. More fundamentally, analogies provide insights into the nature of relationships. To demonstrate, consider these examples of simple analogies:

- Warm is to Hot as _____ is to Cold (Answer: Cool)
- How is a sock like a sweater?

Warm is to hot as cool is to cold makes sense because warm is a less extreme version of hot and cool is a less extreme version of cold. Similarly, a sock is like a sweater because they both keep you warm, they can both be knitted, they can both be made of wool, and so forth. But no one would suggest that warm is the equivalent of hot or that a sock can be exchanged for a sweater. Analogies have their similarities, but they only go so far.

Second, analogy is not confined to language; it also relates to logic. Archimedes did not (so far as we know) get into the tub and, upon displacing the water, say, "Eureka! My body is to a crown as gold is to volume." Without saying it, he understood that his body was displacing water because of its bulk (one wonders whether anxiety about his size might have contributed to this great insight, but it is not my place to cast unjustified aspersions).

Finally, metaphor is the linguistic representation of cognitive frames. Analogy is a more adaptable tool that can put frames in new contexts. Indeed, analogy, by making novel parallels, can help eliminate frames.

∎

Consider relating the following:
- How is a marriage like a matchbox?

Did you instantly rattle off as many similarities as you did to the question, "How is a sock like a sweater?" Likely not. You do not normally think of marriages and matchboxes in the same category. To connect them you must stretch to find parallels. Consider: a marriage and a matchbox can both hold things together; both can catch on fire; both have eight letters; and you can pick them both up in a bar.

Try this one:

- How are dreams like a clothes dryer?

Again, this is a stretch. Consider the following similarities: a dream and a dryer can both cause things to tumble; both can lead you to feel you have lost something; they can mix things up; and their action is fleeting.

■

Metaphor and analogy, says Pulitzer Prize-winning author Douglas Hofstadter, are at the very heart of human cognition. Metaphors define the "chunks" into which we process memories. Analogies help determine what gets chunked. Think of analogy as metaphor's sister – a sister who is more subtle and shrewd. Subjectivity and adaptability are needed to put into context language and memories.

Hofstadter notes that a single idea can be expressed with different levels of intensity:

- He didn't give a flying f***.
- He didn't give a good G**damn.
- He didn't give a tinker's damn.
- He didn't give a damn.
- He didn't give a darn.
- He didn't give a hoot.
- He didn't care at all.
- He didn't mind.
- He was indifferent.

Each would be (at least somewhat) appropriately used in a particular context but inappropriate in another. "He didn't give a flying f***" would be unacceptable in many professional situations, whereas "He was indifferent" might seem an odd phraseology during a rowdy exchange in a barroom. All are metaphors but the appropriate one is chosen so as to match the frame to the circumstance. In choosing the appropriate phrase, you're thinking, "That's how it was said last time I was out drinking but not the last time I sat with the Board of Directors." Dozens of considerations go into your decision about the appropriate use of language. These rely on memories about previous situations and about subtleties of word meaning. Isn't it remarkable that all of this happens within the split-second it takes to plunk down a bottle of beer?

So analogies are an almost constant feature in thinking. They steer you through a jungle of inputs and memories. Socialization demands tight parameters that contain and direct their use, but they remain fluid. Indeed, they are powerful tools in finding new associations. Analogies connect concepts that are different but also similar – such insights allow you to loosely connect things you would not normally connect. It is no wonder then that analogies are used so ubiquitously in scientific creativity.

■

Since time immemorial, analogy has been a central tool for scientific innovation. Bear with me for a moment while I touch on but a few analogies applied to science through the ages. Vitruvius, a Roman architect and engineer, noticed similarities between the behavior of sound and waves of water. As water ricochets off barriers, so echoes might represent a ricochet of sound. A similar analogy was drawn between sound and light in the seventeenth century, leading to the theory of light as wave. Finally, Max Planck and Albert Einstein created the field of Quantum Mechanics through combining two analogies: light as wave and light as particle.

Newton's understanding of forces on celestial bodies came from his use of analogy. His transformational insight about how the moon revolves around the earth came about as follows. Observing an apple falling from a tree, he discovered the concept of gravity. The moon, he argued, is like an apple continually falling toward the surface of the earth. On the other hand, at any position in its rotation, the moon possesses a certain velocity that is perpendicular to the radius of the circle and should cause the moon if it continued along a straight line to fly off into space. Gravitational pull and velocity, Newton realized, counteract each other. Mix in some mathematics from the Pythagorean Theorem and voilá, Newton used the apple analogy to help explain celestial orbits.

Inspiration for the design of the next generation of semi-conductors came from the model of a toy. The semi-conductor industry is forever thirsting for smaller and smaller components. Recently, Jeremy Levy, Physics professor at the University of Pittsburgh found inspiration for a breakthrough from an unusual source: Etch A Sketch®. The decades-old children's toy uses a stylus to scrape lines in aluminum powder from the underside of a glass screen. Levy used an atomic force microscope tip to produce strokes between two layers of insulators (lanthanum aluminum oxide and strontium titanium oxide). The charge from the microscope minutely separated the oxide layers to form a line for semi-conduction. Lines 2 nanometers wide (40 billionths of an inch) or 1000 times smaller than silicon-based transistors, were created. That is, the Etch A Sketch® concept created the tiniest ever platform for designing new semi-conductors.

The parallel between a toy and a technical advance also allowed Michelle Khine to find success. A new faculty hire at a brand-new university, Khine found herself without the needed facilities to make the key tool for her work: microfluidics chips. One evening, while cooking in her kitchen, she remembered the remarkable properties of one of her favorite childhood toys, Shrinky Dinks. The toy's thin plastic surface allows children to create designs and watch them shrink in the oven. To create a microfluidics mold, Khine needed raised lines on small plates of plastic. Shrinky Dinks creates raised outlines when heated. She bought Shrinky Dinks plastic designed for computer printers, printed the needed pattern, and baked it in her toaster oven. Out came the perfect mold. Shrinky Dinks turns out to be a breakthrough application for creating microfluidics chips.

An analogy between drugs and infections is giving hope to cocaine addicts. An estimated 2.4 million Americans currently use cocaine. Although some will ultimately want to get "off" the drug as they spiral into economic deprivation, most find the addiction too powerful to kick. Thomas Kosten and team at the Baylor College of Medicine may have an answer. Kosten has designed a cocaine vaccine. Vaccines eliminate pathogens so why can't they eliminate foreign substances like drugs? Cocaine does not normally elicit an allergic reaction because small molecules do not trigger the immune cascade. But the scientists found that if white blood cells can get a big enough bite (if cocaine is attached to a carrier antigen such as cholera toxin), then vaccinated subjects mount an effective antibody response. In early clinical trials, about one-third of patients mounted antibodies and no longer felt the effects of the cocaine. Of course addicts can overcome the vaccine by simply using more drugs but if sufficiently motivated, vaccinated users may be able to quit.

I could go on and on (as you can see). The German chemist Fredrich August Kekulè envisioned the six-member carbon ring structure of benzene (and thus explained benzene's 1:1 carbon–hydrogen ratio) in a daydream of a snake seizing its own tail, a symbol common in ancient cultures known as the Endless Knot.

Alexander Graham Bell used his experience in recording voice vibrations as a Professor of Vocal Physiology at Boston University when he developed the telephone. His breakthrough discovery was that an electromagnetic current caused reeds at both ends of a wire to similarly vibrate. But how was such a finding useful? Through analogy to his previous voice recordings, Bell realized that the complex pulsation of the reeds set in motion by electromagnetism replicated that of the human voice.

■

Analogies can also be a powerful way to examine similarities and differences across phenomena within a single scientific discipline. Let's call this "horizontal" integration, as opposed to the more traditional examples that we have just seen of "vertical" integration. Vertical integration is the deep understanding of a single phenomenon—let's say voice vibrations as they can be visually observed in a pulsating reed. Horizontal integration involves heuristic insights that come from asking, "How is this disease similar or different from that disease?"

In the eighteenth century, smallpox created devastating epidemics that killed and maimed. A horribly pitted face was the legacy smallpox left to many survivors. When Edward Jenner returned home from medical training to practice in rural Gloucestershire, he noticed something about smallpox epidemics that intrigued him. Milkmaids did not become ill. They came down with a similar yet much more benign disease called cowpox, but they never seemed to suffer from the more devastating affliction. Jenner hypothesized that pus from cowpox lesions might protect against small pox. The theory had been previously proposed, but no one had been bold enough to test it. In the 1780s, Jenner injected cowpox pus under the skin of a few selected research patients, among them his 18-month-old son. Lethal smallpox, when it next swept through the county, affected none of his subjects. The Royal Society refused to publish Jenner's initial 1796 report, ridiculing him as a naïve country bumpkin. But by 1840, the British government formally adopted Jenner's recommendation for immunization. As the vaccine improved, it became the centerpiece for a World Health Organization eradication campaign. In 1980, smallpox was declared the first pathogenic virus entirely eliminated from the face of the Earth.

■

I end my reverie on analogy with one last example, a personal one related to my work on preeclampsia. Preeclampsia is a terrifying, progressive illness that occurs only during pregnancy. It starts with a blip in blood pressure. Next, the woman spills protein into her urine. Then her kidneys begin to fail; blood clots clog vital organs; she seizes; and, if the progression is not stopped, she slides into terminal coma. The only way to save the woman is to deliver the baby, no matter how premature the infant may be. This is a "Sophie's choice" in medicine: mother's health versus baby's prematurity.

Early in my career I became intrigued by the similarities between preeclampsia and heart disease. Although hypertension characterizes both, the scientific community had soundly rejected the link. Yet, there seemed to be too many coincidences. Women who develop preeclampsia are more likely to have had prepregnancy overweight, hypertension, diabetes, and kidney disease, which are all risks for heart disease. So a colleague and I went out on a limb. We floated the audacious proposal that preeclampsia is accelerated cardiovascular disease in pregnancy. To support this idea, we spent a decade showing that preeclamptic women have metabolic syndrome (overweight, hyperglycemia, hyperlipidemia, and hypertension) not just before but during pregnancy. In the meantime, other researchers showed that these women go on within a decade after pregnancy to develop premature heart disease and stroke. Today, most scientists accept the link between preeclampsia and cardiovascular disease. Indeed, a history of severe preeclampsia in a prior pregnancy is now considered a red flag that should prompt clinicians to screen women for cardiovascular risk.

■

Analogies are one of the most commonly used tools for opening the innovation space and generating alternative ideas. While recognizing differences, analogies reveal previously unrecognized similarities. Revealing surprising parallels, analogies can take knowledge about one thing and apply it to another. Analogies generate new insights.

EXERCISES

1. Complete the following sentences and explain the concept that linked the two analogies:

- Wolf is to Mammal as Frog is to   Amphibian; Toad; Tadpole

- Allow is to Permit as Find is to   Lose; Search; Locate

(*continued*)

CONTINUED

- Glove is to hand as software is to   Computer; Internet;
                                            Monitor
- Furs are to Eskimos as Credit is to   Shopper; Card;

2. Try to identify all of the similarities between these things. Don't take a lot of time thinking about this—just write down anything that comes to mind.
   - How is history like a mango?
   - How is temperature like a yo-yo?
   - How is photosynthesis like a symphony?
   - How is a dream like a painting?

3. Analogy is such a common tool in science that you find it everywhere. Go out and find a few examples of scientists either historically or currently using analogies to create innovative solutions.

15

Flip It!

"Discovery consists of looking at the same thing as everyone else and thinking something different."

—Albert Szent Gyorgi

"If the only tool you have is a hammer, you tend to see every problem as a nail."

—Abraham Maslow

Ever play with a Slinky®? It has this wonderful ability to stretch, contract, and reverse directions. When you take a question and broaden it, narrow the perspective, turn it on its head, and marry it with another question, you've turned your mind into a Slinky®. Fun! Just as with analogy, tools that reorganize and rearrange questions and solutions are provided to expand your idea space. The hope is to catapult you out of your frames and to add further generative possibilities to the **PIG In MuD** innovation process. Reorganization and rearrangement expands the number of and originality of alternatives.

Several tools fall into the category of reorganization and rearrangement. They are like hammers and screwdrivers. A hammer is not terribly useful in removing a screw and a screwdriver is not what you reach for to pound in a nail. What you really want are enough different implements in your toolbox so that you can accommodate different situations and take advantage of all opportunities.

■

Broadening your perspective

In Zen Buddhism, a table is not a table. It is the aggregation of all things from which the table came. From the carpenter and the wood, but also the soil and water that nourished the wood, the insect and mammal remains that contributed nitrogen to the soil, and on and on. Buddhists believe that there is no individuality—not even in ourselves—because all living things are connected in an ever-enlarging web. Think about the food you eat, the bed you sleep in, the roof over your head. Where did these things come from? What contributed to the things that those things came from?

Broadening your perspective is an innovation tool that reflects this approach towards mind-expansion. When seeking solutions to a given problem, a common tactic is to narrow the perspective in an effort to gain efficiency and validity. Here you do the opposite. Broadening the perspective produces movement away from standard frames and highlights alternative, untried, and previously unconsidered pathways.

■

In the 1950s, ocean-going freighters were becoming increasingly costly to operate, so much so that shrinking profit margins threatened the industry's very existence. The shipping industry made a series of attempts to reduce costs in addressing the question: "How do we make ships more economical at sea as they transport goods?" They built faster ships that used less fuel and employed smaller and more efficient crews. Still costs remained non-competitive. Finally, in desperation, the industry association hired a consultant who broadened the perspective beyond asking, "How do we make ships more economical at sea?" The enlarged question became, "How might the shipping industry reduce costs?" When put this way, the answer became obvious. Unlike many other industries where personnel are the primary cost-driver, in shipping, the largest sunk cost is the ship itself. So, any time a ship is not traveling means a major erosion of profit margins. Thus, the solution became to reduce ship time at dock. Historically, ships languished at shore awaiting cargo and cargo piled up at dock at risk for theft. Within the new framework, ships needed to be packed before they arrived at port. Container technology does just that: by delivering already-packed goods, containers reduce port time, theft in port, and costs by 60%. Reframing the question from economies at sea to the more general one of overall reduction of cost provided the insight that saved the global shipping industry.

One of the most innovative theories of modern times is evolution. It, too, can be seen as broadening the perspective. Charles Darwin was trained as a naturalist when naturalists viewed the categorization of life within the frame of "deity-guided evolution." He was trained to ask the question, "How does this specific life form fit with other life forms created by God?" In his extensive travels including the historic round-the-world voyage on the Beagle, he studied fossils, tortoises, finches, mockingbirds, and other life forms. His expansion, based on these observations, became a question that was non-sectarian and thus shockingly radical: "How did all life forms come to be?" Upon his return home to the Darby countryside, he continued to ponder this, adding new observations from the farming practice of livestock selective breeding.

Twenty years later, he finally published his magnum opus, *On the Origin of Species by Means of Natural Selection*, proposing the theory that the characteristics of species over time change or evolve. In an even more revolutionary assertion, Darwin proposed that the means by which species evolve is that inherited traits which provide a reproductive advantage gradually become more common in the population. That is, characteristics that make individuals better adapted to their environments are selected, a process he called *natural selection*. Natural selection involves processes of random inheritance and brutal competition for survival. Evolutionary theory could be envisioned only when Darwin expanded beyond the divine.

Broadening the perspective can also mean shifting frame from individuals to populations. If you lived in 1955, your surroundings would have been punctuated by ashtrays on every restaurant table and in every office. Fifty-five percent of American men smoked, as did about one-fifth of women. Camel cigarettes advertised using the tagline, "*More doctors smoke Camels than any other cigarette.*" In 1964, this all changed. *The Surgeon General's Report on The Health Consequences of Smoking* concluded that cigarettes cause lung cancer. Smokers were advised to simply stop. But public health experts quickly realized that many individuals left to their own devices simply could not kick the habit. The Centers for Disease Control and Prevention (CDC) and other agencies instituted a series of population approaches. They regulated tobacco advertising, slapped health warnings on cigarette packs, required disclosure of levels of tar and nicotine on cigarettes, and added taxes.

In the 1970s, the population approach expanded even further. The 1972 Surgeon General's Report identified the health risks of second-hand smoke. It changed the paradigm by framing smokers as not simply a risk to themselves but also to others. Within families and workplaces, smokers were newly envisioned as putting cohabitants at risk. Municipalities, states, and even whole countries outside the United States enacted legislation to ban smoking in public places. Smoking became seen as an environmental toxin. Smokers became social pariahs. Tobacco use morphed from an accepted habit to a killer and then again from a personal demon to a plague on society.

Disease is complex. Scientific methods such as complex systems modeling and systems biology are stretching to capture that complexity by broadening the perspective. One robust example of systems modeling is ARCHIMEDES (developed over a period of more than 10 years by David Eddy) which predicts the natural history of diabetes. ARCHIMEDES is an informatics web of differential equations that start with glucose metabolism. It then adds layers of computer algorithms describing the relationships between elevated sugar and its associated risks (high lipids, high blood pressure, heart attack, etc.). Treatment effects and health economics components of the model overarch all of this. In its complexity, ARCHIMEDES is a whiz at predicting outcomes. In an impressive show of muscle, ARCHIMEDES went head-to-head with nine major glucose-lowering clinical trials. The trial results, involving thousands of patients, dozens of years, and millions of dollars, as compared to the model's predictions, resulted in a correlation of 0.99—almost perfectly identical.

Broadening the perspective can mean expanding a question's scope (á la shipping, Darwin, or tobacco control) or its complexity (á la systems modeling). Always it means reaching beyond the standard frame.

■

Narrowing your perspective

I once saw a fantastic art installation. From a central node emanated an array of yellow, scarlet, and blue fibers, like the spokes of a brightly colored wheel. At the end of each spoke splayed a secondary array of fibers and from each of those yet another array. A bare tap to the center node and the entire installation lit up. A touch to the center of an individual cluster illuminated just that group. A fingertip to one of the endpoints displayed only a lonely point of color.

A problem of great scope or intricacy often needs to be broken down. Isolated elements may lend themselves to individual solutions. The hope is to touch a node that is sufficiently central that it will light up the system. If you doubt that fixing one small piece can impact the whole, consider a bridge. Take out one support or one girder and the whole thing collapses.

The problem of economic advancement in the developing world seems insurmountably complex. Greg Mortenson, former nurse and now internationally respected humanitarian, has said the solution is to educate girls. Years ago, while attempting to climb K2 in Northern Pakistan, he developed altitude sickness and was cared for by villagers in the remote locale of Korphi. The primitive nature of everyday life and the lack of educational opportunity shocked him. He vowed to repay the village for their kindness by building a school. His crusade to raise funds was not easy, but it eventually paid off in the successful international nonprofits Pennies for Peace and Central Asia Institute, which build schools in Pakistan and Afghanistan. Specifically, Mortenson (2006) espouses in his best-selling book, *Three Cups of Tea*, that education of girls brings socio-economic reform, decreases the population explosion, and improves hygiene and health. As such, female education has become a goal for the World Health

Organization. Starting from a multifaceted social problem, Mortenson brought laser focus to a single intervention. To eliminate world poverty, he believes, educating girls is a central node.

Looking for that sentinel node while breaking down a problem is what physicians do when diagnosing medical illnesses. They start with a large number of possible options and then narrow and narrow these until they arrive at the one that, if treated, will cure all the patient's symptoms. In real life, physicians often leap from a set of signs and symptoms to a gestalt impression. Unfortunately, hindsight and context biases may interject error. The more rigorous, evidence-based approach is to use Bayesian considerations. The process goes like this. You consider the initial probability that the patient may have one of several diagnoses. You then look for signs and symptoms or order tests. Each new piece of information increases or decreases the likelihood of each possible diagnosis. Eventually, the probabilities support a single diagnostic contender. That is what you treat.

A 68-year-old man (let's call him Mr. Pitiable) comes to the Emergency Department complaining of "swimming in my head." On exam, the patient is severely dehydrated, with low blood pressure, parched lips, and sunken eyes. After extensive questioning, he admits to you that he is suffering from unrelenting diarrhea.

The differential diagnosis of dizziness is huge. However, already you, as the physician, have limited the diagnostic possibilities by eliciting the key fact that the dizziness is a result of diarrhea-induced dehydration. Still, there are multiple possible causes for diarrhea, including infection, diabetes, tumor, hormonal problems, and so forth. But you notice something unusual.

Mr. Pitiable has darkened, thickened skin on his knuckles, back, and chest. This finding greatly telescopes the possibilities. Celiac disease? Zinc deficiency? Vitamin B deficiency? You draw labs to support or refute any of these possibilities and find a very low level of Vitamin B6, the cause of pellagra (yes, the same pellagra that our hero Joseph Goldberger battled). But with food fortification, pellagra is virtually unheard of in modern America. How is it possible for a modern American man to be suffering from this bygone condition? Mr. Pitiable's unexpected laboratory finding takes you back to his bedside. Has the patient been living outside of the country? Does he follow an unusual diet? No and no. But he is taking several medications, including one for high blood pressure called hydralazine. When you research side effects from hydralazine, it turns out that very rarely it can cause such a syndrome. Upon replacing his hydralazine with another blood pressure medication, the diarrhea, skin condition, and dizziness all go away. Mr. Pitiable sends you an ice chest full of fresh meat to show his gratitude.

The notion that you can dissect a problem and find some node, some sweet spot that, once touched, will have a huge effect, is remarkably intriguing. And it can work. Lowering lipid levels with a single pill prevents many from developing the multifaceted syndrome of heart disease. Vaccination has eliminated a spate of childhood diseases and reduced infant mortality. Fortifying with Vitamin B6 eliminates the range of signs and symptoms that constitute pellagra.

■

Reversal

Public health has saved more lives than all medical treatments combined. The CDC figures that of the 30 years of life expectancy Americans have gained in the past century, 25 are attributable to clean air, potable water, safe food, vaccines, and tobacco control. Yet these facts are almost universally unknown. Why? Because public health is a classic case of reversal and reversals are not intrinsically easy to conceptualize.

Public health is successful when nothing happens. A person suffering a massive myocardial infarction will do anything to survive—even have a stranger (presumably a cardiovascular surgeon) crack open his chest. But that same heart attack victim may have neglected to take the blood pressure medication that would have prevented the life-threatening condition.

When was the last time you drank a glass of ice water and thought, "Gee I'm glad I won't be getting typhoid from my tap today"?

A negative is the goal of public health, not a positive. Medical care is easy to appreciate because it is the presence of disease. Public health is hard to understand because it is the absence of disease. But obliviousness to absence is dangerous. First, to maintain the absence of disease takes federal and state willpower. Would you consider marching on Washington shouting, "We don't have enough absence and we're not going to take it anymore"? You should. Food-borne illnesses are estimated by the CDC to cause a whopping 76 million illnesses, 325,000 hospitalizations, and 5,000 deaths in the United States each year. Asthma has reached epidemic proportions while poor air quality remains a summer constant in several major cities. Head injuries are on the rise as nine states have revoked or limited motorcycle helmet laws. Absence of food-poisoning outbreaks, asthma cases, and head injuries is exactly what you should be fighting for.

Second, obliviousness to absence makes it difficult for many people to practice life-saving prevention. In the best of all worlds, you regularly brush your teeth, eat a healthy diet, use your seatbelt, never smoke, and tap a designated driver when drinking alcohol. Except that often you don't. Even when people have a known risk for illness, many don't make prevention a priority. Of the more than 75 million Americans with high blood pressure, only about two-thirds know it and only half of those have their blood pressure under control. Hypertension is the number one risk factor for heart disease death. But it is hard to take a pill every day so that a heart attack is something you will *not* have.

Reversal can turn a positive to a negative (public health) or change the actor to the action. Edward De Bono, author of *Lateral Thinking*, suggests reversing our thinking about parking cars. Currently, the use of parking meters means that drivers control the amount of time they park their cars. A reversal would be that meters would be eliminated and cars would control the amount of time they are parked. Meaning? Legislation would dictate that all parked cars keep their lights on. Because leaving the lights on will eventually drain the battery, the duration of parking would be limited by the car, not the driver.

Better Place (CEO Shai Agassi), the Israeli start-up company commit-ted to making Israel the first nation free of petroleum-powered automo-biles, flipped the idea of who owns a major component of the car. The company avoids the anchoring effect of price, as we saw in Chapter 9,

Overcoming Bias. Rather than passing on the high price of the battery to the consumer, Better Place sells the body of the car but owns the batteries. The batteries are leased on a mileage-based monthly installment plan. Thus, Better Place reverses car battery ownership.

The office supply division of 3M has benefited to the tune of billions of dollars in sales through a reversal. In 1967, Spencer Silver, a 3M employee, invented a type of glue that as judged by the industry standard of adhesiveness, did not make the grade. Finding an application for this weakling glue was elusive. Finally 3M settled on the Post-It Bulletin Board coated with the glue so it could be used to attach pieces of paper without the need for tacks. Unfortunately, the Post-It Board also attracted unsightly dust. Stellar sales did not follow. Some years later, Art Fry, a colleague of Silver's, became frustrated that bookmarks kept falling out of his hymn book. So using some of the adhesive, he created sticky bookmarks. These morphed into notepaper—and the rest is history. Today, Post-Its are ubiquitous on boards, refrigerators, computers, you name it. So a surface attracting papers became papers adhering to a surface. Turns out this was a double-sided reversal, because Post-Its' poor adhesive qualities, initially thought to be the glue's greatest weakness, also turned out to be its greatest strength.

■

Reversal can be remarkably useful in getting straight to the end of a problem. We generally approach tasks such as getting to work on time using a forward-looking set of steps (such as wake up, brush teeth, take a shower, eat breakfast, and drive). However, many tasks, especially ones with multiple decision points, are better approached backward.

When packing for a trip, you prepare depending on the number of days, the expected weather, and the activities on your itinerary. That's not the starting point, it's the endpoint. Your thinking process might go something like this: "I'll be at the beach five days but since I'll sweat a lot I'd better take seven shirts." What you've just done is to predict an outcome and act on that basis. So you started at the end, stepped back to one step before the end, and you continue to take steps backward until you get to the beginning—your suitcase.

Let's think backward about how you convince the scientific community that your newest breakthrough idea will actually work. Let's say you have invented a new medical device. You want to show that it is safe, effective, and works by a plausible mechanism. To get to these endpoints, you step back and design a series of experiments. For each experiment, you consider all of the possible criticisms that might be mounted against your experimental design. Those anticipated critiques make you step back and redesign some of the approaches. Then for each experiment, you step back to plan the resources needed. What you have done is to start with the desired outcome and from it worked backward.

■

Recombination and rearrangement

Andrea White is a wildly creative writer of adolescent novels. Her gift is to draw imaginative plot lines from story elements that seem unrelated. Who else would write a book uniting a disabled boy, Winston Churchill (his imaginary friend), and an obsession with baseball? Intersections between disparate elements can create points of originality. Her novel combinations lead to striking insights.

In a book entitled *Surviving Antarctica: Reality TV 2083* (2005), White envisions a future world in which children will be schooled via television and a minimum daily intake of TV will be mandatory (a little reversal there?). The televised history course in the book features a reality show. In the 2083 season, a bunch of misfit kids voyage to Antarctica to reenact Robert F. Scott's expedition to the South Pole. If you remember what happened to Scott, then you can just imagine what the kids encounter—blowing snow; dwindling food supplies; and temperatures inviting frostbite. Scott and his crew reached the Pole only to find that they had been preceded by Roald Amundsen's Norwegian team. The starved and exhausted party all froze to death on the arduous trip back. The tension in White's book swirls around the fate of the vulnerable band of children. White combines unrelated elements of reality television, the future of education, exploration, and the exploitation of vulnerable children, to create a surprising and thought-provoking tale.

Combining incongruent people can be funny. Think Will Smith and Tommy Lee Jones in *Men in Black*. Combining incongruent disciplines can lead to invention. An historic meeting of materials chemists and molecular biologists at the Massachusetts Institute of Technology (MIT) led to the engineering of a virus that efficiently converts methane to ethylene. The surface of the engineered virus serves as a catalyst for the chemical reaction. Because viruses are so small, they provide a huge surface area, so the energy needed to drive the reaction is much reduced. The key accomplishment was achieved by Angela Belcher, who engineered the bacteriophage virus to coat itself with metals. The virus can be used in applications as diverse as building more efficient batteries, creating biofuels, and removing CO_2 from the environment.

Or consider a combination of ideas—Joelle Frechette and German Drazer from Johns Hopkins University have developed new microfluidics (manipulation of fluids through tiny channels) techniques for separating mixtures of particles. But if you walk into their lab, you would think they were just fooling around with LEGOs®. To demonstrate the trajectory of microparticles, they distributed LEGO pegs in a board and placed the board vertically in a fish tank filled with the gooey liquid glycerol. Much like playing a game of pachinko, they dropped in various-size ball bearings and watched how the balls tracked around the pegs. What they learned might be useful for designing devices and strategies for medical diagnostics and drug delivery.

As innovation is all about frame-shifting, then combining things that you wouldn't normally put together is yet one other way to get out of the box.

■

The opposite of reorganization and rearrangement is *functional fixedness*. Coined by psychologist Karl Duncker in the 1940s, the term refers to the observation that once we are taught a use for a particular object, we are fixed to that particular usage/function. Thus was born the discipline of gestalt psychology. Replacing the language of gestalt psychology with the vernacular of this book, function becomes our expectation for that object—our frame. To jump out of the fixed frame, you reorganize and rearrange the elements.

To demonstrate your innate tendency toward functional fixedness, try to solve this classic gestalt exercise called the candle problem. On a table you find a candle, a book of matches, and a box of thumbtacks. The task is, using only these things, to attach the candle to a wall next to the table so that the candle does not drip on the table below. Now before you read on, think about how you might solve this.

Most people try to attach the candle to the wall by fixing it with a thumbtack or melting it to the wall (neither of which work). The trick is to take the thumbtacks out of the box, put the candle in the box and attach the box to the wall with a thumbtack. Perhaps not surprisingly, if the context is altered only slightly—if the thumbtacks are found lying outside the empty box, then the solution becomes readily apparent. The more you are forced to rearrange things—particularly if this means altering usage or function—the more readily you get stuck. The need to alter the function of the box (which contains the tacks) so it becomes a candle base stumps most people. It is easy to see how you can break this frame through reorganization and rearrangement.

■

Rearrangement can involve moving around the pieces. But it can also entail changing the sequence, pace, or personnel. How does a research study of the social networks that spread sexually transmitted infections (STIs) gain trust of the prostitutes and drug pushers who are the study subjects? Employ data collectors with criminal records. Ex-cons originally from the same neighborhoods and streets where the research is to be conducted have credibility. Street-based studies by Rothenberg and colleagues on STIs have almost exclusively employed workers with the credential of being an ex-convict.

The Large Hadron Collider, the world's largest high energy particle accelerator, is perhaps also the world's best example of changing the pace. The faster and harder particle beams (protons or lead nuclei) collide, the smaller the elements produced. These super small particles are needed to detect the existence of the hypothetical Higgs boson. As yet unobserved, the Higgs boson is a massive scalar elementary particle with spin-0. It is thought to mediate mass and will help explain the origin of mass in the universe. The Hadron Collider lies under the Franco-Swiss border near Geneva, within a circular tunnel 17 miles in circumference. Funded and built in collaboration with engineers from more than 100 countries, the Collider will attain the greatest speeds known to man. Only at these super-fast speeds can scientists hope to answer fundamental questions in physics.

■

Broadening, narrowing, reversing, and recombining/rearranging all force you to look at a problem differently. They jolt you out of familiar frames and patterns of decision-making and free you to move into new idea space. You can use one, more, or all of these tools. The idea is to hammer and screw until you break down the walls of your habitual in-the-box thinking.

EXERCISES

1. Broaden your perspective and answer the question: How can we get kids to eat better?

2. Design a convenient and low-cost rain jacket. Try approaching the problem by defining sub-challenges and then solving or improving on each:
- What novel materials might work?
- How can we make the rain jacket more convenient to carry?
- What might a fashionable design look like?

(continued)

CONTINUED

3. Design a convenient and eco-friendly trash container. This time find the ways to break down the problem or narrow the perspective, and then answer each sub-question you pose to devise a solution.

4. Most science education games narrow the perspective by creating a smaller, simpler version of some facet of a more complex scientific law or theory. Find or imagine a science toy that narrows the perspective to demonstrate some specific aspect of science or technology. Write an advertisement that markets the fun of learning these scientific elements.

5. Brands can also succeed by total reversal: Rather than assuaging the customer's fears about the product, or trying to fix the negative aspects, some products highlight these negative features. Come up with some examples and ideas to do just that. Apply reversal to encouraging patients to be more compliant with taking their medications.

6. Brands like IKEA reverse the status quo—people hate shopping for furniture (there are too many choices, the salespeople are pushy, etc.), so IKEA made their furniture store a warehouse where people choose, transport, and assemble the furniture themselves. They added frills in other places: a ball pit for children, a good café, a refined simplicity. Science can do the same: design an intervention in which you reverse the prospect of having to exercise to being allowed to exercise.

7. A Rube Goldberg machine involves designing the most complicated way to complete a simple task. It is a crazy form of expansion in which the point is not to attain the outcome but to devise the most interesting route. Try playing a game with friends or colleagues in which the winner is the one who designs a Rube Goldberg machine for tipping over a bucket of water using the most comical set of steps.

16

A Man Walked into a Bar

"If at first the idea is not absurd, there is no hope for it."

—Albert Einstein

"The 'silly' question is the first intimation of some totally new development."

—Alfred North Whitehead

Some innovation tools that can go in your **g**enerative (remember the **PIG In MuD** innovation process) toolbox next to analogy and reorganization are devices for thinking sideways. *Lateral Thinking*, a 1990 book by Edward de Bono, describes methods for generating original ideas by working around cliché mental patterns. De Bono noted that our minds tend to perpetuate stereotypical thinking and resist change (sound familiar—i.e., frames?). The tools he developed were designed to sidestep frames by forcing your mind to follow non-linear paths towards uncertain ends.

Sometimes things do not follow a predictable course; such is the parable of the Chinese farmer's horse. A wise Chinese farmer's horse ran off. When his neighbor came to console him, the farmer said, "Who knows what's good or bad?" When the horse returned the next day with a herd of horses following, the neighbor came to offer congratulations. The farmer said, "Who knows what's good or bad?" Then the farmer's son broke his leg riding one of the new horses and the neighbor came to offer condolences. Again, the farmer said, "Who knows what's good or bad?" A few weeks later the army came for conscripts and the crippled son was not eligible to be marched off to war…Where does the story end? What is good and what is bad?

Science looks for right and wrong answers with the goal of efficiently weeding out the wrong so as to identify the right. But not every question has a single solution and the best path to a solution may be convoluted. Thinking sideways may or may not immediately lead to solutions. But it will surely take your mind where it had not gone before.

■

Jim and Lisa are out at Le Café Expensive celebrating their 30th wedding anniversary. Jim tenderly takes Lisa's hand, leans toward her, and whispers, "Darling, what present would you like for our anniversary? A mink coat? A Lexus? A diamond ring?" Lisa answers, "No need to buy me anything—I want a divorce." "Oh my!" Jim replies, "I wasn't planning on spending that much."

Jokes are the purest form of innovation. They jolt you out of a frame in a way that catches you entirely off guard. The comic campus newspaper *The Onion* is a font of great one-liners. Here are a few of their headlines.

"NASCAR Considers Single 21,500 Mile Race for 2011 Season"

"Obama to Create 17 New Jobs by Resigning and Finally Opening that Restaurant"

"New Google Phone Service Whispers Targeted Ads Directly into Users' Ears"

"Fluid Just Happy to Have Had Opportunity to Build Up in Kobe Bryant's Knee"

"Report: Majority of Government Doesn't Trust Citizens Either"

"Woman Constantly Treating Herself for Once"

"ACLU Defends Nazis' Right to Burn ACLU Headquarters"

"Kellogg's Worker Knew He Was Fired The Moment He Uttered The Word 'Unfrosted'"

"Anecdote Retired After 8 Years Of Stellar Service"

"Cruel Owner Deprives Laptop of Sleep"

"Fitness Researchers Hail Discovery of New Ab"

"Crash Test Dummy Steers Around Wall, Drives to Freedom"

"As Obese Population Rises, More Candidates Courting the Fat Vote"

"Sierra Leone Diamond Miner Devastated By News of Broken-Off Engagement"

"Massive Earthquake Reveals Entire Island Civilization Called 'Haiti'"

"New Law Forces CEOs to Humbly Shrug Before Receiving Massive Bonuses"

"Rich Guy Feeling Left Out of Recession"

"Report: 23% of Population Just Sort of Like That"

What makes jokes funny? Jokes are counterfactuals—ideas that are absurd. Sometimes they get you to anticipate some particular line of reasoning and then trick you by interjecting a logically inconsistent shift. Other times they are just plain reversals of widely held truisms or belief systems. Jokes are simultaneously both logical and illogical. But, at their core, jokes get you to trip over a cognitive frame.

Sorry but you're going to have to indulge me in a few more laughs. Whereas jokes from *The Onion*, generally rely on mixing frames, the following jokes from *Demotivators* are belief system reversals.

"Arrogance: The best leaders inspire by example. When that's not an option, brute intimidation works pretty well too."

"Blame: The secret to success is knowing who to blame for your failures."

"Blogging: Never before have so many people with so little to say said so much to so few."

"Corruption: I want either less corruption or more opportunity to participate in it."

"Despair: It's always darkest before it goes pitch black."

"Perseverance: The courage to ignore the obvious wisdom of turning back."

"Planning: Much work needs to be done before we can announce our
total failure to make any progress."

■

Why are jokes funny? No one really knows, but systems scientist Donald
Burke thinks it is because of evolution. His explanation is that humans
have developed uncontrolled reactions to threats. An infection threatens
your lungs and causes sneezing or coughing. A counterfactual threatens
your normal patterns of thought (frames) and causes laughing. So humor
is to illogicality as sneezing is to getting a virus up your nose. This explanation may make you feel better about laughing when you see people
jumping into shallow pools or slapping each other around. It may also
rationalize why people sometimes inappropriately begin to laugh upon
seeing a loved one hurt themselves. Such inappropriate reactions might
all result from your innate response to frame breaks.

■

This brings us to Ireland in the mid-1700s. The population had risen to
more than 1.5 million people. Streets were thronged with women, strings
of children at their backs, begging for crumbs of food. It was a time
when the rich turned a blind eye to the poor and the poor were starving.
Jonathan Swift, famed satirist, wrote the essay, *A Modest Proposal for
Preventing the Children of Poor People in Ireland from Being a Burden to
Their Parents or Country, and for Making Them Beneficial to the Public.* In
a masterpiece of flawless logic, Swift exposed the barbaric frame toward
the poor by proposing, as audacious as it sounds, that unwanted children
be sold as a foodstuff.

Children born to women of the lower classes, so Swift explained, had
only three options as they matured: to "turn thieves for want of work,
leave their dear native country to fight for the Pretender in Spain, or sell
themselves to the Barbadoes." In a cynical reversal of ethics, Swift proposed selling 1-year-olds into the meat market as a delicacy for the rich.

It would give work to the butchers; provide a renewable and profitable commodity for the poor; and reduce the number of Roman Catholics in the kingdom. *A Modest Proposal* is an unmatched example of using a counterfactual to highlight a frame. It is unlikely that we will ever choose eating our children as a reasonable solution to starvation. Nevertheless, there is no better way to blast your mind out of the box than to consider a completely outrageous idea as though it were reasonable.

■

Provocative Orientation

Jokes are amusing, but how do they contribute to novel ideas in science? One of de Bono's tools for creative thinking, Provocative Orientation (PO) relies, as do jokes, on counterfactuals. A PO puts forth a counterintuitive contention and asks you to defend it. As with jokes, you respond to any counterfactual with incredulity. But counterfactuals also force you to imagine new alternatives.

PO is designed to create movement in idea generation, independent of whether the idea makes any sense. One PO is, "Cups should be made of ice." This assertion is, of course, absurd because on a hot day a cup made of ice would melt. But consider the advantages. Ice cups would contain no waste; are comprised of a renewable and readily available material (water); are inexpensive to manufacture; do not shatter; and keep a drink cold. In Texas in the summer, a cup made of ice would be ridiculously impractical. But how about the manufacture of cups made of ice for use in Vermont in the winter?

Try another one—PO: "Women should serve in the military." Can you promote this idea? Most likely your initial reaction is to giggle because this counterfactual opposes every ounce of your social norms. But consider the benefits. Women are thought to be more peaceful and so may try to avoid wars. They often keep the household budget and thus might hold down military spending or at least put an end to the procurement of those thousand dollar toilets the military was once infamous for buying. Women can carry less, so fields of engagement would be more limited—as might casualties. Plus armies would only need to stock uniforms for a single gender. The Israeli army, which conscripts men and women equally, has the most collaborative military structure in the world. Perhaps the participation of women in the military has its benefits.

Now for a science PO: "First grade math should avoid counting." This surely is counter-intuitive. The pride of young children and their parents is not just that they can count but how high they can count. But consider that the underlying concepts in early mathematics are around quantitative relationships. More powerful than getting hung up on memorizing numbers and learning rote calculations would be to demonstrate such connections. Objects such as balls or cups could replace counted numbers. Figures, graphs, and geometric forms could be used to impart quantities and associations. Whereas rote skills are work, pictures and toys could be made to create curiosity and fun.

■

Alternatives, Possibilities, and Choices

Imagine you see a glass full of water sitting on a table. You cannot tilt the glass and you cannot damage the glass. Think of all of the ways you might be able to get the water out of the glass. APC is another de Bono tool that explores alternatives, possibilities, and choices beyond the obvious. "Think of all the ways to get water out of the glass," is a statement that asks you to consider all possible APCs. See how many solutions you can think of.

Now see if you get further with the help of these hints: You were not discouraged from using devices to remove the water. You were not told the resultant water had to be drinkable. You were not even warned that you had to capture the water. In other words, remove your preconceived constraints and expectations (i.e., your frames) and see if that does not improve your ability to devise various solutions (*see* answers in the back of the book).

Here is another exercise: for the objects in the list below, consider all of the alternatives, possibilities and choices for their use (*see* answers in back).

- brick
- wheelbarrow
- incubator
- comb
- pipette

In a movie called *Rock Round the Clock*, a powerful talent manager played by Alix Talton and an aspiring dancer played by Lisa Gave are competing for the same love interest. Talton tells the younger and sexier Gave that to secure a 3-year contract that will launch her career, she must agree not to marry (of course the man in question) during the duration of the contract. Think of all the alternative possibilities as to how Gave might snag both the contract and her man? (*see* answer in back).

You commonly attribute another person's behavior to underlying personality traits rather than to situations, particularly when you don't know the other person well. So, rather than thinking, "Joe must have had a fight with his wife before coming into this meeting," you think, "Joe is such a so-and-so—how could anyone be married to him?" Say you are at a gas station late on a Saturday night and you happen to notice a young man pouring beer into the gas tank of a car. Your first attribution might be that the man is such a drunkard that he has no idea what he is doing. What are other alternative, possible explanations? (*see* answers in back)

■

Here is a novel alternative solution to the daunting problem of global warming. An estimated 14% of the world's greenhouse gases originate in agriculture. A large portion of these gases come from the methane released by the world's 1.5 billion cows. Methane is a markedly potent greenhouse gas (about 25 times more potent than carbon dioxide). In Australia, as a new alternative to the consumption of beef and mutton, people are beginning to raise and eat kangaroos. Kangaroo gastrointestinal flora turns out to produce virtually no methane. Biologists have latched onto this insight by trying to replicate the gastrointestinal flora in kangaroos and transplant those bacteria into the guts of cows.

How about these possibilities related to the intractable global problem of malaria? Mankind's battle to control *Plasmodium falciparum* dates back to at least Egyptian times. Nonetheless, at present it appears that in the war between malaria and man, malaria is coming out the victor. Resistance to antimalarial drugs is emerging even with the very newest agents, the expensive artemisinin medications. Vaccines are nowhere near prime time, and alternatives are desperately needed. Consider two possibilities. First, the 2008 report on Malaria from the World Health Organization estimated that 247 million people contract malaria each year and 881,000 die. This is a lot of deaths but way more disease than death (0.4% of people affected die). Almost all malaria-related deaths occur in children under age 5 years in Africa. What if the limited resources available for control efforts were focused solely on birth to 5-year-olds in Africa and no one else? Surely it would be politically difficult to see other cases of disease remain, but deaths would greatly decline. Second, a new observation that laser beams trap mosquitoes raises the possibility that insecticide-laced bed nets might someday be replaced with laser beam community nets. A Star Wars against malaria? Interesting idea!

■

Plus, Minus, Interesting
Another de Bono tool is plus, minus, interesting (PMI). Using this tool means not only evaluating the good and the bad in an idea but finding movement to a new idea by considering what is interesting.

An interesting scientific progression has occurred in stem cell research. In November, 2009, scientists at Kyoto University and the University of Wisconsin published in the world renowned journals *Science* and *Nature* that they had reprogrammed skin cells to behave as embryonic stem cells without cloning or destroying embryos. This breakthrough potentially overcomes the gridlock around embryonic stem cell research created by religious and ethical concerns. Although it remains unclear whether reprogrammed skin cells will be as useful as embryonic cells, the *Science* and *Nature* reports constitute a leap forward in regenerative medicine's hopes for curing diseases such as Parkinson's.

This 2009 stem cell research news was particularly reassuring because earlier reports (in 2007) using programmed skin cells turned out to have a dark side. Cancers arose from the regenerating tissue. The initial research groups used an adenovirus as the "vector" for the genes needed to turn skin cells into stem cells. Adenovirus causes the common cold, but in this case, the infectious agent was causing even greater collateral damage. Fortunately upon switching to a different virus vector, scientists discovered that the benefits could be retained while cancers were averted.

Stem cell research is an area of tremendous potential. But it has had more ups and downs than most roller coasters. The pluses and minuses from reprogrammed skin cells were clear: the hope of regenerative medicine and the fear of transmitting cancer. What was most intriguing was the "interesting." Changing the virus vector solved the cancer risk. Given that adding genes to cells has many applications (beyond skin cells), the discovery of a new, apparently safe virus vector has broad implications for tissue engineering.

A few people, when exposed to HIV (the virus that causes AIDS), do not get infected. How can the holy grail of resistance to HIV be harnessed? Bone marrow transplants are used to treat many blood diseases, and a Berlin doctor, Gero Huetter, transplanted bone marrow from an HIV-resistant donor to a man with leukemia. The patient's leukemia was cured. But the patient also experienced an unexpected plus—the transplant eliminated his HIV infection. Bone marrow transplantation has many minuses. It requires a hair-raising destruction of the recipient's immune system and long-term use of post-transplantation immunosuppression. It seems unlikely that transplantation will become a widely applicable solution for transferring resistance to HIV.

Instead, Gero Huetter's discovery provided the momentum to pursue something interesting. Gene editing is a process of conferring the same kind of genetic changes to cells that can be transferred by bone marrow transplantation but without the same risks. HIV resistance occurs when a person has two mutant copies of a gene called *CCR5*. A new technology called zinc finger nucleases can induce that mutation. Rather than transferring bone marrow, scientists can transfer the specific *CCR5* mutations. Perhaps with more research this technique will contribute to a cure for AIDS.

PMI presses beyond an idea's strengths and weaknesses to look for what is interesting. The good is the enemy of the great. A good theory may prematurely attract attention away from the push toward something better. Each finding has some kernel that is interesting enough to lead to further innovation.

■

Change your point of view
Novel points of view open unconsidered possibilities. It is like the classic story of the blind men and the elephant. One blind man sees the tail and says the elephant is a snake; another sees the side and says the elephant is a wall, and so forth. If you think like an economist, then you will answer a question differently than you would as a behavioral scientist. If you think like an engineer, then you will take a different approach than a physician.

Even better, imagine points of view of people who are not scientists at all. Consider how a scientific question might be seen from the point of view of a child. Children ask fundamental "Why?" questions that adults would not think to ask or would be embarrassed to ask: "Why is the sky blue? Why are there tides?" Consider how a scientific question might be seen by a poet; a politician.

■

Romantic love has always been a subject of artistic fascination. How is this most basic and universal experience understood within science? Recently, love moved into the laboratory. Fisher, Aron, and Brown (2006) used functional MRI to scan the brains of 37 people who were madly in love and 15 people who had just been dumped. In those who were madly in love, Fisher and team found activity near the base of the brain, which releases dopamine to other brain centers, literally engulfing the brain in pleasure. This part of the brain is associated with motivation and craving. It is, in fact, the brain location that experiences the rush from cocaine. In subjects who were recently dumped, the dopamine-producing base of the brain remained active but was joined by two other areas: one associated with calculating losses and the other associated with deep attachment. That painful yearning in the aftermath of a break-up now has a neurological explanation. It is not be as poetic as Shakespeare. Nonetheless, such observations may be important in the treatment of pathological grief.

■

Sports exist within the frames of the entertainment industry and popular culture. In South Africa, the frame for sports became transformed into a vehicle for political healing. Before the presidency of Nelson Mandela, the South African national rugby team, the Springboks, had always represented the divide between Blacks and Whites. Springboks' team members were uniformly White and mostly racist. Blacks in South Africa would protest their own team by cheering for the opposition. When the World Cup was held in South Africa in 1995, many newly enfranchised Blacks wanted to shut down the games. But the just-elected President Nelson Mandela had a different idea. Mandela, a political prisoner for 27 years and later winner of the Nobel Peace Prize, looked at the games as a tool for reconciliation. Instead of shunning the team and the White supremacist history they represented, Mandela wore the Springboks jersey. He encouraged Springboks team members to get out into the Black community and teach young people how to play the game. When, against all odds, the Springboks managed to become a contender in the finals,

Whites and Blacks in unison joined in cheering on their team. And the Springboks won! Winning the 1995 Rugby World Cup on home turf inspired hope and unity in the new Rainbow nation. Understanding the game from a different point of view allowed Mandela to snatch peace from the jaws of discord.

"Do not judge a person until you have walked a mile in their mocassins" is an old American Indian saying that applies to seeing questions from others' points of view. Employing other perspectives expands alternatives.

■

PO, APC, PMI, alternative points of view, and even satire allows you to be freed from the limits of a single frame. The tools for thinking sideways increase the scope of your ingenuity.

EXERCISES

1. Defend the following counterfactuals:
- Women should get paid more
- All dogs should be taxed
- Corn products should be taxed
- Corn products should be free
- Tenure should not exist
- All academic positions should be tenured upon hire
- Universities should have no physical campuses
- Web-based courses should be outlawed

2. Work through these problems using the APC method:
- What alternative approaches might there be for reducing consistent smoking among young people?

- Imagine a sudden rise in the rates of homicide in a large American city. What alternative to standard criminal justice explanation might be given for this?
- The American commute is becoming overwhelming and unbearable (not to mention that cars produce hundreds of millions of tons of greenhouse gases). What alternatives can you think of?

3. Use PMI to think through these innovative suggestions:
   - Everyone should wear a badge showing his or her mood.
   - Every child should adopt a senior citizen to look after.
   - Everyone should be required to work on a farm for a summer during college.
   - Military service should be mandatory in the United States.

4. Consider the problem from two different points of view: scientists and nonscientists
   - Design a better method of testing environmental toxicants from the point of view of a microbiologist; a toxicologist; an engineer; an epidemiologist.
   - Design a better method of testing environmental toxicants from the point of view of a mayor; a policeman; a professional athlete; a school child.

17

The Power of Group Intelligence

"The way a team plays as a whole determines its success. You may have the greatest bunch of individual stars in the world. But if they don't play together the club won't be worth a dime."

—Babe Ruth

Ever played the game, "Guess how many jelly beans there are in a jar"? Try this: Fill a jar with jelly beans. Label both the dimensions of the jar and of the beans (e.g., jar dimensions: 6" tall, 11" circumference; each jelly bean 5/8" long and ¼" wide). Now get guesses from a whole group of people. The one who guesses closet to the actual number gets a prize. And that is the end of the game.

Except—instead of ending there, take this game one step further and you will uncover something surprising. If you average everyone's guesses so you have a single "best" estimate, this average guess turns out almost always to be closer to the true number of beans in the jar than any individual guess. No matter how many times the experiment is repeated, the group assessment is closer to the true number of beans than are 80% or more of individual respondents' guesses. This suggests that groups often make better judgments than individuals.

Groups can be more intelligent, more efficient, and even more innovative than any single person. Another way to create new ideas within the **G** (generative) step of the **PIG In MuD** innovation process is to harness the engine of the collaborative. The power of numbers as well as the synergies among people with different types of expertise can accelerate discovery.

■

When no sign could be found of the U.S.S. Scorpion, a skipjack class nuclear submarine that was a week late in returning to Newport News from a tour of the Atlantic, the Navy presumed that the ship must have sunk. Vanishing nuclear submarines are not an everyday occurrence. In June 1968, it had happened only once before in all of peacetime U.S. history. Immediate search operations were activated by both the public and the Navy to try to locate any sign of the 99 crewmen, a treasure trove of classified spy manuals and gear, and two nuclear-tipped torpedoes. Not a scrap of evidence emerged. Although the Navy knew that the location of the last communication from the Scorpion was near the Azores, they did not know the time between that signal and the ship's submersion. Thus, they were forced to search in an area so vast that the likelihood of finding the vessel seemed hopeless.

Dr. John Craven, the Chief Scientist of the U.S. Navy's Special Projects Division, was allowed to spearhead his own search. His strategy was to harness the power of group intelligence. He assembled experts with a broad range of expertise in submarines, mathematics, salvage, and acoustics. The team had a secret weapon—Bayesian mathematics. The term Bayesian may sound vaguely familiar. You encountered it in Chapter 15: *Flip It!* being used by physicians in evidence-based diagnosis. As described by Sherry Sontag and Christopher Drew in their 1998 book *Blind Man's Bluff*, Craven's team worked like this. First, they dissected the elements of the disaster. There must have been an instigating event, a location, a rate of descent, a slope of descent, and so forth. Craven and group concocted scenarios as to how each event may have occurred based on the limited available evidence. Their acoustics expertise turned out to be the particularly important because Gordon Hamilton, pioneer of the use of hydroacoustics, added key clues. Next each authority within the team had to say for each scenario how likely it was to be correct. To spice things up, the men bet on their guesses with bottles of Chivas Regal. Finally the collective wisdom of the group was entered into a Bayesian model, which uses each new piece of information to adjust the likelihood of the outcome.

At the end of October, after 5 months of intensive effort, the Navy's oceanographic research ship, Mizar, located sections of the hull of Scorpion in more than 9,800 feet of water about 460 miles southwest of the Azores. Craven and his team had directed them right to it. In his best-selling book, *The Wisdom of Crowds,* James Surowiecki (2005) argued that this is one of many examples wherein the judgment of the collective was superior to that of the individual. "The location that Craven came up with was not a spot that any individual member of the group had picked. In other words, not one of the members of the group had a picture in his head that matched the one Craven had constructed using the information gathered by all of them." The distance between the location that Craven's team selected and where the Scorpion's hull was detected was 220 yards.

■

In addition to being smarter than individuals, groups can be more productive. In the twenty-first century, the social collective is king. Social networking, self-organizing collectives, and open source have become highly prized centerpieces of daily life. Networks of loosely connected individuals accomplish tasks with great speed. One dramatic feature of networked individuals is their ability to conquer tasks requiring great reach across geography and complexity.

Group expertise is perhaps nowhere better demonstrated than by the online encyclopedia *Wikipedia*. In 2005, the accuracy of this highly cited source was put to the test. The news team of the eminent international science journal *Nature* asked: Is *Wikipedia* as accurate a source of information as *Encyclopedia Britannica*? *Encyclopedia Britannica* is the gold standard: a 32-volume set printed once every several years. In 2007 *Wikipedia* was estimated to be equivalent to 1250 volumes and is edited daily. But of course *Wikipedia* is the work of volunteers with unclear levels of expertise, separated by miles and oceans, and interfacing only virtually. Experts selected by *Nature* compared 50 entries in each encyclopedia on the same set of topics, representing a broad range of scientific disciplines. Only entries that were approximately the same length in both encyclopedias were selected. Experts did not know which article came from which source. They were asked to identify factual errors, critical omissions, and misleading statements. Eight serious errors were found—four from each source. The conclusion: the two sources are equally valid. So experts can edit a gold standard every several years. But groups can edit an equally accurate resource every few minutes.

Volunteer, self-organizing networks are working on everything from improving Google Maps to deciphering the genetic code. In a project called Open Street, individuals and social groups armed with GPS devices take Google Maps and fill in the location of bike racks, park benches, and running paths. Doing so transforms a general navigation tool into a user-friendly aid for living in neighborhoods.

International Hapmap is an open-source project involving scientists from Japan, the United Kingdom, Canada, China, Nigeria, and the United States to identify and catalog genetic similarities and differences among disparate populations. All of the information generated by the project is made available in the public domain. Hapmap has become a platform for discerning the meaning of the genetic code that is used by thousands of scientists around the world. Whether it be through mapping neighborhoods or mapping the genome, groups are an efficient and effective engine of progress.

■

With so many examples, everyone must believe in the power of group intelligence. But to be scientifically valid such beliefs must be rigorously demonstrated and the very fact that groups can be intelligent had never been proven. Until now. Woolley et al. (2010, publishing in *Science*) studied 699 people working in groups of two to five. Groups were set to intelligence tasks like the ones on IQ tests. Surprisingly, group intelligence (which Woolley termed the "c" factor), defined as performance on these group tasks, was not strongly correlated with the intelligence quotas of participating individuals. In other words, smarter people did not necessarily comprise smarter groups. Group intelligence was, however, correlated with the group's social sensitivity. It was also correlated with equality. Groups that spent the most time engaging in turn-taking and listening, thereby using the totality of their aggregate brain clout, were the "smartest."

∎

So groups can be smart and efficient. But can they be innovative? Decades of brainstorming, practiced within business and industry, argues that the answer is "Yes." Moreover, scientific breakthroughs are increasingly happening at the intersection of disciplines. But before you get to all of that, let me tell you how the very basis for our modern explosion of social networks is an example of group invention.

This story starts with the two letters: L and O. The date was October 29, 1969, and at UCLA, a student named Charlie Kline was trying to communicate with his counterpart at Stanford. Before Kline was cut-off, those letters made history.

In 1962, Bob Taylor, Lawrence Roberts, and a team at the Defense Advanced Research Projects Agency (DARPA) began a multisite test of the first packet-switching network. The system was based on the work of Paul Barran who beginning around 1959 designed a radically novel departure from the traditional communications framework. Historically information, such as over telephone wires, was transmitted via circuit switching, in which one party on one end communicated to another party on another end through a dedicated circuit. In packet-switching, data are dissembled into datagrams and then gathered in packets that are deposited into a system like a letter would be placed in a postbox. Each packet from the system (think postbox) can be routed through a different destination and then reassembled upon reaching a receiver. This allowed multiple machines to communicate in a way that was markedly more efficient and robust than any system that had gone before it. Data-switching was at the heart of the system called ARPANET built by Taylor and Roberts at DARPA and a team of university and private partners. ARPANET is the precursor of the Internet.

DARPA awarded the contract to implement ARPANET to a seven-man team at BBN Technologies after most contractors refused to even bid on the proposal, thinking it too outlandish. UCLA, Stanford, UC Santa Barbara, and the University of Utah were the first to link to the system. "L" and "O" were the first two letters of "Login," typed during the first attempt to communicate over the network. Before transmission was complete, the system crashed. Obviously, subsequent testing was more successful. By 1970, nine computers were connected; by 1971, 18; by 1972, 40; and by 1981, another host was being connected every 20 days.

The invention of the forerunner of the Internet is a classic example of team science. Although we attribute the invention to scientists in the United States, the breakthrough idea of packet-switching might also reasonably be claimed by Donald Davies at the National Physical Laboratory in the United Kingdom, who almost simultaneously with Barran came up with the idea. So the key concept of packet switching was simultaneously simmering in scientific circles separated by the Atlantic Ocean. Moreover, the actual invention of the Internet was a team effort, first at DARPA, then at BBN Technologies, then at an ever-enlarging cadre of academic computing centers. With all due respect to Al Gore (the vice president who took credit for its invention), the Internet, likely the most revolutionary innovation of the 20th century, was invented by a group.

■

DARPA's greatest accomplishment is surely the creation of the Internet. But their mission is broader than that. It is to promote military innovation. As they put it, "We create technological surprise in our adversaries." DARPA funds advances in technology and operations (think stealth aircraft) that come out of large, multidisciplinary groups. With the many military advances they have produced, it would seem that DARPA has no need to prove the intelligence of groups. But they set out to do so anyway and ended up proving more than they had hoped for.

A contest funded by DARPA challenged anyone to find 10 8-foot-tall red helium balloons in plain view placed at random sites around the United States. Balloons were tethered in Centennial Park (Atlanta, GA); Union Square (San Francisco, CA); and Glasgow Park (Christiana, DE); among other locations. A reward of $40,000 was offered for the first person or team to identify the location of all 10 balloons. The winning team, with a core of five people from MIT, took only 8 hours and 52 minutes to find all 10 balloons. This remarkable accomplishment, completed in dramatically less time than the organizers thought possible, was achieved through an Internet site that was set-up to recruit volunteers and report results. As an incentive, the MIT team used an ingenious pyramid reward structure: $2,000 to each finder of a red balloon; $1,000 to a referrer of a finder; and $500 to the referrer of the referrer of the finder, and so forth. By employing hundreds or perhaps thousands of volunteers, they instantly placed balloon detectives in every corner of the United States. But the MIT team did more. They demonstrated the power of groups to innovate. The team had just conducted a real-time experiment in behavioral economics with excellent results. The use of the Internet was perhaps a given, but the incentive scheme was pure genius.

∎

A particularly powerful incubator for originality exists at the intersections between disciplines. Evolutionary biology meets regenerative medicine. That should have been the title of a recent paper in *Cell Stem Cell* chronicling an inventive new technique that could make stem cell research obsolete. A team at Stanford University led by Helen Blau and Jason Pomerantz and conducted by Kostandin Pajcini in 2010, used team science to combine concepts from two disciplines (molecular biology and evolutionary biology) to generate a breakthrough idea in tissue regeneration. They looked not to human embryos, but to newts. Newts can regenerate limbs, fins, and even part of the heart. This process occurs when adult cells at the site of the damage revert to an embryonic stem-like state and then grow in to recreate the missing tissue. Adult humans have almost no regenerative capacity.

Evolutionary biology explains why this is so. Genes responsible for regeneration are the same ones that regulate cancer. So humans, with our much longer lifespans, likely evolved mechanisms to limit the effect of regenerative genes. Blau's team inactivated two genes that suppressed tumors and thus got mouse cells to revert to a multipotential state that could repair tissue. One of these genes is *Rb*, which newts can turn off to regenerate tissue. Mammals have not only the anti-regenerative *Rb* but a back-up anti-regenerative gene called *Arf*. By suppressing both genes with silencing RNA, scientists got mouse muscle cells to renew themselves. Evolutionary biology thus lit a path toward a holy grail of medicine—our newt within. A multidisciplinary approach achieved what neither discipline could have done alone.

Today labs share cell lines and reagents, but if they are smart, they also share intellectual talent. In most parts of science, the era of the white-coated doctor working in an isolated laboratory is a thing of the past. Team science provides the opportunity for collaboration among individuals with different training, different backgrounds, and different experience. In *The Medici Effect* (2004), Frans Johansson provides a wealth of research and multitude of examples suggesting that "an explosion of insight happens at the intersection of different fields, cultures, and industries." Whole fields of science have been founded at the juncture of diverse disciplines. Bioengineering; chemical engineering; systems biology; behavioral economics; artificial intelligence; and neuropsychology are disciplines that derive novelty from making surprising connections.

■

If you want to know how ant self-organization informs us about telecommunications, look to the crossroads of two disciplines. This recent fusion of computer science and ecology is called "Swam Intelligence". Ants and bees, flocks of birds, and swarms of fish follow simple behavioral rules and signals from the environment such that their individual behaviors become remarkably coordinated. Humans are, of course, more individualized, but check out teenagers at a dance and see if you think their behaviors are self-organized. Swarm behavior insights now inform computing and systems science, and computing insights inform biologic research.

For example, "Ant colony optimization" is actually a class of computer algorithms directed at finding the most direct path to a goal. A classic experiment by Deneubourg and colleagues in 1989 showed that ants chose the shorter of two paths to get home from a food source through following the most intense pheromone trail. The more ants, the stronger the trail. In the computer program "Ant colony optimization," artificial ants (computer algorithms) move through a virtual computer space and lay down virtual pheromones to optimize decisions. So ants inform computer programs. Then too, computing can inform ecology. For example, synchronized robots have been used to validate models that ecologists use to describe biologic systems.

Swarm intelligence has been applied to describing why rivers take certain paths; to animation (the movement of bats in the 1992 Tim Burton movie *Batman Returns*); and to telecommunications. Your future phone calls may be transmitted using an algorithm called "Ant Based Routing."

■

When groups who should be working together aren't, critical opportunities can be missed. September 11, 2001, proved to be a painful reminder of this fact. The tragedy, it seems, may have been prevented if, at the time, a trail of signals had been recognized by intelligence agencies. A central problem was this: The intelligence community, with its alphabet soup of agencies including the CIA, NSA, NRO, DIA, and all three military services simply did not talk to each other. Supposedly, the director of the CIA had authority over this hodge-podge of organizations. But most of the budget for intelligence work came from another agency— the Department of Defense. The CIA Director's theoretical oversight was only that—theoretical. Moreover, the FBI, which handled potential terrorists operating in the United States did not work with any of these groups. Senator Richard Shelby, one of the intelligence agencies' sharpest critics, argued for agency centralization. Of course, centralization is a step backward from social networking.

Ultimately, Congress legislated collaboration. If intelligence organizations would share information and judgment, starting with a common informatics platform, they could work as a smarter network. In an attempt to foster agency collaboration, Congress passed *the Intelligence Reform and Terrorist Prevention Act of 2004*, which created the Director of National Intelligence.

So, in 2011, how is it going? Well, the fourth director in 5 years was recently hired, and some pundits argue that the director's office simply adds a layer of bureaucracy without the authority to orchestrate cooperation. On the other hand, the computer systems of the intelligence agencies are beginning to "talk" to each other. So progress is occurring but American intelligence still has room to fully achieve the power of groups.

Scientists are often slow to share ideas for fear of losing their individual intellectual property. Yet, an unwillingness to work within groups can limit productivity. How many times has a junior scientist been told, "Don't let anyone steal that idea," or a company spent millions to protect against industrial espionage? Scientists often wonder: Do the benefits of working in groups outweigh the potential loss of the fruits of their scholarly labors?

Introducing ADNI. In August 2010, after decades of failure in producing diagnostic tools for Alzheimer's disease, researchers reported a spinal fluid test that is touted to be 100% accurate in diagnosis. Just months before, a brain imaging technique, since approved by the Food and Drug Administration, was validated for its ability to detect Alzheimer's disease at an early stage. Amyloid-beta, a protein fragment known for years to form the telltale plaques in the brains of Alzheimer's patients, is the basis of both tests. How did this crop of remarkable advances suddenly arise out of a research area that had been so barren for so long? The answer is that these breakthroughs represent the harvest from an historic collaboration based on group innovation. It started with the exchange of shared frustration between scientific colleagues. Neil Buckholtz, chief of the Dementias of Aging Branch at the National Institutes on Aging, was driving to the airport in 2000 with his friend William Potter, who had recently left the National Institutes of Health (NIH) to work for Eli Lilly. The two were commiserating about the glacial progress of developing diagnostic tools and therapeutics for Alzheimer's sufferers. "We wanted to get out of what I called [nineteenth] century drug development—give a drug and hope it works," said Potter. Scientists needed to be able to look inside the brain to find out how the disease progresses and to develop detection tools. But laboratories around the world were each using different tests and different methods, none of which correlated with each other. It was the tower of Babel. The effort to get everyone to speak the same language would be huge—too great for even the NIH to tackle. Suddenly the two had an epiphany. If they could convince the players that no one—no matter how great the individual payoff—could do it alone, then maybe they could get everyone to do it together. From that conversation was born a consortium between the NIH, industry, and academia called ADNI.

ADNI is a revolutionary concept. In ADNI, no one owns the data; no one gets to submit a patent. All results are made immediately available over the Internet to the public. To appreciate just how disruptive this is, consider the metaphors for ideas: *"They'll never buy that idea." "You need to sell your ideas." "That idea is worthless." "Don't waste your thoughts."* Our traditional frame is that ideas are valuable commodities and individually owned.

ADNI represents a frame-shift in which commercializing discoveries will reap rewards but there is no winner-takes-all. Yet, ADNI accomplishes a goal that no party could achieve on its own: breakthroughs in a debilitating illness from which all of mankind will profit. Who would ever have thought that industry would buy into this let alone support it? But indeed they did, to the tune of a combined $24 million from 20 companies and 2 nonprofits. The NIH Foundation, set up by Congress to raise private funds for federal research, put up another $41 million. In the end, Buckholtz and Potter convinced their colleagues that there was simply no other way. Today, more than 100 projects are funded from ADNI with the hope for many other discoveries within the foreseeable future. A new initiative using this same collaborative model is being planned for Parkinson's disease.

Perhaps collaboration can help scientists tackle other threats to mankind. ADNI is the proof that in science, transformation can be driven by the power of groups.

■

When people come together—particularly when people from different disciplines come together—the group can be highly intelligent, efficient, and innovative. Isn't it heartwarming when a widely repeated aphorism proves true? The whole really can be greater than the sum of the parts.

18

Getting the Most from a Group

"Honest criticism is hard to take, particularly from a relative, a friend, an acquaintance, or a stranger."

—Franklin P Jones

Love is blind, especially when it is the love of a new idea—but if we love one idea to the exclusion of all others, then we may miss out on a better alternative. Groups can motivate members to reach for novelty and can also provide a reality check. The Western Psychiatric Institute and Clinic of the University of Pittsburgh is head and shoulders above any other department of psychiatry in the country in terms of federal funding. Their post-docs and junior faculty have unusually high rates of success. What are they doing right? Since 1994, Charles (Chuck) Reynolds has run a post-doctoral training program wherein young scientists engage in regular and rigorous group vetting of grant proposals. Every couple of weeks, the cohort of young scientists, mentored by experienced, senior faculty, meets so the trainees can present work in progress. The sessions are designed to be tough but supportive, providing guidance but also criticism and redirection. In the first 4 years of the program, 16 of 30 fellows succeeded in obtaining NIH funding, a remarkably high hit rate considering that at other institutions, success rates were running at less than 1 in 5. The group that Western Psychiatric created is particularly effective. Not so with all groups. What makes some groups better than others? Are there strategies to get the most out of group innovation?

■

In their 2001 book, *The Art of Innovation: Lessons in Creativity from IDEO, America's Leading Design Firm*, Kelley and Littman describe what they call HOT Teams. These multidisciplinary groups have a goal to achieve a high energy, high performance passion for their work. They have:

- total dedication to and belief in achieving the goal
- slightly ridiculous timelines
- nonhierarchical structure
- many individual strengths, which make them well-rounded
- respect for each other
- a belief that they can obtain whatever is needed to succeed but also that they are ultimately responsible for getting the job done.

In science, a HOT Team may be working toward a grant, a paper, a symposium, or some other collaborative effort. They may have self-assembled just for some quick turn-around opportunity, or they may have long experience working together. Either way, a critical strategy for ensuring the productivity of HOT Teams is to build trust and value. Each team member has to feel that they will personally benefit and that the overall team is doing something important. HOT Teams build a sense of belonging through relationships and shared fun. In a multi-disciplinary, international collaboration to which I belong, semi-annual meetings are held at enjoyable destinations around the world (London, Australia, New York City, Chicago), and each host tries to out-do the last in building-in some enjoyable highlight (ever sipped champagne on the London Eye?).

■

Groups can also balance psychological strengths and weaknesses. Scott Belsky, author of *Making Ideas Happen* (2010), categorizes team members as Doers, Dreamers, and Incrementalists.

Joe, despite doing well in his courses, has been working on his dissertation for 10 years (now part-time). He is a font of ideas that have excited his committee but none seem to get off the ground. Joe is a dreamer. Dreamers are forever imagining new projects but never completing them. Although Joe is a great guy to hang out with, you hope you'll never have to count on him to meet a deadline.

Doers, in contrast, are generally rule-bound, rigidly organized, and highly task-oriented. Sue is the business director for the laboratory. When her staff report to her, they know they had better have their ducks in a row. In brainstorming sessions, Sue will punctuate the discussion with questions about feasibility and implementation. She is laser-focused on the step-by-step logistics.

Incrementalists do it all. They can both conceive and execute ideas. Jeff Staple, founder of Staple Design, is described by Belsky as one of the great Incrementalists. At any given time, he is running a gallery, designing a new clothing line, and directing a design studio that creates brand strategies for Nike and Burton. Although Incrementalists are Renaissance people, they often suffer from having too many irons in the fire. Doers and Dreamers are best when paired. Incrementalists can work with either or both.

Balancing personality types on a team is enormously useful; in fact, when working on a complex, long-term project, it can be essential. To wit, "To thine own self be true" but to be truest, get feedback from others and balance your weaknesses with others' strengths.

■

Brainstorming is one of the central tools used by HOT Teams at IDEO. First devised by Alex Osborn in the 1960s, brainstorming is likely the most commonly used tool in business for idea generation. In brainstorming, a group generates as many ideas as possible on a defined topic within a defined period of time. Despite its extensive use in business, there is some skepticism about the use of brainstorming. Studies have shown that more ingenious solutions to a problem are devised by individuals than by groups. However, this result comes from an experimental situation involving motivated research subjects. Brainstorming provides the motivation to get group members thinking. It is meant to be generative; if it does not always lead to novelty, then the sheer numbers can be a platform for later originality.

Typically a brainstorm group is not terribly large (less than 20 people) and the time does not go over an hour. A key commodity in any brainstorm is a skillful leader, commonly called a facilitator. Particularly if the group has not previously worked together or if the question is a technical one, assigning homework, such as background reading, before the brainstorm can help to enhance productivity. In *The Art of Innovation,* Tom Kelly puts forth "secrets of brainstorming":

- Sharpen the focus—create a pointed, actionable question.
- Playful rules—don't let the critics rule (defer judgment: one conversation at a time).
- Number your ideas—try for 100 ideas per hour (go for quantity).
- Build and jump—a good session will lead to ideas building on ideas as momentum grows.
- Combine fluency (fast flow of ideas) and flexibility (ideas with different viewpoints).
- The Space Remembers—write on paper taped to the walls or tables.

To sharpen the focus, a group must clearly state the problem without excessive narrowness. An example of a bad brainstorm idea given in *The Art of Innovation* would be: Design better bicycle cup holders. This limits the range of ideas (maybe the container shouldn't be a cup). A good brainstorm idea might instead be: Help bike commuters to drink coffee without spilling it or burning themselves.

Playful rules involve discarding any sense of judgment and forgoing any hierarchy. I was at a high-level advisory committee a couple of years ago and our task was to articulate the following years' grant opportunities. Happily, the committee agreed to focus on innovative applications, but what did that mean? To expand and specify our thoughts, we decided to brainstorm. Members of the group made great, imaginative suggestions. After each, the committee chair commented, "We've tried that before and it didn't work," or "The resources we would need would make it impossible to do anything else." In less than 5 minutes, the discussion petered out. Only after the chair was reminded of the rule, "Don't let the critics rule," did the brainstorm become reinvigorated. It ultimately resulted in a novel approach to incenting particularly creative investigators to enter the field.

Brainstorming is all about going for quantity. By numbering ideas, the team can see their progress and progress is a great motivator. A good brainstorm generates 100 ideas an hour. When I told this to my first *Innovative Thinking* class, the statement drew complete silence. Finally, one of the bolder students asked, "To generate 100 ideas an hour, how many people were there?" Then another asked, "Were those 100 *separate* ideas?" Forty-five minutes later, the 18 students had generated 90 ideas and were going strong. At an hour, they were speeding past 120 suggestions. What a joyful surprise it was to them when they took a breath and realized what they had done!

Build and jump is where the facilitator really makes her salary. In a brainstorm, typically the momentum builds as participants get rolling on a particular idea, but then it plateaus. A good facilitator can see when energy is leveling and help the group switch to another aspect of the question. The skill is in leading the group to a new dimension without offering a solution or injecting a bias. In this way, the facilitator helps to combine fluency and flexibility.

Ever taken a test in which you remembered the answer because you could actually see where the information was on the page? Or worse, you couldn't remember the answer but you could remember where it was on the page? Spatial memory is a characteristic we all have, and it can be a help in brainstorming. Whether you use Post-Its or big white pages, you should plaster these all over the wall—ideas are then linked to physical locations. You will find yourself returning to the actual location of an idea. Moving around the room as the facilitator writes also helps to keep the group alive and active.

IDEO also warns you to avoid "six brainstorm killers":

- The boss gets to speak first—This "no-no" makes for a sense of domination. IDEO recommends bosses taking a back seat during idea-generation sessions.
- Not everybody gets a turn—A single, dominant member can turn brainstorming into a solo performance rather than a group activity (focus should never just be on one person).
- Experts only—Everyone has something to share. Cross-pollination among individuals from different backgrounds leads to authentic breakthroughs.
- Brainstorms only happen off-site—Great ideas should come in daily work, not just on the rare occasion that the team gets out of the office
- No silly stuff—Instead, encourage wild ideas (brainstorming = fun).
- Write down every detail—Obsessive note-taking can be toxic. Instead, the facilitator uses short notes to preserve a thought

Brainstorming is yet another tool for jolting yourself out of your normal cognitive frames and generating alternatives. Whether it be brainstorming or blowing the question up, pulling it apart, turning it on its head, combining it with something else, rearranging the pieces, finding analogies, or jumping out of frames, it is all about altering the normal script. Brainstorming can be practiced alone but it is often more effective when employed in a group. Having a toolbox that includes tools for individuals as well as ones for groups adds to the likelihood of successfully innovating.

EXERCISES

Embark with some friends on a 45-minute brainstorm. Before starting, engage the group in constructing the question. Choose a facilitator from the group. Cover the walls with large Post-Its or butcher paper. Then let the fun begin! Make sure you keep things completely judgment-free and idea-filled.

19

Incubation

"I know when I have a problem and have done all I can to figure it out, I keep listening in a sort of inside silence until something clicks and I feel a right answer."

—*Conrad Hilton*

What was the last idea that just "popped into your head?" When did you last have a "light bulb go off?" Or "an epiphany?" These are your metaphors for inspiration. They suggest something instantaneous. An idea arrives in your brain preformed and out-of-the-blue. But that is a misperception. Epiphanies really reflect a time lag. Somewhere in the innovative process between the prolonged process of generating novelty and the insight that you hope will transform science is a pause. This pause is called incubation. Incubation is the **I** in the stages of innovation: **PIG In MuD**. Almost always, incubation occurs during a period when you simply don't seem to be getting anywhere—nothing seems to be happening. Ideas have to gestate. Incubation is literally what it sounds like—finding a nice warm, closed space for things to grow. To achieve uninterrupted, unstressed mental relaxation, you may want to look for a time/place to be free of other concerns. On the other hand, it need not be a special place or special time; eureka moments commonly occur in the shower, on a plane, in dreams, or after wakening. No matter where or when it is found, incubation implies a stress-free mental state that allows you to simply clear your mind and let those neurons connect.

■

Henri Poincare, the famed mathematician and physicist who made fundamental contributions to algebra, geometry, electromagnetism, and relativity, in describing (but not using the word) incubation, wrote:

> Most striking at first is this appearance of sudden illumination, a manifest sign of long, unconscious prior work. The role of this unconscious work in mathematical invention appears to me uncontestable... Often when one works at a hard question nothing good is accomplished at the first attack. Then one takes a rest, longer or shorter, and sits down anew to the work. During the first half hour, as before, nothing is found, and then all of a sudden the decisive idea presents itself to the mind... these efforts then have not been as sterile as one thinks; they have set going the unconscious machine and without them it would not have moved and would have produced nothing. (1952)

■

More than 2,500 years ago in India, a man named Gautama, the son of a king, lived in great wealth. One day, when he was a young man, already with a wife and child, he went for the first time to walk outside of the walls of his insular family conclave. To his shock, he saw the pain and suffering of daily Indian life. For 6 years thereafter, he wandered in the valley of the Ganges River, learning the practices of great religious teachers and experiencing the real world. One day, while sitting under a Banyan tree, he experienced enlightenment. When later asked to sum up his teaching in a single word, he said, "awareness."

Gautama had become the Buddha. The Buddha is a state of being to which millions have since aspired. In fact, the term *Buddha* means the "awakened one."

This may well be the most legendary example of incubation in the history of mankind. Gautama observed and studied and thought about a problem. Then, after resting under a tree, he had a transformational eureka moment and created a new religion.

The central tenant of Buddhism is "mindfulness," meaning full awareness of what is going on both inside yourself and outside. To be mindful means to pay attention to everything and to live entirely in the present. This is a particularly important tool for observation, wherein mindfulness means concentrating full attention and noticing every detail anew. Buddhism is not about cultural trappings, prayers, beliefs, or doctrines. It is just about being alert to actual moment-to-moment experiences. To achieve mindfulness, Buddhists practice meditation. It allows you to clear your mind, to free your thinking from daily concerns. Meditation is a constructive tool for incubation.

■

One of the clearest consequences of meditation is its ability to decrease stress. Chronic stress has been shown to have all sorts of detrimental effects on the mind and body. It can change brain chemistry so as to leave you vulnerable to anxiety and depression. It can raise blood pressure, increasing the risk of heart attack and stroke. It can directly suppress the immune system.

My grandmother used to warn me, "Don't get so stressed or you'll get sick." Well, in 1991, Sheldon Cohen, professor at Carnegie Mellon University, proved my grandmother right. He and his colleagues provided 394 British men and women with an all-expenses-paid week-long vacation in spacious rooms in Salisbury, England. The downside was that the rooms were at the Medical Research Council's Common Cold Unit. Cohen's experiment started out in a quite mundane way. Each participant filled out an extensive set of questionnaires about recent stressful life events; the extent to which current demands exceeded his/her ability to cope; and an index of negative mood. These were summed into a single stress scale. Then something quite remarkable was done. Each subject (all consented to this, mind you) had drops inserted into their nose containing adenovirus, the infection that causes the common cold. For 6 days, participants were set behind closed doors to wait to see if they would get the stuffy nose, sneezing, sore throat, and other unpleasantries of a cold. About 40% of them did.

Were the ones who got sick under stress? In fact, yes! Colds attacked a higher percentage of subjects who reported being stressed out. Among those who reported being at the lowest end of the stress scale, about one-fourth became ill, whereas among those with a high level of stress, one-half got a cold. The study, published in the *New England Journal of Medicine*, ignited the field of stress research and underscored the power of your emotions.

Meditation can substantially reduce clinical anxiety and stress. In one study, patients with mood disorders and patients with cancer, even after just 8 weeks of training, saw sizable improvements in mood. Adapting to college is a high-stress experience for many students. College students who engaged in mindful meditation are better able to adapt to the new environment and handle the stresses of college life.

■

Novel thinking is inhibited by stress. Have you ever had a moment of insight while running for a bus?

Meditation's impact on brain function suggests it may improve imaginative thinking. Concentration and reaction times improve with meditation. Brain scans of people meditating show better blood flow between diverse parts of the brain, suggesting stronger connections. As you discovered previously, complex creative thinking tasks activate a multitude of brain regions. Novel thought may rely on the strength and magnitude of those connections; mediation may enhance brain region connectivity.

More directly, mediation has been demonstrated to enhance insight. A study of transcendental meditation (one of the most popular forms of meditation, in which a mantra is used to focus concentration inwardly) found that regular practitioners as compared to controls significantly improved their scores on tests of creativity. Scores improved on average between 25% and over 100%. Interestingly, the practitioners were not experts. They were simply subjects who had completed 5 months of practice.

■

Meditation does not require a major investment of time to achieve benefi-cial results. Although best accomplished in a quiet place when you can be assured that you will not be interrupted, certain techniques can be used anywhere. During meditation, you try to achieve complete awareness of the moment. You do not try to block your reflections. Instead you simply let these pass through your mind without examination. Meditation has been compared to clouds passing over a mountain. The person meditat-ing is aware of the thoughts but does not become emotionally involved with them.

One kind of meditation, called Vipassana, emphasizes a "simple aware-ness." The Vipassana practitioner notices and recognizes personal feelings and details of the environment without fixating on any one thing. The mind drifts without becoming attached to any specific emotion. Other techniques of meditation include focusing on all of the senses (smell, hearing, sight, touch, and smell), sometimes in succession, to concentrate on the environment rather than on thoughts. Another involves calming the breath, such as by doubling the length of the inhalation to exhala-tion (breathe in for 4 seconds, out for 8; in for 6 seconds, out for 12, etc.). The body is kept relaxed, and the breath is kept deep and even. Finally, meditation can involve focusing on a mantra (a word or words repeated over and over) or an object (a fountain, a rock, a garden). No matter what the vehicle, the idea is similar: to become aware of the moment without becoming distracted by intrusive thoughts.

■

Meditative techniques are useful tools for promoting the incubation stage of creativity. Freeing your thoughts so as to make unusual new cognitive connections can be accomplished by a relaxed mental state. Such a state can be achieved using calming methods like meditation. Meditation counteracts anti-innovative stress and promotes original and novel thinking. After the hard work of generating new ideas, a little brain relaxation can lead to that sudden insight that solves a difficult problem.

EXERCISES

Let's try a simple exercise in meditation. Start with a comfortable posture either in a chair or on the floor. Cross your legs, put your hands in your lap, clasping your fingers together, and close your eyes. Now relax. Observe your breathing. Just witness the breath—don't inhale or exhale consciously. Just let it happen on its own, but observe your pattern of breathing.

When you notice a thought, cut it short, and go back to the breath. After a while, the density of your thoughts diminishes. Breaths become thinner and shorter until the breath disappears like a flash and you become breathless and thoughtless. This is the meditative state. This state will not be reached the first time you meditate. In fact, it may take weeks or even months to achieve this. The more meditation practice you do, the more readily you can find this state of contemplation.

20

Testing Your Ideas

"Always look for a second right answer."

—*Charles Thompson*

When my son Joel was a toddler sitting in his highchair, he took great delight in throwing an empty plastic cup on the floor, then squealing and gesticulating until I picked it up. Joel would seemingly have repeated this experiment forever, except that mom eventually got too exasperated and stopped picking up the cup. In *The Magic Years*, Selma Fraiberg (1959) characterizes children as continually exploring and probing their world to make sense of the objects and events around them. Children are budding scientists. They learn by exploration and action to predict the ways of the world. On a grander scale, science has codified a process for evaluating and validating explanations for the workings of nature. This is called the scientific method.

So far, in learning the **PIG In MuD** method, you have **P**hrased a question; **I**dentified frames and found alternatives; **G**enerated all sorts of ideas and solutions; and Incubated. Now is the time to **M**eld your single-best idea back into the process of normal science. This step is where the rubber meets the road. The challenge is to take your best novel idea and prove it. To do this you will need to spend far more time than you did generating the idea. You will need to get meticulous about design, obsessive about every experimental detail and its documentation, and consumed with avoiding the pitfalls around which your results could be picked apart.

In short, like all other scientists, you will have to embark on a rigorous life's work.

What differentiates dreamers from scientific discoverers is the drive to action. In *Chapter 11: The Brain and Creativity: Getting Out in Front*, we met Joseph Goldberger who believed that nutritional deficiency is the cause of pellagra. It was an insight that compelled him to tirelessly design one experiment after another, take personal risks, challenge authority, and refuse to admit defeat. With the greatest tenacity, Goldberger pursued this passion, this quest.

Proving that your best idea is valid, critically assessing, "Am I sure I have hit on something with the desired effect or that is the true cause?" is the core of science. It is a long and arduous road. Nonetheless, without the dedication that science demands, an idea is just a fantasy.

■

The approach science takes to deciding that an idea is valid has an interesting history. As technologic invention began accelerating in the seventeenth century, science needed better principles for explaining what things would likely work and what would not. Up until that time, the frames for understanding the world were the divine and the supernatural. In 1620, Francis Bacon wrote the paradigm-shifting treatise *Novum Organum*. In it, he proposed the theory of scientific thinking called *induction*. Bacon's thesis was that observations induce the formulation of a hypothesis in the mind of the scientist. So, for example, according to Bacon's theory, Jenner's observation of a lack of smallpox among milkmaids actually caused Jenner to say, "Aha—cowpox provides immunity to smallpox." Induction became the underpinning for all of modern science.

Unfortunately, inductive reasoning was not a perfect theory. In 1739, Hume pointed out that one could create a hypothesis based on observing a connection between an exposure and an outcome, but this did not prove cause-and-effect. Imagine, as Bertrand Russell did in 1945, that you hear two clocks. Each clock chimes on the hour but one is set 5 minutes ahead of the other. So in perpetuity, one clock chimes, then, 5 minutes later, the other clock chimes. Although the two clocks are inexorably linked and one always precedes the other, there is no causal connection. Disappointing as it sounds, Hume argued that observation alone can never prove causality.

To add fuel to the fire, Russell pointed out that inductive reasoning leads to logical fallacies. To quote directly from him:

> "If pigs have wings, then some winged animals are good to eat; now some winged animals are good to eat; therefore pigs have wings. This form of scientific inference is called 'scientific method'"

Induction as a way to prove cause could not survive. Yet, there was no better construct to replace it. Then, in 1959 along came Karl Popper. Popper granted that scientific hypotheses can never be proven true. However, he realized that hypotheses can be proven false. Observations can never constitute proof even if they pile up until you are buried. Yet a single observation that is inconsistent with a hypothesis will irrefutably invalidate it. Say you are a scientist in Delaware and you have just made the discovery that water consistently boils at 100°C. You have repeated the experiment a hundred times and gotten the same result, so you grandly announce to the world that you have solved the mystery of water's boiling point. But your colleagues remind you that your observation, even if repeated, is no proof. In fact, a competitor cleverly takes the experiment to Denver, which is about a mile above sea level, and there water boils at 95°C. You feel humiliated. Don't. That's just how science works.

■

Popper's theory suggests that science starts with a hypothesis, from which we expect certain observations. If those are the observations we see, then we infer that our hypothesis was correct. But our hypothesis is only correct insofar as it continues to provide a reasonable explanation for how the world works.

At any time, an observation may come along that refutes our hypothesis and replaces it with an alternative. The loop looks like this:

Innovative thinking adds a wrinkle to this already complex weave. An idea, as a pure leap of insight or as a result of new observations may create a new expectation or inference. If that leap is then supported by observation, the new idea refutes and ultimately replaces the standing hypothesis. So, the loop can be injected with an idea that temporarily resets it at any point. If an idea if supported by consistent observation, it can thus lead to a new view of the world:

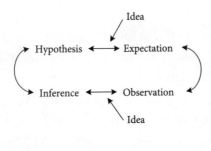

■

Even in the absence of proof, science moves on—medicine treats and cures. To move forward in the absence of absolute certainty, science uses a method wherein a body of evidence consistently supporting a hypothesis, without serious evidence to the contrary, is used as a surrogate for proof of cause. Scientists talk about the number of experiments that would be needed to overturn the accumulated evidence. If that number is large, then the hypothesis is believed.

To conduct the experiments that prove or disprove hypotheses, you need lengthy training in biology, physiology, epidemiology, or whatever is the relevant discipline. This is typically not "stuff that can be done at home." Moreover, you must have certifications and approvals for the use of animals or humans in studies. The discussion here, therefore, is not meant as a roadmap on how to conduct empiric experiments. It is simply meant to make the point that ideas must be tested to be accepted as valid representations of reality. Moreover, the point to remember is that ideas can be overturned when better, tested propositions arise.

There are many different modalities for testing an idea. These include in vitro studies—that is, "at the bench," which includes a broad array of approaches from test tubes to tissue cultures to computer simulations. Testing in animals includes a range of techniques and subjects that go from one-cell organisms to primates. Finally, anything that will ultimately be used for humans should be tested in humans or even in communities.

■

As evidence in favor of an idea mounts, scientists begin to wonder when they can answer the question, "Am I sure the idea will have the desired effect or is the true cause?" How does science reach a high level of confidence that something actually works in a predicted way?

A commonly used set of criteria used in the biological sciences for developing that confidence were put forth in 1965 by Sir Bradford Hill. When observations meet the high bar set by Hill's tenets, science has a good deal of reassurance that an intervention or exposure causes an effect. Said another way, if the cumulative scientific decision is "Yes," that Hill's tenets have been met, then an intervention is judged to be useful. The Food and Drug Administration (FDA) thus uses such criteria for approval. Hill's tenants have been modified a bit by time and consensus to include:

- Strength of association (exposure or intervention and outcome are strongly associated)
- Consistency (observations from different studies generally agree)
- Temporality (the cause must precede the effect)
- Biological gradient (the greater the exposure in duration or dose, the larger the effect)

- Biological plausibility and coherence (known biology supports the idea)
- Experimental evidence (human experiments—that is, clinical trials, if ethical, concur that the intervention or exposure triggers the outcome)

■

Let's work through an example. The question is whether endometriosis causes ovarian cancer, a worrisome specter given ovarian cancer's high rate of fatality.

Endometriosis, in itself, is a dreadful, although fortunately not fatal, disease. Affecting an estimated 5% to 8% of reproductive age women, it cannot be appropriately described except by the women who are affected. From one patient's blog:

> For so long I thought I was all alone. I had a complete hysterectomy at age 27...I was so excited especially because I believed that would end all my pain.. Boy was I mistaken. That was only the beginning. A year later the pain was back...I had a laparoscopy done, and I was full of adhesions. He cleaned me out and I was Okay. Well, for about 6 months. Then it all started again. The pain!!!!!

No one knows what causes endometriosis. It occurs when tissue that should only be found lining the uterus instead embeds itself into the ovaries, bowel, and other internal organs. There the endometriosis undergoes a menstrual cycle just as it would if it had stayed inside the uterus, but the blood collects inside the main body cavity and causes pain and infertility. Often symptoms are resistant to treatment.

When pathologists look at tissue from affected women, they can sometimes see a spot of cancer within a patch of endometriosis. In early reports, this was noted infrequently, but a more recent pathology series of up to 1,000 endometriosis patients found ovarian cancer in 5% to 10%. Two specific subtypes of ovarian cancer are regularly found within areas of endometriosis. Conversely, among the biopsies from women with these subtypes of ovarian cancer, pathologists quite often (up to 40%–50% of the time) find endometriosis admixed.

One unfortunate woman had a biopsy of her ovary that showed endometriosis with some atypical cellular changes that, still benign, were not removed. Three years later, a biopsy of the same site revealed that she had developed ovarian cancer in the same location. Although surely this is not proof, the possibility that cancerous cells developed out of the atypical endometriosis is suggestive of malignant transformation.

Several epidemiological studies have quantified the rates of ovarian cancer among women with a history of endometriosis. Louise Brinton and colleagues (1997) searched through medical records of 20,686 women in Sweden who had been hospitalized with endometriosis. After a mean of more than 11 years of follow-up, women with endometriosis had a twofold excess in the development of ovarian cancer. Those women with a long-standing endometriosis had a fourfold excess risk. This suggests that rather than a 1 in 75 normal lifetime risk of developing ovarian cancer, the lifetime risk for women with endometriosis could be 1 in 18. Other studies, including a recent international consortium involving more than 21,000 ovarian cancer cases and controls, support these findings. Looking at the question backward (not how many women with endometriosis develop cancer but how many women with cancer had prior endometriosis), two to three times as many women with ovarian cancer versus controls had experienced endometriosis. Indeed, among the epidemiological studies conducted, virtually all have found that women with endometriosis have a risk of ovarian cancer that is two to four times higher than the average woman.

Until recently, scientists were unable to examine the mechanism by which endometriosis may be carcinogenic for lack of an animal model. Dinulescu and colleagues (2005) were able to manipulate the biology of the mouse to create an animal model linking endometriosis to ovarian cancer. By causing two local gene mutations (activation of *Kras* and suppression of *PTEN*), they created a mouse that first developed endometriosis and then went on to ovarian cancer. This has provided the insight that genetic insults can transform endometriosis to cancer.

So does endometriosis cause ovarian cancer? By Hill's tenets, the answer would be, "Yes...But."

The strength of the association between endometriosis and ovarian cancer is sizable. It is not a 20% or a 50% increase in risk—it is at least a 100% increase (a doubling or twofold elevation) and a fourfold increase among women with long-standing disease.

Consistency is demonstrated by the numerous, indeed universal demonstration in epidemiological studies of risk for a specific subtype of ovarian tumor.

Temporality requires a study in which the cause is measured before the effect. In the Brinton study, women had endometriosis recorded in their medical records and only later had a diagnosis of ovarian cancer. Moreover, at least one woman has had endometriosis that appears to have transformed into cancer.

Biological gradient means that longer-standing disease should be more strongly associated with cancer risk. And it is.

Biologic plausibility is shown by the rodent model in which endometriosis transforms into ovarian cancer.

The, "But" in the, "Yes...But" is that experimental evidence is absent. The best "proof" would be a clinical trial. But ethically it would be difficult to defend providing surgical treatment for some women but not others. Neither is it possible to give some women endometriosis and not others. Thus, of Hill's criteria for which data can be generated, all are met. However, without experimental evidence, the "Yes" is tentative.

So as not to excessively alarm women with endometriosis, the risk for ovarian cancer remains small. Even if a woman's risk of ovarian cancer is raised to 1 in 18, that means that 17 of 18 will *not* develop cancer. Something about the duration of disease, treatment, and physiology causes one woman harm while another remains harm-free. Unfortunately, the current state of science cannot predict which woman is which. Yet the evidence for the link between endometriosis and ovarian cancer is sufficiently compelling that it impels science to find ways to prevent possible cancer progression.

■

Why are scientists such wimps? Why do I feel compelled to say, "Yes...But;" "the evidence is tentative"? Of course, Popper never allows us to make claims of proof, but can't I just say, "Yes, the link is sufficiently likely," and move along?

The hesitation is this: an idea can meet almost all of Hill's criteria and be wrong. Take post-menopausal hormone replacement therapy (HT), which in the 1990s was the largest selling medication in the United States. Dozens of large epidemiological studies showed sizable associations between HT (containing estrogen with or without progestin) and lower heart disease risk. The consistency was textbook. HT use came before the heart attack. The longer a woman took HT, the lower the heart risk. Mechanistic studies reinforced the notion that HT caused cardiovascular disease: HT lowers lipids, blood pressure, and glucose—all risk mechanisms for heart disease. In 1990, Deborah Grady, an icon in the field of women's health, recommended that all post-menopausal women, other than those with breast cancer, should take HT because it would actually gain them months of life expectancy. At its zenith, more than three-fourths of post-menopausal female gynecologists were taking HT.

So after 50 years on the market, the National Institutes of Health undertook a mammoth randomized clinical trial, an experimental study to finally establish cause. The *Women's Health Initiative* was the largest human health study ever conducted—an $800 million trial randomizing more than 16,000 post-menopausal women to HT or placebo and following them to document reductions in heart attacks and strokes.

Except the study did not find what it expected. In stunning results published in 2002, the *Women's Health Initiative* found that those women treated with HT compared to those taking placebo suffered a 29% excess in heart attacks, a 41% increase in stroke, and a twofold greater risk of blood clots. HT did not reduce cardiovascular disease—it increased it. All of the prior studies were wrong. Why? Because they were all wrong in the same way—healthier women were more likely to take HT. It was not the HT but the underlying heartiness of HT takers that led to the appearance of benefit. Moreover, scientists overlooked important aspects of biology. The mechanistic experiments that had supported enthusiasm for HT had focused on the advantageous outcomes and ignored those that were detrimental.

HT turned out to be Hume's two clocks: one clock consistently chimed before the other, but that clock did not cause the other to chime. Takers of HT consistently had lower rates of heart disease and stroke but HT did not cause these reductions. The idea that HT caused a reduction in cardiovascular disease was a fallacy. The HT experience serves to underscore the philosophy that the most informative experiments are ones that would disprove, rather than confirm, a hypothesis.

Unfortunately scientists are not dispassionate. As you can imagine, entire careers often go into proving an idea; frames and cognitive biases support the norm. As Thomas Kuhn so eloquently argued in his 1962 classic *The Structure of Scientific Revolutions*, even when an idea begins to show its flaws (he called these anomalies), it is hard to change.

Were there warnings that HT could be harmful? Unfortunately there were many. HT was widely known to increase the risk for blood clots and uterine cancer. Science and medicine discounted the former risk because blood clots are unusual. The latter was considered manageable because it was confined to the use of estrogen alone, so with the addition of progestin, women with a uterus could still use HT safely. HT was then found to increase the risk of breast cancer. This anomaly was surely more concerning. Yet, many scientists and doctors argued that heart disease is the greater killer, and breast cancer can generally be detected early by mammography. Some mechanistic studies had, by this time, shown that inflammation and blood-clotting markers were adversely affected by HT; such studies were simply overlooked. When finally studies began showing that women taking HT were healthier and so the link between HT and heart disease might be a fallacy, a vocal group of scientific innovators began demanding funding for a major clinical trial.

Trying to argue away anomalies is common in science. In the case of HT, there was an additional reason the belief in its benefit was so resilient. Its advantages were shrouded in fantasy. Starting in the 1960s, R.A. Wilson in his book *Feminine Forever* (1966) wrote, "Breasts and genitals will not shrivel. Women will be much more pleasant to live with." R.A. Wilson had initiated a cult that subtly embedded in the psyches of women that HT was the "fountain of youth." As the popularity of the medication increased, more and more women came to believe that the medication improved their mood, softened their skin, improved their libido, and might even save their memory (none of which turned out to be true).

After the publication of the results from the *Women's Health Initiative*, a disturbing truth about the use of HT emerged. As prescriptions for HT fell so also did rates of breast cancer. This occurred not just in the United States but around the world. Suddenly it became apparent that this leading medication prescribed to improve women's health had contributed to a decade's long run-up in rates of breast cancer.

■

Science is forever in a continuous loop of striving to establish certainty. Its lot is to endlessly replace one hypothesis with another through new discoveries and new insights. Each emerging hypothesis undergoes rigorous testing and, if successful, may become part of the dominant paradigm. As you generate new ideas, realize that it is a long and hard road to be able to establish the answer to the question, "Am I sure my idea will have the desired effect or will turn out to be a true cause?" Only after years of evidence-building can science feel some level of confidence.

Even then, being king of the hill is often ephemeral. New ideas are ever replacing older ideas. Innovation is forever moving science forward toward finding more valid explanations within nature. Curiosity and flexibility accelerate the pace of progress. But in this complex universe in which we live, none of us can ever know with absolute certainty what will turn out to be truth.

EXERCISES

1. The care and feeding of ideas exists in a world of constraints: budgets; deadlines; who you know (or might get to know). Let's say you have only a million dollars over the next 5 years (not a lot of money for population studies) to answer the question as to whether fertility rates are declining in the world. The current state of evidence is conflicting, with some studies showing sperm counts tumbling over the past decades but others showing that among couples trying to get pregnant, they are just as successful now as they have always been. How might you approach this question? What would be the strongest study type you could use to address the question?

2. Read the following brief review about the relationship between salt and hypertension: *Ness, R. B. (2009). Controversies in epidemiology and policy: salt reduction and prevention of heart disease. Annals of Epidemiology, 19, 118–120.* Do you think the relationship is causal? Make a chart enumerating Hill's tenants and list the data that you think support or refute each.

21

That Right Idea

H ard as it is to "get the answers right," science has clearly made and continues to make enormous strides toward improving the health and prosperity of humankind. The innate uncertainty of science is exactly the reason to forge ahead with ever more innovative ideas. At the same time, the need for precision and validity makes it essential to converge on the idea that will most likely provide a valid understanding of reality.

In *The Structure of Scientific Revolutions*, (1962) Kuhn makes an analogy between science and evolution. Both, he says, maximize advancement through generating large numbers of random mutations or ideas. Most mutations die, as do most ideas. But when mutations or ideas flourish, they ultimately modify the norm. Innovative thinking involves learning to produce masses of original ideas, but to commit the resources to generate the evidence to turn your idea into a reality you must select a single one.

Idea generation can be like *The Sorcerer's Apprentice*. Before you know it, you have spun so many dreams that you begin to wonder if you are controlling them or they are controlling you. Deciding how to prioritize can be tricky.

There are two primary rules: *(1)* do not rush to judgment; and *(2)* whittle down to only the number of conjectures you can handle. Just because you have not yet accumulated enough evidence to support an idea, if that idea seems interesting and plausible, then it is best to keep working on it. On the other hand, if you try to juggle too many proposals, then you may find yourself trying to successfully keep in the air a tire iron, a basketball, and a light bulb. Holding on and at the same time peeling off seems difficult, if not downright incompatible. Balancing is indeed delicate. But it is not impossible.

The first way to safely exclude ideas is to jettison ones that can be rejected by evidence. The most likely hypothesis is usually the one with the least evidence against it, not the one with the most evidence for it. Think like Popper: Try to find evidence that refutes an idea. For example, some ideas will show themselves as biologically implausible in in vitro or animal studies. Observational epidemiology may refute others. Clinical trials may show the intervention is not safe, either because of side effects or because the dose that leads to efficacy is uncomfortably close to the dose that causes harm.

At the same time, while assembling data, it is best to avoid prematurely forming impressions. Once your mind is made up, you are biased and cannot weigh evidence dispassionately. If, after assembling limited information, you find yourself thinking you know the answer, then ask yourself what information you could generate that would change your mind.

Let's play a game. I give you three numbers—1, 3, and 5—and ask you to find the pattern underlying the numbers. The game is won by correctly identifying the arrangement but you get only one guess. You can improve your chances of correctly guessing the pattern by proposing other numbers. Most people guess 7, and I say, "Correct." Then they guess 9, and again, I say, "Correct." Then they say, "It is ascending odd numbers." And I say, "Wrong!" Now, how did that happen? The way to play the game and win is not to guess what you think may be correct numbers in the sequence but, instead, to guess at numbers that you imagine may be incorrect. So, if your first guess was "6" (which you thought was wrong because your hypothesis was ascending odd numbers), then I would have said, "Correct," and, although you would have been caught up short, you would also have changed your hypothesis. The correct answer is simply: "Ascending numbers."

A second way to limit the ideas you will commit to moving forward is to restrict yourself to those that are most plausible, actionable, and useful.

Plausibility implies that to your knowledge, there are no data that exclude your idea—nothing that has clearly disproven it. Actionable in this case means that you are likely to be able to bring the idea to a useful solution. For example, as a chemist, you have two ideas: a personal flying machine and an enzyme that will speed the growth of oil-producing bacteria. The flying machine is cool but neither you nor anyone you know can really pursue this because of lack of expertise. On the other hand, you've got a pretty good notion about how to synthesize the enzyme for oil-producing bacteria.

A third approach for prioritizing ideas is rapid prototyping. Remember when Ted Koppel from *ABC Nightline* challenged IDEO to redesign the all-American shopping cart? A wall full of drawings came out of two brainstorming sessions, from which teams extracted the best designs and built models. The best model features were then combined into a beautiful curvaceous frame on futuristic casters. Rapid prototyping is a lower risk way to check out designs or ideas before you've made too great an investment.

Rapid prototyping underlies the process of drug discovery. The pharmaceutical industry tests new drugs within a hierarchy of trials (Phases I, II, and III), each larger, more comprehensive, and more costly than the former phase. If public health research were conducted that way (it isn't), then it might look like this: Let's test the hypothesis that menu labeling changes consumer food choices. A Phase I (dosing type) study might examine this proposal in a single food outlet, altering the type, placement, and content of signage until you have achieved the largest effect. Expanding to a restaurant chain in a single geographic setting might become the Phase II (safety) study. At this stage, the study would be designed to test whether food labeling might have any unexpected adverse consequences. Finally, a full-fledged Phase III (efficacy) study could involve multiple food outlets within a large population setting. In current public health research, we typically race straight to the expensive demonstration projects in multiple food outlets. Using a stepped approach allows engagement in the Israeli concept of constructive failure with its associated limited cost.

A fourth approach to prioritization is to interact with the world. You may learn from others that the hypothesis you propose has already been shown not actionable, having been tested and roundly rejected. Others may identify flaws in plausibility. The technology may simply have not been developed. You may discuss your idea with the target audience, and they may hate it or (worse) find it boring. Alternatively, everyone you talk to may be intrigued, and some may become inspired advocates. Although this approach can be very useful, I repeat something I said earlier, "To thine own self be true." If you really believe in an idea, then do not be easily dissuaded. With some tweaking or within a different setting, you may get a more favorable response.

Sales of PDAs were an initial failure. Marketing positioned them as a replacement for desktop computers and in that market, they competed poorly. But when developers realized that the PDA is not a replacement but, rather, a complement to the desktop the rest, of course, became (lucrative) history.

Finally, the decision may not be an either–or. With more resources, you can do more. Science funding is scarce in general and even scarcer for really out-of-the box ideas. The groups of scientists (called study sections) that evaluate projects for federal funding tend to prioritize normative, feasible science and generally play it safe. However, the best idea-generating laboratories get funded for the obvious and squirrel away enough for the innovative. Private investment in novel intellectual property is even scarcer. But if such a person or persons can be found, then an enlightened Angel Investor can allow an innovation to come to maturity.

■

These suggestions may leave you still uncomfortable. What happens if you lose the idea that would have turned out to be "The One?" Unfortunately, trying to juggle too many ideas will leave you dropping them all. Ideas are not babies. Throwing them out is not heinous—it is necessary.

Walt Disney is known as one of the greatest creative thinkers of our time, but he developed a ruthless strategy for ensuring that his creative teams were redirected when they veered down a path toward wasting time. Keith Trickey (2011) has described how Disney developed three rooms for idea generation and elimination. In room one, a project team promoted the generation of unlimited numbers of ideas without judgment. Ideas were aggregated and organized in room two, resulting in storyboards and character descriptions. Room three, known as the "sweat box," was a place of unrestrained critique. Here, characters, storylines, or any other element were ferociously altered or eliminated. No hard feelings. Just business.

An essential element in generating and selecting ideas is the drive to forward action. It sounds simple when the King of Hearts in *Alice in Wonderland* benignly explains, "Begin at the beginning and go'til you come to the end, then stop." But it's often not. In his book *Making Ideas Happen* (2010), Scott Belsky asks, "How many times have you had a great idea for a new product or device or even for a book, but never moved it to fruition?" With lots of steps between the beginning and the end, you can find yourself doggy-paddling as fast as possible and getting nowhere. The only way to save yourself from drowning is to get organized.

Belsky suggests that the way to organize a complicated project is to break it down. Your work falls into three areas: Action Steps, Backburner, and References.

Action steps are the project-specific, concrete tasks that move the innovation project forward. Your first set of action steps is to phrase your question. Within this, there are multiple tasks, each consisting of multiple steps. A "to-do" list becomes the backbone of your action steps. The list breaks down each stage of the project into a series of steps and each step into bite-sized actions. So for finding and phrasing the question, some of the steps may be: make a list of questions you are passionate about; map out a search strategy, go to the source to observe, and so forth. "Map out a search strategy" might have under it: look up a particular fact; read a particular book; e-mail an expert. Each action should start with an action verb, such as "call," "write," or "research." If you are working within a team, then you still write all action items on your list but they get identified with the lead person's name so as to identify responsibility and ensure follow-up. Each task should have a due date and get checked off when completed. When the to-do list gets too ratty or, even better, is all checked off, it is time to generate the next one.

While pursuing action steps, other ideas pop up. Rather than setting off immediately in those directions, Belsky recommends putting these into a Backburner. The Backburner is a running list of possible future projects. The trick is to stay focused while not cutting off exciting new avenues. If you keep your Backburner on the side so it is not distracting but make sure to review it regularly, then you can pull off useful insights or solutions. If time allows, then you can even start to work on something new.

References are the totality of information you acquire. Some are specific to a project. Others you simply pick up as part of normal worklife. These may be notes from a particularly intriguing seminar or a handout from a meeting. The organization of these, just like action-items, should be project-specific. The folders or lists you create to maintain references may be linked to "to-do" items. But keep them separate. References should not muck up your action list.

Action steps, Backburner, and References may seem overly anal, but they are better than landing on your posterior. Like hiking up a mountain, you take one action step and then another and another. You avoid distractions (putting these in the Backburner) and keep track of where you are (with References). Without looking too far up or too far down, you keep moving until—ah ha—you have reached the summit.

■

A visual way to organize your thinking and the tasks needed to complete your innovation project is a "Mind Map." Mind Maps can also be used to diagram brainstorming (i.e., as a visual tool to generate ideas). In the center of the Mind Map, you place a central concept or word. Around it, you arrange concepts with those intuitively most important placed closest to the center. The idea is that by placing ideas in a radial, nonlinear pattern, you overcome normal patterns and trigger connections.

In his book, *Use Your Head* (1974), well-known author Tony Buzan suggests the following guidelines for creating Mind Maps:

- Place the central concept or word in the middle of the page.
- Use several colors to categorize a group of ideas.
- Use images and symbols to stimulate imagery.
- Select key words radiating from the central concept and print these in capital letters.
- Connect each key word/image with a single line to the central concept and then each of these to more peripheral concepts.
- Use emphasis to show strength of associations.

■

Tough problems are often complex. *Occam's Razor*, a central concept in science recommends: Keep things simple. The rule states that when two hypotheses appear to be equally good, the best one is the one that introduces the fewest assumptions. A mathematical proof by Marcus Hutter (2005) demonstrated that theories requiring less computation are more useful than the more complex process of estimating across all computable theories. It might seem that accounting for all computable data would be better but not so. Said another way, if there is a way to simplify, then do it; if there is a short-cut, then take it.

■

Nike's classic admonition, "Just do it," is a particularly important philosophy in idea generation. Generating a really good, novel idea is as hard work as physical training. In both cases, after a few minutes of exercise (muscles or brain), it is natural to want to stop. In training for a marathon, you may wake up dreading and even putting off those first

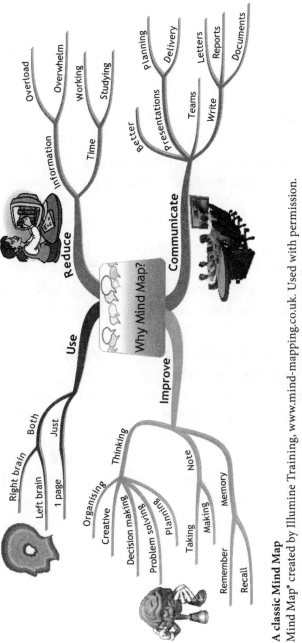

A classic Mind Map

Mind Map® created by Illumine Training, www.mind-mapping.co.uk. Used with permission.

strides. So, too, with creative thinking. Before getting into the work, your desire to watch an hour of TV may overpower you, or 15 minutes into the effort, your desire to check your e-mail may prove overwhelming. Sitting down and hour-after-hour, engaging in the heavy-duty mind lifting needed to answer a truly important and complex question is hard. Great mathematicians and physicists who spend weeks or years solving a single theoretical problem may not be the ones who are so brilliant so much as they are the ones who doggedly persist. To tackle a creative problem requires uninterrupted time. You will need to turn off your e-mail, refuse to answer your phone, and close your office door. Here are some useful time-management strategies for time-management courtesy of Belsky:

- *Don't horde urgent matters.* Share or delegate. Multiple small tasks needing rapid attention will eat your time, so work within a group (if you don't have one, then find one), and share urgent tasks. Sue takes questions about certification of the lab; David handles acute ordering needs; Grace deals with customers who have technical complaints; and you deal with customers with personnel or interpersonal problems. Within these clear boundaries no one oversteps.
- *Be selfish.* Decide what is necessary and what is nice. Not everything needs to be perfect. A hospital administrator I knew once said that he wanted to pass accreditation by just one point—no more, no less. If less then they wouldn't get accredited. If more then they would have wasted precious time that could have been spent on other important matters.
- *Don't dwell on decisions.* Make them and move on. Said another way: Live in the present and future and never in the past wondering what you might have done wrong.
- *Spend the least possible time moving between tasks.* Can people really multitask? We certainly cannot text and drive at the same time. The risk of accident while doing both is equivalent to the risk associated with driving drunk. What we can do and do all the time is serially task. But the more time you spend switching, the

less time you spend on task-oriented work. A trick is to intersperse mind-consuming jobs with mind-numbing ones. For instance after a complicated negotiation or an exhausting brainstorm, move to deleting junk e-mails or looking up a reference.

- *Relentlessly move forward.* Never stop accomplishing Action Steps. Each week, have a goal of what can reasonably be accomplished and finish that. If you don't, then consider how you can be more efficient next week or whether the goal was reasonable. Better to have smaller steps but keep your own deadlines as a way of developing discipline and trust in yourself.

- *Don't wait before you act.* Don't wait too long on others—if someone else is slowing you up and you cannot do the task yourself, then find another collaborator. If you truly believe in something, then don't wait for others—just act.

Plus, always, always believe in yourself. Innovative projects can take a long time, and time instills self-doubt. When fear of failure rears its ugly head, see it for what it is. So get organized, be decisive, delegate, and move forward. Trust that you are on the right course, and go baby go!

EXERCISES

1. Make a "distraction list" consisting of the following headings: e-mails, text messages, Tweets, Facebook or other social network sites, other non-project-related time spent on the computer. Estimate the number of times you check each of these, on average, per day. Then estimate how many minutes you think you spend on each of these each day. Now double and triple that estimation (because most of us underestimate).

2. Devise a personal plan for time management that sets aside blocks of time for innovation generation or innovative project pursuit.

(continued)

CONTINUED

3. Spend a day decisively, not taking more than 10 seconds to make any choice. Afterward, write about how you felt about the experience; catalog which choices you were pleased with and which you regretted. Decide whether any of the choices you made will significantly affect you in the future.

4. Consider someone you know well: your mother, father, sister or brother, best friend, office mate. List all of the projects that, to your knowledge, he/she is currently working on (include home, work, service). Using the rules of plausible, actionable, and useful, how would you prioritize those projects and advise reallocation of their time?

22

The Stodginess of Science

"Whenever you see a successful business someone once made a courageous decision."

—Peter F Drucker

You have now come to the last step in **PIG In MuD: Disseminate** your innovative idea. Finally all your hard work has resulted in something important—something that will surely lead to fame and fortune. But acceptance may be harder than your think. Society and science can be idiosyncratic in its acceptance of new information and ideas.

Consider the discovery of one of the great miracles of modern science: anesthesia. Although his method for finding a cure for tuberculosis was peculiar, if not downright dangerous, Sir Humphry Davy, baronet and President of the Royal Society of London exercised his creative genius at the turn of the nineteenth century by inhaling different gases, hoping to improve respiration. Experimenting with nitrous oxide, now known as "laughing gas," he reported, "I was now completely intoxicated...inconceivably pleasurable." Humphry's discovery that laughing gas caused a drug-induced high made him the toast of British society when, upon providing the gas to well-heeled friends, it became the social drug of the era (who would have thought in 1799?). Then one day, Davy had a toothache and upon taking nitrous oxide, something completely unexpected happened. The pain temporarily subsided. Davy subjected his new observation to further experimentation. After a series of tests, he ultimately came to believe that nitrous oxide might cause a transformation in surgery, making it more tolerable. At the time, unfortunately, the accepted medical frame was that pain was beneficial. Suffering was considered to be evidence of the body's fight for health. Doctors often tried to induce or enhance pain during invasive procedures.

Davy had found the first anesthetic. He knew it. He was a world-famous scientist. Yet his discovery was simply not accepted. Only 40 years later was it translated into standard clinical practice.

Unfortunately the story of Davy and the discovery of anesthesia is no historical oddity. In December 2002, the widely anticipated results of the $130 million clinical trial entitled ALLHAT were released. This historic study of first line treatment for hypertension had found that a class of anti-hypertensive medications that costs a few cents a day were just as effective as ones that cost up to 20 times as much. A solidly conducted, large, randomized trial had found that inexpensive diuretics are a safe and inexpensive solution to treating one of the most common conditions among Americans. With great fanfare, clinical guidelines changed. Yet, research published a decade later showed that the use of diuretics before versus after the trial increased only marginally (30% of all patients using before versus 40% after). Not surprisingly, the Big Pharma companies that make the medications costing 20 times more than diuretics had a lot to do with burying this important and cost-saving research. Thousands of drug representatives blanketed clinical offices to convince doctors that their more costly offerings were superior. Nonetheless, the disappointing lack of uptake of the ALLHAT trial results represents a not uncommon problem in science.

■

How people evaluate new information and make decisions is not only based on individually oriented, empirical information. Humans are social creatures. Social standards have a marked impact on your thinking, and widely held norms limit the acceptance of new ideas. A cognitive bias called the "bandwagon effect" describes how social beliefs—beliefs that are strongly influenced by commonly held frames—influence what we choose to do and think. Humans tend to do what others do. For example, when told that a political candidate is leading in the polls, you are more likely to switch your vote to that candidate. What causes bandwagon bias is not entirely clear. Perhaps it is your universal desire to be accepted—to avoid seeming different or foolish. Perhaps it is something more "hardwired" that has allowed humans to live in large social groupings.

Mankind, unlike any other animal, transmits culture and norms so faithfully that we "over-imitate." When young chimpanzees and children are shown how to retrieve a reward from a box using a series of both relevant and irrelevant steps, the chimps skip the unnecessary actions, whereas the children repeat every little thing. Even when children are told to avoid "silly" steps, they continue to do things that clearly have nothing to do with releasing the reward. For example, they will repeat the act of rubbing a feather across the lid of the box in addition to the requisite act of removing the lid, slavishly following every observed detail. Scientists hypothesize that over-imitation is the means for transmitting culture. That is, humans likely maintain complex cultural and social norms over generations because we are so good at doing exactly what everyone else is doing, staying on the bandwagon.

■

Although the bandwagon effect is critical to the function of human societies, it also limits the adoption of novelty. Remember our earlier discussion of the very long lag between the demonstration of efficacy and the acceptance of medical innovations? From the time research supports a medical intervention to the time that intervention becomes part of routine clinical care is one or two decades.

In science, shifts in tradition are sometimes poorly accepted. There are many likely explanations, but let's consider a particularly powerful one: the frame for science is that it moves forward in a straight line. This "linear movement," frame is represented by metaphors such as "*science marches forward*" and "*scientific progress.*" What happens during frame-shifting is that it disrupts normal science and thus creates a hiccup in scientific linearity. "Normal science," as described by Thomas Kuhn (author of *The Structure of Scientific Revolutions*) involves delving into discrete scientific problems with great precision. Such painstaking work should not be disparaged; as you have seen, observation and experimentation are essential to the primary goal of science: to creating a valid understanding of the natural world.

Nonetheless, normal science seeks to validate and refine existing hypotheses and this has two anti-innovative draw-backs. First, scientific observations derive from the design of experiments that are informed by the existing paradigm. Attention to details and even the design of instruments are narrowly focused. What is often missed is anything unexpected or unmeasured. When the hypothesis and the observations are all confined to the "box," it becomes less likely that surprises will be discovered "outside-the-box." Second, anomalies in existing paradigms are often explained away. There are always small irregularities and glitches when matching-up emerging data with existing understandings, but these can sometimes be, and generally are, attributed to experimental error. If researchers allowed themselves to be stopped by every glitch, they would never progress. In normal science, linear movement trumps imagination.

Another frame that opposes paradigm shifts is that science is hierarchical. Academic scientists are referred to as "junior faculty" and "senior faculty" so as to differentiate between those who have and have not attained the achievement of tenure. "Expert panels" and selective scientific societies abound. Authorities who occupy the top rung of the hierarchy control resources, acceptance, and prestige by dominating the process of peer review. Kuhn noted, "The successive transition from one paradigm to another via revolution is the usual developmental pattern of mature science." And yet, he also comments, "To desert the paradigm is to cease practicing the science it defines." Paradigm shifts make a whole cadre of expert authorities irrelevant.

For a paradigm to shift, anomalies must be detected over and over. Scientists must "lose faith" in the traditional norms. But the battle over paradigms is more contentious than this statement would imply. Often paradigm shifts involve raw, high-stakes combat. Recall Needleman's battle to clear his name after accusations of scientific misconduct; Semmelweis's dismissal by Professor Klein after proving that hand-washing eliminated puerperal fever; Goldberger's vilification in the South for campaigning for higher quality food for the poor.

■

Skepticism about the *Women's Health Initiative*, the high-stakes study that demonstrated the ill effects of taking hormone therapy (HT), started the day the results were released. Detractors argued that the research had not studied the right women. Enrolled women, they claimed were too old even though the study's huge size meant that it had included the largest number of younger, post-menopausal women ever randomized. Critics also argued that study women were not healthy enough since some women will always have undetected heart disease. Finally, there was the argument that the clinical trial had not used the right formulation of estrogen plus progestin even though it was the medication used by more than 90% of U.S. women taking HT at the time.

How could it be that the results of a massive trial among tens of thousands of women, costing almost $800 million could be considered by many physicians to be unconvincing? The bandwagon effect had allowed the popularity of HT to mount for decades. The lure of HT had become such a powerful influence on medical thinking that it would take years to alter no matter how definitive the conflicting data.

■

Yet, not all science is immediately rejected. In fact, technology is often gobbled up like a much anticipated Thanksgiving dinner. Mobile (cell) phones, for example, were only made commercially available in 1983. Between 1990 and 2010 subscriptions grew from 12.4 million to more than 4.6 billion. In the developed world on average, the number of mobile phone subscriptions per 100 inhabitants is 97 (guess that means that all but infants have one), and in some industrialized countries cell phones out-number population. Even in the developing world, half of the population has a cell phone subscription. From Zaire to Afghanistan, young and old people have global communications even when they have erratic access to electricity and go without indoor plumbing. The face of entertainment, law enforcement, medicine, and much else has been forever changed by mobile phones. This is one invention that has most surely gone viral.

New surgical techniques can also spread quickly and broadly. Guidelines for bariatric surgery performed to treat morbid obesity were formalized only two decades ago. By 1998, an estimated 20,000 pro-cedures were performed; by 2010 bariatric surgeries in the U.S. were performed on ten times that number of patients (200,000). Similarly, lap-aroscopic surgery, which only came into broad use in the early 1990s, has become the standard of care for an increasing array of applications. Cholecystectomy, appendectomy, hysterectomy, tubal surgery, and even liver and adrenal surgery are now standardly performed using this less invasive method. There are many other examples of the rapid spread of surgeries for joint replacements, cardiac procedures, and others. Like information and communication technology, surgery is a field in which innovation dissemination often inspires rapid uptake.

So although dissemination of important scientific ideas can be greatly slowed by the bandwagon effect and by entrenched interests, some science and technology is readily adopted. In order to disseminate your own idea, you must understand why some innovations hit a societal wall, whereas others are quickly and broadly diffused. That is the subject of the next chapter.

23

Overcoming the Stodginess
of Science

"Be curious always. For knowledge will not acquire you, you must acquire it."

—Anonymous

Although barriers to new ideas can sometimes be daunting, they are not insurmountable. New ideas can and are adopted every day, and even revolutionary ideas eventually shatter paradigms. To overcome the inertia against innovation, start with yourself. See if you can answer this brainteaser.

Emperor Akbar once ruled over India. He was a wise leader but one who demanded respect and obedience. He had five advisors, each brilliant, but the wisest of all was Birbal. One day the emperor asked his advisors: "If somebody pulled my mustache, what sort of punishment should be given to him?"
"He should be flogged!" said one courtier.
"He should be hanged!" said another.
"He should be beheaded!" said a third.
But Birbal replied, "He should be given sweets."
"Why do you make light of my question, Birbal?" asked the emperor.
What do you think was Birbal's answer?

To solve the riddle, you must analyze the implications of absolute authority. Social norms, Birbal realized, would make it impossible for the emperor's mustache to be touched by any old citizen. Only someone not following social norms could have pulled the emperor's mustache—a child, and more likely a child from the royal household.

Try this one:

> One day, Emperor Akbar, while walking in the Royal Gardens, stumbled on a misplaced stone. His embarrassment at appearing clumsy caused him to order the arrest and execution of the chief gardener. Birbal went to the gardener's prison cell and pledged to help. He advised the gardener that he must do something that he would normally never do. Reluctantly, the gardener agreed. The day before the execution, the gardener was given an audience with the emperor, as was the custom. The gardener shuffled up to the throne, and when he was within reach, he lurched forward in an attempted attack. After the guards had pulled the prisoner off and begun to take him away, Birbal stepped forward to explain. The emperor then ordered the release of the gardener. What did Birbal say?

Anyone other than an emperor would be held to the social standard that the punishment must fit the crime. Birbal's explanation reminded the ruler that even emperors should meet this norm. "Surely the royal subjects will protest a man being executed for mislaying a stone," Birbal said, "but they would understand the death penalty for a man who attacks an emperor." So Birbal explained that he had instructed the gardener to initiate an attack to provide a rationale for his harsh punishment. With this, the emperor, being a reasonable monarch, released the prisoner. Stepping outside of the social frame presented the explanation.

■

A willingness to buck societal norms can help you train yourself to accept change. But what gets society enthusiastic about new ideas? Think about microwave ovens, the Internet, DVD players. As soon as they became reliable and accessible they were gobbled up.

Let's say that you are now the proud inventor of a great new idea that has been rigorously tested and found to be useful and effective. You may have found a new behavioral approach for smoking cessation, developed a more efficient procedure for isolating DNA, mutated a bacterial species to synthesize Vitamin D, or developed a stronger amalgam of steel. How do you get the world to adopt your ground-breaking innovation?

First, you must identify your audience. Are you "selling" to the scientific community—that is, are you trying to get others to replicate and expand on your idea? Or are you trying to get adoption by the public? Are you advising lawmakers on policy or marketing to industry?

Many scientists feel comfortable only when talking to scientists and that is understandable. But if science wants innovation to be actionable, then it must go beyond its own community and try to achieve high impact. These statistics suggest that scientists must get better at telling their tale to the public:

- Scholarly books in the United States contributed only 1.3% to all books sold by U.S. publishers.
- The most common way for scientists to transmit their findings is through journals and meetings. These avenues reach only hundreds to perhaps a few thousand persons and almost never the people who are most critical for getting an idea into policy.
- Many really important findings, certainly in public health, are not implemented (indoor smoking bans, helmet laws, lower speed limits), and politicians say this is because in the competition between scientists and advocacy groups, advocacy groups are simply the most vocal and compelling.

■

Whether you want your idea to be adopted by scientists, by legislators, or by the public more broadly, how do you do it? In his sensationally popular book, *The Tipping Point: How Little Things Can Make a Big Difference* (2002), Malcolm Gladwell argues that ideas are spread like epidemics. Epidemics have some intriguing qualities. They can spread from a few people to thousands or millions of people over a very short time.

How does this relate to promoting your idea? Gladwell argues persuasively that just as disease can spread wildly to quickly overtake a population the uptake of novelty seems to occur everywhere and all at once. To get your idea into practice, you must create a social epidemic—you must reach a tipping point

Epidemiologists use three variables to describe and predict infectious disease spread: host, pathogen, and environment. In explaining social epidemics, Gladwell converts these parameters to: the right people, "The Law of the Few;" the right idea, "The Stickiness Factor;" and the right environment, "The Power of Context."

Gladwell's "Law of the Few" suggests that a small number of the "right people" spread social epidemics. These people have extraordinary personal characteristics that make them highly influential and thus capable of inciting attitudinal change. The right people are highly connected, knowledgeable about new trends, great at selling dreams, or all three.

To demonstrate the influence of people who are highly connected, Gladwell recounts a classic experiment by Stanley Milgram that established the moniker "six degrees of freedom." Milgram's experiment was designed to see how difficult it would be to get a letter from Omaha, Nebraska, to a stockbroker in Massachusetts by way of social networks. Of the 160 letters sent, on average, the letters reached the stockbroker in six steps. Now here is the clincher. Half of all deliveries were handed to the stockbroker by Mr. Brown, Jones, or Jacobs. In other words, fully half of all responses came through three individuals who were highly connected.

People who are connected, knowledgeable, and convincing quickly spread novelty because they know lots of people, are a respected source of information, and are compelling. The silliest-seeming You Tube videos, for example, become overnight phenomena when highly connected thought leaders promote them as favorites to large numbers of friends.

■

The right idea, as described by Gladwell, suggests that tinkering with the message can make a big difference in creating a market for new inventions and innovations. Innovations need not be earth-shattering. They can be product improvements (phones with camera features, music features, Internet features); product segmentations (a shampoo for dandruff, dry hair, greasy hair, colored hair); better packaging; and so forth. Finding a market for novel ideas can occur either by differentiating the idea or by hitching it to socially valued attributes.

Girls seem to be forever forgetting to take their birth control pills, raising their risk of pregnancy. What if birth control pills came with a free cell phone app that appealed to a young woman's frame about the value of freedom. Imagine that every morning the first thing a pill user hears on her phone is the Akon song, "Everything I have, everything I own, all my mistakes man I already own. I want to be free...." Then the girl sees a liberated young woman taking her birth control pill. Who knows if this reminder would work, but it might—and if it doesn't, some other messaging will. Social marketing suggests there is a simple way to package each particular type of information, but you have to find the right frame and leverage it to make an idea stick.

■

Finally, Gladwell discusses the right environment. Epidemics are sensitive to the time and place in which they occur.

One of the enduring demonstrations of the powerful influence of the environment was conducted by Philip Zimbardo in the 1970s at Stanford University. In the basement of the psychology building, Zimbardo fabricated a prison made up of 6-by-9-foot cells. He selected 21 subjects who

appeared particularly normal on psychological testing, divided them half
into guards and half into prisoners, and dressed each group in appropriate garb. Almost immediately, the guards became rigid martinets. They
awakened prisoners at 2 A.M. and forced them to do push-ups. When the
prisoners rebelled, the guards sprayed them with fire extinguishers and
threw the ring leader into solitary. By day six, guards were consistently
behaving in a way that was cruel and dehumanizing. Prisoners went from
crying and rageful to docile and immobile. It was then that Zimbardo
prematurely called off the experiment. Good kids from a good school had
become transformed by circumstances.

■

How do the right people, the right idea, and the right environment apply
to scientific innovation? Let's answer this question with a question: What
does Robert McNamara, infamous as secretary of defense during the
troop build-up in Vietnam, have to do with seat belts? Before McNamara
was named by President Kennedy to his later maligned cabinet position,
he was President of Ford Motor Company. Joining the mammoth organization in 1946 as a former World War II officer who had earned a Legion
of Merit, he soon became known as a Whiz Kid for his analytic approach
to management. A major focus for McNamara was safety.

In 1950, with 40 million cars on the road, 33,000 people died in traffic
accidents. Sixty years later, while the number of cars had exploded to 248
million, the crude number of highway fatalities had actually fallen. Age-
adjusted death rates from motor vehicle accidents per 100,000 population
in the U.S. fell from 22 in 1976 (the earliest calculation seemingly available) to 14 in 2007. McNamara initially offered seatbelts as an optional
package on Ford cars but later had all Fords outfitted with a safety package called the Lifeguard as standard equipment. The Lifeguard included
a seatbelt and a dished steering wheel, replacing the cone steering center
that had impaled many drivers. According to Levitt and Dubner in their
book, *Super Freakonomics: Global cooling, patriotic prostitutes, and why
suicide bombers should buy life insurance* (2009), McNamara recalled,

"I flew down to visit an assembly plant in Texas. The manager met me at the plane. I buckled my seat belt and he said 'What's the matter, you afraid of my driving?'"

That pervasive frame that seatbelt use equated to mistrust of the driver was hard to change. Although McNamara did what he could, seatbelt use did not seriously increase. Finally car manufacturers gave up on volunteerism. They added warning lights and bells to the dashboards of cars in the mid-1970s so as to annoy customers into compliance. In 1984, influenced by dummy crash experiments as well as studies showing that seatbelts reduced highway fatalities by almost 50%, the first state (New York) instituted legislation making seatbelt use mandatory. Others followed. By 2007, The U.S. National Highway Traffic Safety Administration estimated that 15,147 lives were saved by seatbelts that year alone. As compared to 1960, when 11% of Americans wore seatbelts, the rate of seatbelt use had climbed to 90%.

The right person in this story was McNamara, although many others promoted the same idea at the time. The right idea was to make seatbelts universally accessible (standard); comfortable (retractable); and memorable (bells and whistles). The right environment was the accumulating data consistently showing that seatbelts saved lives and the willingness of federal and state legislatures to pass policies that favored public health over individual rights.

The use of seatbelts was ultimately the result of a frame shift. In 1960, use of a seatbelt equated to insulting the driver's competence. In 2011, lack of use of a seatbelt equated to pointlessly risking your life. None of these influences alone—not McNamara nor retractable belts nor governments— tipped use patterns. But all of them together caused seatbelt use to become normative.

■

Other important innovations have been adopted when the right people, the right idea, and the right environment have pushed them past the tipping point. Folic acid, which today you will find fortifying your bread, cereal, and pasta, tipped because of Godfrey Oakley. While employed at the Centers for Disease Control and Prevention (CDC), Oakley learned of the newly released results from a small clinical trial by Smithells and colleagues (1989) in England showing that among women who had a previous child with the birth defect spina bifida, the use of high-dose folic acid almost eliminated the risk of bearing a subsequent child with a similar congenital condition. Spina bifida is one of the more common birth defects, and because it represents a lack of closure of the spinal canal, it can cause devastating disability.

To prevent spina bifida, a woman must have a high blood level of folic acid in the first weeks of pregnancy, generally before she is aware she is pregnant. Oakley thus argued that prenatal vitamins containing folate were taken by most women too late in pregnancy to ever work. He went on a one-man campaign to get the Food and Drug Administration (FDA) to legislate the addition of folate to one of the most commonly eaten foods in the United States—flour. At first, his argument met resistance because of a concern that folic acid (Vitamin B9) can mask deficiency of Vitamin B12. However, Oakley found himself in the right environment. First, cereal companies had begun to add vitamin fortification, and this had become widely accepted. Second, studies were emerging showing that higher folic acid intake might reduce the risk of heart disease.

Folic acid fortification was mandated by the FDA in January, 1998. In 2004 and 2007, large population studies demonstrated that after the addition of folic acid to flour, the rate of spinal defects had dropped by 25% in the United States and 46% in Canada.

The right person (Oakley), the right idea (flour fortification), and the right environment (the analogy to cereal fortification and the emerging hope that folate might prevent heart disease) tipped the government to require folate fortification. It turned out to be the right thing to do.

■

If electric cars (which we met when talking about Cognitive Biases) tip, it will be because of the right person, idea, and environment. The driving force behind Better Place, the Israeli company launching the effort, is Shai Agassi (CEO). But it doesn't hurt that Agassi has been backed from the beginning by Ehud Olmert, former Israeli Prime Minister. Olmert has helped bring funding and cooperation from corporate partners, including Dor Alon, one of Israel's leading gas station operators, which will host battery switch stations, and Renault, which has agreed to convert a portion of more than 45,000 internal combustion engine cars to electric. The right idea is Agassi's plan for the battery to be leased through a monthly use fee. The right environment is the creation of a national grid of battery replacement stations that are as conveniently located as gas stations. Better Place is actively building such a nationwide grid. If Israel can pull this off, then electric cars will dominate the market there, and this may begin a tipping away from the world's dependence on oil.

■

The right people, if convinced to become passionate advocates, can make your idea spread wildly. These may not be people you already know. You may have to find them through social networking—through friends of friends, professional organizations, internet groups, and so forth. You will likely have to court them. Ideas do not sell themselves—they need to be sold.

When I was a wet-behind-the-ears assistant professor working as an emergency department doc, I had an idea to study whether hospitalization is necessary for the treatment of pelvic inflammatory disease (PID). PID occurs when sexually transmitted diseases infect the pelvic organs, and it often results in infertility. No one knew whether simply giving these women antibiotics and sending them home, as was usual practice, would damage patients' future reproductive potential. Although I had the training to design the study, I had no idea how to get it funded. While pondering this, I read everything I could. One name, a senior official at the CDC, kept popping up. Ward Cates was his name and he seemed to be *the* guy writing about PID. So I cold-called him. When I told him what I had in mind, he said, "You know, the CDC has wanted to do that clinical trial (comparing inpatient versus outpatient treatment for PID) for years but we figure it will cost $12 million and we don't have those kinds of resources." To which I casually replied, "I bet I can do it for less." Perhaps my audaciousness simply amused Ward Cates because by all rights he should have hung up. Instead, he connected me to the top clinical researchers across the country. With his seal of approval, they all joined in, we ultimately we got the study funded, and the result (outpatient treatment works just as well as inpatient treatment at 10% of the cost) became a backbone of treatment guidelines. The "Law of the Few" had taken my idea from nowhere to everywhere with one right person.

The idea must be right—it must have attributes that make it attractive. Packaging and targeting are the expertise of marketers, but frequently you don't have the resources for such hired guns. Focus groups representing the target audience can provide insights into what will stick. In my study of PID, I relied on more knowledgeable epidemiologists who had conducted such trials to figure out how to get the experts on board. The backing of Cates was a huge help but likely not enough to get these very busy gynecologists to devote their scarce time. To make the trial intriguing and desired, I asked each clinical researcher to administer a site where the subjects would be recruited. This expanded the scope of the trial to locations around the country representing different cultural and racial groups. More importantly, it shared the credit and funding among collaborators. Having some skin in the game made assisting in the trial an idea that stuck.

Finally, the environment must be supportive. This is much like establishing that the question you pose is actionable. Technology and society must be in a position and in a place to accept your idea. With the PID trial the question was one that represented a long-standing clinical quandary. As an emergency doc, I found myself frequently at odds with the gynecology residents who rarely wanted to admit a woman with PID. I, on the other hand, worried that sending the woman home would do her real harm. The context of uncertainty was ripe for embarking on the proposed study.

Sometimes the context must be helped to become ripe. To nudge people toward readiness for an innovation may mean engaging professional groups or engaging other "insiders" through a blog, Twitter, Facebook, or YouTube. A specific group might be particularly adapted to or accepting of your idea. From there, it can spread further.

So finding the right people, the right idea, and the right environment can bring your idea to action. Your best tools toward success are flexibility, tenacity, and, of course, a strong belief in yourself.

EXERCISES

1. How you respond to something depends on how you define it. We see it as acceptable to wear bikinis outdoors, but not underwear. We are willing to accept disobedience from small children that we would never accept were they only a year or two older. Redefining a category can be as effective as reinventing it. Think of new uses for old products, either by finding a right environment or by modifying the product to make it the right idea.

2. President Kennedy invigorated a generation of American children to become scientists by creating the U.S. space program. What might the current U.S. president do to become a champion for innovative solutions to some of our most pressing problems?

24

Innovation Incubators

"Free the child's potential, and you will transform him into the world."

—Maria Montessori

"We especially need imagination in science. It is not all mathematics, nor all logic, but it is somewhat beauty and poetry."

—Maria Montessori

N ow that you have learned how to answer questions with novel and actionable scientific ideas, will you and an army of other passionate innovators overcome the greatest threats to health and prosperity? Will you solve the problems of emerging infections, obesity, global warming, limited water supplies? You may. But only if the establishment allows you to.

If America were to build environments at school and at work that consistently encourage innovation, what would those environments look like?

■

Amabile, one of the country's foremost researchers on organizational innovation, has studied workplaces all of her career. She is an activist for creative business environments. Some of her advice is to avoid rigid oversight, refrain from judgment, and build an environment that is generally pleasant.

Here are some of Amabile's specific recommendations:

- Allow professionals a "network of possible wanderings" wherein they can explore and solve problems
- Freedom of choice in approach
- Supervisory encouragement (managerial recognition of new ideas)
- Transparent and consistent goals
- Time, although under certain conditions real time constraints can heighten creativity
- Money at a threshold of sufficiency, but task-contingent monetary incentives can dampen creativity
- Mutually supportive teams

■

For two glorious pre-kindergarten years, my daughter, Sara, went to a Montessori school. The Montessori Method, developed by the Italian physician and educator Maria Montessori at the beginning of the twentieth century, is grounded in a philosophy of self-directed development. Children choose their own activities and work at their own pace. When strictly implemented, Montessori pre-school, as compared to other schools, has been shown to result in superior performance on standardized tests of reading and math as well as advanced social skills. Older Montessori students reported a greater sense of motivation and community than students from other schools. And Montessori students in a randomized comparison to other students wrote more creative essays.

What are the similarities between what Amabile suggests and the Montessori Method? Clearly both involve "possible wanderings" and "freedom of choice in approach." This is not about removing structure. Instead, Montessori identifies the child's "job" as development and she rigorously describes the conditions under which that job can be best accomplished. At the same time, within the supportive Montessori environment, the child is given unprecedented flexibility. Each child has remarkable independence in their approach to learning.

A second notable parallel to Montessori is Amabile's "transparent and consistent goals." The Montessori Method employs well-defined goals, although these are not prescribed by checklists or algorithms. Instead they are directed by the environment. For example, a child may play with a counting tool, but that tool is not offered until the child is prepared. First there is an explanatory lesson. Then the environment is carefully outfitted with a set of materials that practitioners of the Montessori Method call "the apparatus," organized by subject and complexity. Setting limits on availability of learning tools shapes the direction and pace of learning.

Third, both Amabile and Montessori have a common vision for super-vision. Amabile describes supervision as supportive, and Montessori describes the teacher as an observer and guide. The authority figure is neither directing nor judging but instead enabling.

A fourth common feature is the inducement to work in teams. Montessori classrooms typically contain mixed age groups as broad as ages 2 to 6 years. Children provide support and challenge to each other. Pairings form naturally as less experienced children learn and more expe-rienced children learn to teach.

Finally, Amabile talks about the need for internal over external moti-vation. Although it may seem counterintuitive, task-contingent external rewards hamper creativity. In one experiment, a set of children mak-ing paper flowers were told theirs would be judged. Another group was simply left to create. Who made the more creative patterns? The chil-dren who did not expect they would be externally evaluated. In another experiment, preschoolers who were promised a "good player award" if they played with a magic marker to complete a task shifted from playing with the marker creatively to playing only as a means toward the reward. Similarly, in several studies of employees, those given task-based financial incentives (beyond salary) made less creative decisions than those whose compensation was not linked to achieving specific tasks. If employers are trying to increase productivity, task-based incentives are useful. If they are trying to encourage innovation, money is not what speaks.

In traditional Montessori environments, there are neither grades nor other external incentives. Children's motivation to work comes from designing materials and environments that are attractive and alluring. Children, Montessori believed, are intrinsically curious if provided with objects that spur their curiosity. The method cultivates a sense of motivation from within.

Overall, Montessori provides a model environment for fostering creativity. It is not an environment that allows complete freedom. Rather, it supports self-direction and self-motivation bounded by realistic environmental constraints. It enables supervisory guidance but not control and it values support from peer groups. Montessori models the very attributes Amabile described for creative workplaces.

■

In science, how do environments measure up to these aspirational attributes? Many scientists gravitate to academic settings in the hopes of having the freedom to pursue "possible wanderings." Indeed, academia has historically been the crucible for discovery and remains the best hope for future innovation.

Is academic science organized to support innovative endeavors, which are often slow, meandering, and high-risk? Surely academic science continues to represent one of the highest accomplishments of humankind and much exciting research is coming out of modern universities. Yet (as reviewed in Chapter 1: *Don't Read this Book*) pundits worry that the pace of scientific innovation could use acceleration.

Academia has become a business like any other business, with financial bottom lines and quarterly income statements. Administrators, Boards of Directors, and lawmakers want efficiency and results. Funding is the coin of the research realm. Most academic research is funded by industry or the federal government. Industry funding is usually highly controlled and outcome-based, with little room for intellectual drift. Federal funding contains the opportunity to nurture the seedling of innovation but the question is whether the process of granting federal science dollars meets the potential for maximizing creativity. The peer review committees that determine where the money goes are typically risk averse. Failure is considered by many committees to be unacceptably costly. A—if not *the*—major consideration in accepting or rejecting proposals is feasibility. Surely scientific activity must focus on rigor and the need to understand the realities of natural processes. Yet, the hope is to inject in this discipline a shot of creativity. This situation may be improving somewhat with the National Institutes of Health's new peer review scoring system which puts a premium on innovation. Nonetheless, a colleague on a review panel once complained that for a novel idea to be funded it must first be proven and it cannot be proven until it is funded. This catch-22 limits many out-of-the-box ideas.

As Amabile posits and experiments have shown, external motivation weakens innovation. Yet, incentives, both positive and negative, are the backbone of academic science. The way to professional status is through garnering grants. Consistent rejection of grant proposals is antithetical to academic advancement. How can young people remain motivated to pursue uniquely novel ideas, which are often unfundable, require years of misses, and have uncertain payoffs?

It took Edison 12 years of failures before he returned to a carbon filament and patented the light bulb. The Wright Brothers spent 7 years and several hang-glider crashes to achieve the first powered human flight. Tom Starzl, father of liver transplantation, spent 20 years failing again and again until he finally found a surgical recipe that was dependable and safe. In modern-day science, there is little room for costly misses—the best and brightest work at the edge or normal science but do not get too far ahead.

■

There are both financial and structural limitations to the ability of students and trainees—the next generation of scientists to pursue "possible wanderings" and "freedom of choice in approach." The frame of linear scientific progress means that the goal becomes the destination (graduation) rather than the journey. Funding also limits the approach that young people can pursue. Most often, traineeships require work that is within the confines of the work of their mentor. For students hoping to avoid excessive debt there is limited choice beyond walking the straight and narrow.

■

Some academic institutions and funding agencies are only too aware of these limitations and are working hard to do something about them. From these attempts and other thoughts, come the following 10 modest suggestions.

First, the anti-wandering climate in academia seems well-established. But history tells us that science is forever changing. Israeli businesses, perhaps the most innovative in the world, embrace constructive failure. Rather than considering failure too costly, they instead judge lack of innovation as too costly. When short-term gains are the yardstick, certain behaviors are favored; when novelty is the yardstick, entrepreneurs may well behave differently. If science were to embrace the Israeli frame whereby innovation is valued as highly as linear progress, the trajectory of discovery might well accelerate.

Second, federal funding models that are used and successful in some settings could be extended more broadly to support scientists' flexibility and originality. In most of American academia, financial support must be obtained for every separate set of scientific experiments through the arduous and lengthy (often taking years) process of peer-reviewed grant submissions. The funding, if and when it finally comes, supports only those limited ideas. In contrast, inside the National Institutes of Health and in the United Kingdom, scientific funding supports whole laboratories, consisting of senior scientists and their trainees, over periods of time. The idea is that if the laboratory remains successful, then the many experiments within the laboratory pay off. Stable infrastructure funding to "winners" provides sustenance for laboratories with proven track records in innovation. Perhaps some hybrid model of infrastructure and grant-specific funding is worth a little experimentation.

Third, a critical element to accelerating the pursuit of scientific innovation comes from an old joke: "The answer is money...Now what's the question?" Enhancing innovation will take a financial commitment. The National Institutes of Health should be applauded for investments in the NIH Common Fund focusing on high risk-high gain initiatives, resources, and scientists. Some critics have noted that the proportion of the NIH portfolio committed to such activities (a few percent or less) is too modest and presumably more would be better. A complementary approach might be to separate implementation from ingenuity. Such a program would reward potentially earth-shattering ideas as ends in themselves. Ideas would need to be realistic only in theory. At a later stage, funding would be separately awarded to test whether those ideas could be executed. Imagine this as an architect is to an engineer. The architect drafts something beautifully functional, and the engineer ensures that the structure is physically sound.

Fourth, a cadre of scientists with particularly great creative potential should be identified during training and supported through at least early career, with no strings attached. McArthur genius awards provide sustained support to future knowledge leaders without the expectation of immediate productivity. According to the Foundation's website, "The fellowship is not a reward for past accomplishment, but rather an investment in a person's originality, insight, and potential." Each year, McArthur awards 5 years of support to 20 to 40 artists, musicians, and scientists. But such a small program has only a limited impact. Expanding this conception to provide the luxury of fiscal support for a much larger number of young scientists with exceptional potential is worth more than a few moments of thought.

Fifth, character is consistent in persons and in organizations. Laboratories that turn out original discoveries generally do so repeatedly, and they also repeatedly turn out the next generation of innovators. The best training sites should be financially encouraged to train the best and brightest. After all, Nobel Prize winners tend to train in the labs of former Nobel Prize winners.

Sixth, to socialize young people into an innovative work world, early expectations should be less about outcomes and more about ideas. This would require a change in the metrics used to judge early success—from an orientation around products (e.g., scientific papers) to one around thought content.

Seventh, "possible wanderings" are less risky if science learns to fail faster and smarter. The design industry (á la IDEO) incorporated this into their processes long ago by way of prototyping. Prototyping means quick and dirty testing. Small studies on the way to more definitive ones, novel methods for screening targeted outcomes, and computer-based systems-models on the way to human studies all speed innovation. Failing small reduces the pain of trying out new ideas.

Eighth, the hierarchical structure of science must be overcome to foster ingenuity. Peer review, central to scientific acceptance and success, intensifies the bandwagon effect. What if peer review were reframed from reliance on the judgment of authorities to reliance on the power of groups? Recently the prestigious literary journal *Shakespeare Quarterly* tried such an experiment. The journal posted four essays online prior to acceptance and invited a sizable group to comment. By simply registering one's contact information on the website, anyone else could chime in. In the end, 41 people posted more than 350 comments. Decisions on print publication were based on these comments.

Ninth, science will progress more rapidly in some areas through supportive teams. Collaboration and open source are coming into their own in science with initiatives such as ADNI (the Alzheimer's disease consortium) and HapMap (the genetics open source website). However, initiatives that result in a shared prize run against the frame of idea ownership. Currently, academic promotion and reward are based almost entirely on individual accomplishment. How do team members get recognized when the impact is not attributed to the parts but to the whole? In confronting this dilemma, academic institutions have been quick to discuss but slow to act. Almost surely, the answer will lie in changing the metrics for academic success such that team contributions are sincerely valued. Balancing the primacy of independent thought with the priority of group contributions will be tricky, but the time has come to at least attempt clever strategies to do so.

Tenth, scientists and science administrators should be trained in innovative thinking. Such training will, I believe (biased as I am) enhance the likelihood of embracing suggestions one through nine.

■

Maximizing scientific creativity is critical to advancing discovery and improving health and prosperity. The breakthroughs that will sustain humanity will come, not from simply flogging scientists to work harder but from building systems in which they can work better.

Innovative thinking can be taught. What would America look like if "possible wanderings" were incorporated into curriculum starting in kindergarten? What if methods-based innovative training were standard in high school science courses and continued through doctoral education? What if promising creative minds were consistently supported and professionally advanced as they struggle to reach their potential for productivity?

The first and perhaps the most important step to innovation generation is to acknowledge the limits of human thinking. Jumping outside frames will take a collective will to recognize the boundaries and find creative alternatives. The world has enormous and formidable challenges, but science has a remarkable track record of turning disaster into success.

Science has achieved the most impressive set of accomplishments of any endeavor in human history. Its continued triumph requires maximizing what each of us brings to it. The greatest hope for science's future is you. I urge to you to regain your inner toddler—re-kindle your curiosity; follow your dreams; ask the most audacious questions. In short, pull out your crayons and feel free to color outside of the lines.

Don't Read this Book:

1918 Influenza outbreak: *Kolata, G. (1999). Flu: The Story of the Great Influenza Pandemic. New York: Simon and Schuster; Taubenberger, J. K., & Morens, D. M. (2006). 1918 influenza: the mother of all pandemics. Emerging Infectious Diseases. 12, 15–22.*

2009 H1N1; vaccine manufacture: Leroux-Roels, I., & Leroux-Roels, G. (2009). Current status and progress of prepandemic and pandemic influenza vaccine development. *Expert Review of Vaccines. 8*, 401–423; Tang, J. W., Shetty, N., & Lam, T. T. (2010). Features of the new pandemic influenza A/H1N1/2009 virus: virology, epidemiology, clinical public health aspects. *Current Opinion in Pulmonary Medicine. 16*, 235–241; H1N1 Influenza Timeline. Accessed October 24, 2011 from http://en.wikipedia.org/wiki/2009_flu_pandemic_timeline;

Gain of 30 years in life expectancy: Centers for Disease Control and Prevention. (1999). Ten great achievements – United States 1900–1999. *Morbidity & Mortality Weekly Report. 48*, 241–243.

War on Cancer: Jemal, A., Thun, M. J., Ries, L. A. G., Howe, H. L., Weir, H. K., Center, M. M., et al. (2008). Annual report to the nation on the status of cancer, 1975–2005, featuring trends in lung cancer, tobacco use, and tobacco control. *Journal of the National Cancer Institute. 100*, 1672–1694.

Creativity Slow-down and Crisis: Bronson, P. & Merryman, A. (2010, July 10). The Creativity crisis. Newsweek, Accessed February 24, 2010 from http://www.newsweek.com/2010/07/10/the-creativity-crisis.html; The New York Times. Opinion Pages. Where are the jobs? David Brooks. (2011) Accessed October 25, 2011 from http://www.nytimes.com/2011/10/07/opinion/brooks-where-are-the-jobs.html; Cowen T. (2010) *The Great Stagnation: How America Ate all the Low Hanging Fruit, of Modern History, Got Sick, and (Eventually) Will Feel Better.* New York: Penguin.

American slippage in research productivity: SJR. County Scientific Rankings, 1997. Accessed December 4, 2009 from http://www.scimagojr.com/countryrank.php?areaZ0&categoryZ0&regionZall&year Z1997; Science News: Handful of U.S. Schools Claim Larger Share of Output (2010). Accessed October 27, 2011 from http://www.sciencemag.org/content/330/6007/1032.full

American children lose creativity with age: TED. Ideas Worth Sharing. Ted Robinson says schools kill creativity (2006) Accessed August 23, 2008 from http://www.ted.com/talks/ken_robinson_says_schools_kill_creativity.html.

Creativity program evaluations: Clapham, M. M. (2003). The development of innovative ideas through creativity training. In Shavinina, L. V. (Ed.) *The International Handbook on Innovation* (pp. 366–374). Oxford: Elsevier; Scott, G., Leritz, L. E., & Mumford, M. D. (2004). The Effectiveness of Creativity Training: A Quantitative Review. *Creativity Research Journal 16,* 361–388; Basadur, M. S., Graen, G. B., & Scandura, T. A. (1986). Training effects on attitudes toward divergent thinking among manufacturing engineers. *Journal of Applied Psychology, 4,* 612–617; Basadur, M. S., & Finkbeiner, C. T. (1985). Measuring preference for ideation in creative problem solving training. *Journal of Applied Behavioral Science, 21,* 37–49

Torrance 50 Year results: Torrance, E. P. (1993). The beyonders in a thirty year longitudinal study of creative achievement. *Roeper Review15,* 131; Plucker, J. A. (1999). Is the proof in the pudding? Reanalyses of Torrance's (1958 to present) longitudinal data. *Creativity Research Journal 12,* 103–114.

Ericsson experiment: Syed, M. (2010). *Bounce.* New York. Harper Collins.

It All Depends on How you Look at It

General discussion of frames: Schiffrin, D., Tannen, D., & Hamilton, H. E. (Eds.) (2001). *The Handbook of Discourse Analysis.* Malden, MA: Blackwell.

Koch and Pasteur germ theory: McGraw Hill. Online Learning Center. Interactive Time Line. Discovering the microbial world. Accessed December 2009 from http://highered.mcgraw-hill.com/sites/0072320419/student_view0/interactive_time_line.html..

Jane Goodall: Greene, M. (2005). *Jane Goodall: a biography.* Westport, CT: Greenwood Press; Goodall, J. (2002). *My Life with the Chimpanzees. The Fascinating Story of the One of the World's Most Celebrated Naturalists.* New York: Aladdin Paperbacks; Goodall, J. (1986) *The Chimpanzees of Gombe: Patterns of Behavior.* Boston: Bellknap Press of the Harvard University Press; Goodall, J. (1990). *Through a Window: 30 years Observing the Gombe Chimpanzees* Boston: Houghton Mifflin.

Overcoming Frames

Kuller: University of Texas School of Public Health Conference: *Social and Environmental Solutions to Obesity.* March 16, 2010. Austin, TX.

Kelly Brownell soda tax: Brownell, K.D., Farley, T., & Willett, W.C. (2009). The public health and economic benefits of taxing sugar-sweetened beverages. *New England Journal of Medicine.* 361, 1599–1605.

Einstein special theory of relativity: Einstein, A. (1961) *Relativity: The Special and General theory.* New York: Crown Publishers

Herbert Needleman: Needleman, H.L. (2009). Low level lead exposure: history and discovery. *Annals of Epidemiology. 19,* 235–238; Denworth L. (2009). *Toxic Truth: A Scientist, A Doctor, and the Battle Over Lead.* Boston: Beacon.

Say it Like you Mean It

Sapir Whorf hypothesis: Boroditsky, L. Wall Street Journal 7/24/10 pW3.

Language affects frames and frames affect language: Fausey, C. M. & Boroditsky, L. (2010). Who dunnit? Cross-linguistic differences in eye-witness memory. *Psychonomic Bulletin & Review* 17:644–650; Fausey, C. M., Long, B. L., Inamori, A. & Boroditsky, L. (2010). Constructing agency: The role of language. *Frontiers in Cultural Psychology* 1:162.

Types of metaphors: Lakoff, G., & Johnson, M. (2003). *Metaphors We Live By.* Chicago: The University of Chicago Press.

Cooking metaphors: A Language of Metaphors: Cooking metaphors. Accessed October 24, 2011 from http://knowgramming.com/cooking_metaphors.htm.

Hofstadter: Hofstadter, D. R. (2006). Analogy at the core of cognition: Stanford presidential lectures in humanities and the arts. Accessed September 1, 2010 from http://prelectur.stanford.edu/lecturers/hofstadter/analogy.html

Overcoming Metaphors

Advance directives: Agency for Healthcare Research and Quality. (2003). *Research in Action. Advanced care planning: Preferences for care at the end of life. 12,* 1–20. AHRQ Pub No. 03-0018; Aries, P. (1991). *The hour of our death.* 2nd ed. Oxford, UK: Oxford University Press. N. Tucker, S. Jones, R. Reynolds, & J. D'Amore (Eds.) *Honor My Wishes: Advancing Choices in Death and Dying for More Effective End-of-Life Care and Organ Donation.* Innovative Thinking class project.

War on cancer metaphor: Schiffrin, D., Tannen, D., & Hamilton, H.E. (Eds.) (2001). *The Handbook of Discourse Analysis.* Malden, MA: Blackwell.

Mammographic screening in 40–50 year olds: U.S. Preventive Services Task Force. (2009). Screening for breast cancer: U.S. Preventive Services Task Force recommendation statement. *Annals of Internal Medicine. 151,*

716–726; New York Times: Mammogram debate took group by surprise. Accessed October 24, 2011 from http://www.nytimes.com/2009/11/20/ health/20prevent.html

Life metaphors and discovery metaphors: Lakoff, G., & Johnson, M. (2003). *Metaphors We Live By.* Chicago: The University of Chicago Press.

Check this Out!

Walk through daily routines: Nierenberg, G. I. (1982). *The Art of Creative Thinking.* New York: Simon & Schuster.

C. Elegans: Rose, J. K., & Rankin, C. H. (2001). Analyses of habituation in Caenorhabditis elegans, *Learning and Memory. 8,* 63–69.

Visual megapixels: Curcio, C. A., Sloan, K. R., Kalina, R. E., & Hendrickson, A. E. (1990). Human photoreceptor topography. *Journal of Comparative Neurology. 292,* 497–523.

Diallo: Gladwell, M. (2007). *Blink: The Power of Thinking Without Thinking.* New York: Back Bay Books.

Aoccdrnig to rscheearch: Psyblog. Understand Your Mind: Aoccdrnig to a rscheearch at Cmabrigde Uinervtisy. Accessed October 24, 2011 from http://www.spring.org.uk/2005/08/aoccdrnig-to-rscheearch-at-cmabrigdehtm.php

Visual tendencies: Mendell, R. L. Observation still matters: how to increase your powers of observation. Accessed October 24, 2011 from http://www.pimall.com/ nais/n.obser.html

Barry Marshall and Robin Warren. Marshall, B. J., & Windsor, H. M. (2005). The relation of Helicobacter pylori to gastric adenocarcinoma and lymphoma: pathophysiology, epidemiology, screening, clinical presentation, treatment, and prevention. *Medical Clinics of North America. 89,* 313–344; The Nobel Prize in Physiology and Medicine (2005). Barry J. Marshall and J. Robin Warren. Autobiographies. Accessed October 24, 2011 from http://nobelprize.org/nobel_prizes/ medicine/laureates/2005/warren-autobio.html#

Alexander Fleming: Brown, K (2004). *Penicillin man. Alexander Fleming and the antibiotic revolution* London: Sutton; The Nobel Prize in Physiology or Medicine 1945. Sir Alexander Fleming, Ernest B. Chain, Sir Howard Florey. Biography. Accessed October 24, 2011. http://nobelprize.org/nobel_prizes/medicine/ laureates/1945/fleming-bio.html

Percy LeBaron: Gallawa, J. C. Microtech. Who invented microwaves? Accessed October 24, 2011 from http://www.gallawa.com/microtech/history.html

Becoming a Keener Observer

NYPD goes to Frick: Herman, A. E. *The art of observation. How the long arm of the law is reaching the Frick Collection.* American Association of Museums. Accessed July 9, 2010 from http://www.aam-us.org/pubs/mn/frick.cfm.

Leonardo daVinci: Phillips J. (2008) *World History Biographies: Leonardo daVinci. The Genius Who Defined the Renaissance. (National Geograhic World History Biographies)* New York, NY: Random House; Suh, A. (2005). *Leonardo's Notebooks* New York: Workman Publishing.

Drawing: Edwards, B. (1999). *The New Drawing on the Right Side of the Brain: A Course of Enhancing Creativity and Artistic Confidence.* New York: Jeremy P. Tarcher/Putnam.

ABC Nightline: ABC Nightline: IDEO shopping cart. Accessed October 24, 2011 from (http://www.youtube.com/watch?v=M66ZU2PCIcM;

IDEO: Kelley, T. (2001). *The Art of Innovation: Lessons in Creativity from IDEO, America's Leading Design Firm.* New York: Currency Doubleday.

Ness: Inflammation and ovarian cancer: Ness, R. B., & Cottreau, C. (1999). Possible role of ovarian epithelial inflammation in ovarian cancer. *Journal of the National Cancer Institute 91,* 1459–1467.

How Biased Are You?

Expected Utility Theory: Mogin, P. (1997). Expected utility theory. In Davis, J., Hands, W., & Maki, U. (Eds.) *Handbook of Economic Methodology.* (pp. 342–350). London: Edward Elgar.

Context bias: Ariely, D. (2008). *Predictably irrational: The hidden forces that shape our decisions.* New York: Harper.

Richard Wilkinson: Wilkinson R., & Pickett, K. (2009) *The Spirit Level: Why Greater Equality Makes Societies Stronger.* New York, London: Penguin.

Christakis and Fowler: Christakis, N. A., Fowler, J. H. (2007). The spread of obesity in a large social network over 32 years. *New England Journal of Medicine. 357,* 370–379.

Variability in surgery by geography: Patel, M. R., Greiner, M. A., DiMartino, L. D., et al. (2010). Geographic variation in carotid revascularization among Medicare beneficiaries, 2003–2006. *Archives of Internal Medicine 170,* 1218–1225; Halm, E. A. (2010). The good, the bad, and the about-to-get ugly: national trends in carotid revascularization. *Archives of Internal Medicine 170,* 1225–1227.

Anchoring bias: Ariely, D. (2008). *Predictably Irrational: The hidden Forces that Shape Our Decisions.* New York: Harper.

Context in medicine decision-making: (Redeimeier D. A., Shafir, E. (1995). Medical decision making in situations that offer multiple alternatives. *JAMA* 273, 302.

Anchoring: Ariely, D. (2008). *Predictably Irrational: The hidden Forces that shape Our Decisions.* New York: Harper.

Joshua Bell: Weingarten, G. Pearls before breakfast. Washington Post. Sunday April 8, 2007. Accessed October 24, 2011 from http://www.washingtonpost.com/wp-dyn/content/article/2007/04/04/AR2007040401721.html

Placebos: Silberman, S. "Placebos Are Getting More Effective. Drugmakers Are Desperate to Know Why." *Wired Magazine* 24 Aug. 2009. Accessed October 24, 2011 from http://www.wired.com/medtech/drugs/magazine/17-09/ff_placebo_effect?currentPage=all; De Craen, A. J., et al. (1999). Placebos and placebo effects in medicine: historical overview. *Journal of the Royal Society of Medicine* 92, 511–515.

Hindsight bias: Central Intelligence Agency: Chapter 13. Hindsight bias in intelligence reporting. Accessed October 24, 2011 from https://www.cia.gov/library/center-for-the-study-of-intelligence/csi-publications/books-and-monographs/psychology-of-intelligence-analysis/art16.html#rft150

Exercise: placebo effect: de la Fuente-Fernandez, R., Schulzer, M., & Stoessl, A. J. (2004). Placebo mechanisms and reward circuitry: clues from Parkinson's disease. *Biological Psychiatry.* 56, 67–71.

Overcoming Bias

Lateral thinking, DeBono: de Bono, E. (1990). *Lateral Thinking: Creativity Step by Step.* New York: Harper Perennial.

The Brain and Creativity: The Seat of Inspiration

JW split brain patient: Funnell, M. G., Colvin, M. K., & Gazzaniga, M. S. (2007). The calculating hemispheres: Studies of a split-brain patient. *Neuropsychologia,* 45, 2378–2386; Gazzaniga, M. S., Holtzman, J. D., Deck, M. D., & Lee, B. C. (1985). MRI assessment of human callosal surgery with neuropsychological correlates. *Neurology35,* 1763–1766.

Work of Gazzaniga and Sperry: Nobelprize.org. Nobel Prize in physiology or medicine 1981. Roger Wolcott Sperry. Accessed Sept 1, 2010 from http://www.nobelprize.org/nobel_prizes/medicine/laureates/1981/sperry-autobio.html#; Gazzaniga, M. S. (2005). Forty-five years of research and still going strong. *Nature Reviews.* 6, 653–659.

Mihov meta-analysis: Mihov, K., Denzler, M., & Förster, J. (2010). Hemispheric specialization and creative thinking: A meta-analytic review of lateralization of creativity. *Brain and Cognition 72*, 442–448.

Carlsson: Carlsson, I., Wendt, P. E., & Risberg, J. (2000). On the neurobiology of creativity: Differences in frontal activity between high and low creative subjects. *Neuropsychologia 38*, 873–885.

Studies of regional blood flow and functional MRI: Bechtereva, N. P., Danko, S. G., & Starchenko, M. G. (2001). Study of the brain organization of creativity: II. Positron-emission tomography data. *Human Physiology 26*, 516–522; Chavez-Eakle, R. A., Graff-Guerrero, A., Garcia-Reyna, J.-C., et al. (2007). Cerebral blood flow associated with creative performance: A comparative study. *NeuroImage 38*, 519–528; Howard-Jones, P. A., Blakemore, S.-J., Samuel, E. A., et al. (2005). Semantic divergence and creative story generation: An fMRI investigation. *Cognitive Brain Research 25*, 240–250; Bechtereva, N. P., Korotkov, A. D., Pakhomov, S. V., et al. (2004). PET study of brain maintenance of verbal creative activity. *International Journal of Psychophysiology 53*, 11–20; Seger, C., Desmond, J., Glover, G., & Gabrieli, J. (2000). Functional magnetic resonance imaging evidence for right-hemisphere involvement in processing unusual semantic relationships. *Neuropsychology 14*, 361–369.

Complex tasks require bilateral integration: Bronson, P., & Merryman, A. (2010, July 10). The Creativity crisis. Newsweek, Accessed October 24, 2011 from http://www.newsweek.com/2010/07/10/the-creativity-crisis.html.

Seat of creativity is not on the right side: Dietrich, A. (2004). The cognitive neuroscience of creativity. *Psychoneuroscience Bulletin Review 11*, 1011–1026.

Different tasks require different brain regions: Bechtereva, N. P., Korotkov, A. D., Pakhomov, S. V., et al. (2004). PET study of brain maintenance of verbal creative activity. *International Journal of Psychophysiology. 53*, 11–20; Seger, C., Desmond, J., Glover, G., & Gabrieli, J. (2000). Functional magnetic resonance imaging evidence for right-hemisphere involvement in processing unusual semantic relationships. *Neuropsychology 14*, 361–369.

Leading hypothesis in the field: Ward, T. B., Smith, S. M., & Finke, R. A. (1999). Creative cognition. In R. J. Sternberg (Ed.), *Handbook of Creativity* (pp. 189–212). Cambridge: Cambridge University Press; Weisberg, R. W. (1993). *Creativity: Beyond the Myth of Genius.* New York: Freeman.

The Brain and Creativity: Getting Out in Front

Studies of regional blood flow and functional MRI: Bechtereva, N. P., Danko, S. G., & Starchenko, M. G. (2001). Study of the brain organization of creativity: II.

Positron-emission tomography data. *Human Physiology 26,* 516–522; Chavez-Eakle, R. A., Graff-Guerrero, A., Garcia-Reyna, J.-C., et al. (2007). Cerebral blood flow associated with creative performance: A comparative study. *NeuroImage 38,* 519–528; Howard-Jones, P. A., Blakemore, S.-J., Samuel, E. A., et al. (2005). Semantic divergence and creative story generation: An fMRI investigation. *Cognitive Brain Research 25,* 240–250; Bechtereva, N. P., Korotkov, A. D., Pakhomov, S. V., et al. (2004). PET study of brain maintenance of verbal creative activity. *International Journal of Psychophysiology 53,* 11–20; Seger, C., Desmond, J., Glover, G., & Gabrieli, J. (2000). Functional magnetic resonance imaging evidence for right-hemisphere involvement in processing unusual semantic relationships. *Neuropsychology 14,* 361–369.

Phineas Gage: Damasio, A.R. (1994). *Descartes' Error: Emotion, Reason, and the Human Brain.* New York: Avon Books.

Frontal lobe syndrome: Milner, B. (1995). Aspects of human frontal lobe function. *Advances in Neurology 66,* 67–84; Shallice, T, & Burgess, W. (1991). Deficits in strategy application following frontal lobe damage in man. *Brain 114,* 727–741; Zangwill, O. L. (1966). Psychological deficits associated with frontal lobe lesions. *International Journal of Neurology, 5,* 395–402.

Damasio: Descartes' Error: Damasio, A.R. (1994). *Descartes' Error: Emotion, Reason, and the Human Brain.* New York: Avon Books.

Prefrontal connections: Robin, N., & Holyoak, K. J. (1995). Relational complexity and the functions of prefrontal cortex. In Gazzaniga, M. S. (Ed). *The Cognitive Neurosciences.* Cambridge, MA: MIT Press.

Prefrontal function: Dietrich, A. (2004). The cognitive neuroscience of creativity. *Psychoneuroscience Bulletin Review 11,* 011–1026; Frith, C. D., & Dolan, R. (1996). The role of the prefrontal cortex in higher cognitive functions. *Cognitive Brain Research 5,* 175–181; Goldstein, K. (1994). The mental changes due to frontal lobe damage. *Journal of Psychology 17,* 187–208; Rangel, A., Camerer, C., & Montague, P. R. (2008). A framework for studying the neurobiology of value-based decision-making. *Nature Reviews. 9,* 545–556.

Perseveration: Boone, B. K. (1999). Neuropsychological assessment of executive functions. In B. L. Miller & J. L. Cummings (Eds.), *The Human Frontal Lobes: Functions and Disorders* (pp. 247–260). New York: Guilford.

Relational complexity: Robin, N., & Holyoak, K. J. (1995). Relational complexity and the functions of prefrontal cortex. In M. S. Gazzaniga (Ed.). *The Cognitive Neurosciences.* Cambridge, MA: MIT Press; Damasio, A. R. (2001). Some notes on brain, imagination and creativity. In K. H. Pfenninger & V. R. Shubik (Eds.), *The Origins of Creativity* (pp. 59–68). Oxford: Oxford University Press.

Memory with cultural modifiers: O'Gorman, R., Wilson, D. S., & Miller, R. R. (2008). An evolved cognitive bias for social norms. *Evolution and Human Behavior 29*(2), 71–78.

Kuhn: Scientific Revolutions: Kuhn, T. S. (1962). *The Structure of Scientific Revolutions.* Chicago: The University of Chicago Press.

Goldberger: Harris, H. F. *Pellagra;* Kraut J. Dr. Joseph Goldberger & the war on pellagra. Accessed February 24, 2011 from http://history.nih.gov/exhibits/gold-berger/docs/ackn_8.htm

Theory of freeing the frontal cortex: Martindale, C. (1999). Biological bases of creativity. In R. J. Sternberg (Ed.), *Handbook of Creativity* (pp. 137–152). Cambridge: Cambridge University Press; Bristol, A. S., & Viskontas, I. V. (2006). The dynamic processes within memory stores: Piecing together the neural basis of creative cognition. In J. Kaufman, & J. Baer (Eds.), *Creativity and Reason in Cognitive Development.* (pp. 60–80). Cambridge: Cambridge University Press.

The Joy of Science

Characteristics of creative people: Feist, G. J. (1999). The influence of personality on artistic and scientific creativity. In R. J. Sternberg (Ed.). *Handbook of Creativity.* (pp. 273–296). New York: Cambridge University Press; Renzulli, J. S. (2003) The three-ring conception of giftedness: its implications for understanding the nature of innovation. In Shavinina L (Ed) *The International Handbook on Innovation* (pp 79–96). Oxford: Elsevier; Amabile T, Gryskiewicz, S. (1987). *Creativity in the R&D laboratory.* Greensboro, NC: Center for Creative Leadership Press.

Edison quote: Think Exit.com. Thomas Alva Edison quotes. Accessed September 1, 2010 from http://thinkexist.com/quotation/i_haven-t_failed-i-ve_found-ways_that_don-t/346094.html.

Israeli innovation: Senor, D., Singer, S. (2009). *Start-up Nation: The Story of Israel's Economic Miracle.* New York: Hachette Book Group.

Richard Feynman: Feynman, R. P., & Leighton, R. (1985). *Surely You're Joking Mr. Feynman.* New York Norton & Company; Feynman, C., & Feynman M. (1999). *The Pleasure of Finding Thing Out.* Cambridge, MA: Perseus; Gleick, J. (1992). *Genius: The Life and Science of Richard Feynman.* New York: Vintage Books.

Asking the Right Question

KS Joseph and epidemic of low birth weight: Joseph, K. S., & Kramer, M. S. (1997). Recent trends in infant mortality rates and proportions of low birth weight live births in Canada. *Canadian Medical Association Journal. 157,* 535–541.

Jules Verne: Butcher, W. (2006). *Jules Verne: The Definitive Biography*. New York: Avalon.

Semmelweis: Nuland, S. B. (2003). *The Doctor's Plague: Germs, Childbed Fever, and the Strange Story of Ignaz Semmelweis*. New York: WW Norton.

Hitchhiker's Guide to the Universe: Adams, D. (1994) *Hitchhiker's Guide to the Universe*. New York: Ballantine.

How is a Marriage like a Matchbox?

Achimedes: Gamow, G. (1961). *The Great Physicists from Galileo to Einstein*. New York: Dover.

Hofstadter: Hofstadter, D. R. (2006).Analogy at the core of cognition: Stanford presidential lectures in humanities and the arts. Accessed September 1, 2010 from http://prelectur.stanford.edu/lecturers/hofstadter/analogy.html.

Vitruvius: Vitruvius, Pollio (transl. Morris Hicky Morgan, 1960), *The Ten Books on Architecture*. Courier Dover Publications.

Newton: Gamow, G. (1961). *The Great Physicists from Galileo to Einstein*. New York: Dover.

Jeremy Levy: RSC. Advancing the Chemical Sciences. Chemistry World. Atomic Etch-A-Sketch. Accessed October 25, 2011 from http://www.rsc.org/chemistry-world/News/2008/March/03030801.asp

Michelle Khine: Scientific American. Thinking outside the box: 4 children's gizmos that inspired scientific breakthroughs. Accessed October 24, 2011 from http://www.scientificamerican.com/article.cfm?id=toy-box-tech

Tom Kosten: Kosten, T. R., Rosen, M., & Bond, J. (2002). Human therapeutic cocaine vaccine: safety and immunogeniticy. *Vaccine. 15, 20*(7-8), 1196–1204; Orson, F. M., Kinsey, B. M., Singh, R. A., Wu, Y., & Kosten, T. R. (2009). Vaccines for cocaine abuse. *Human Vaccines. 5,* 194–199.

Fredrich Kekule: Roberts, R. M. (1989). *Serendipity: Accidental Discoveries in Science*. New York: John Wiley and Sons.

Alexander Graham Bell: Bruce, R. V. (1990). *Alexander Graham Bell and the Conquest of Solitude*. Ithaca, NY: Cornell University Press.

Newton affinity: Aubusson, P. J., Harrison, A. G., & Ritchie, S. M. (Eds.) (2006). *Metaphor and Analogy in Science Education*. Dordrecht, The Netherlands: Springer.

Jenner: Scott, P. *Edward Jenner*. Accessed June 1, 2010 from http://www.sc.edu/library/spcoll/nathist/jenner.html; *Edward Jenner and the Discovery of Vaccination*. Thomas Cooper Library, University of South Carolina. (1996). Accessed June 1, 2010 from http://www.historylearningsite.co.uk/edward_jenner.htm.

Ness preeclampsia: Ness, R. B., & Roberts, J. M. (1996). Heterogeneous causes constituting the single syndrome of preeclampsia: a hypothesis and its implications. *American Journal of Obstetrics & Gynecology 175,* 1365–1370; Ness, R. B., & Sibai, B. (2006). Shared and disparate components of the pathophysiologies of fetal growth restriction and preeclampsia. *American Journal of Obstetrics & Gynecology 195,* 40–49.

Flip It!

Buddhism: Hagen, S. (1997). *Buddhism plain and simple.* New York: Broadway Books.

Ocean-going freighters: Michalko, M. (2006). *Thinkertoys: A Handbook of Creative-Thinking Techniques* (2nd ed.). Berkeley: Ten Speed Press.

Darwin and evolutionary theory: Desmond, A., & Moore, J. (1991). *Darwin: The life of a Tormented Evolutionist.* New York: WW Norton.

Tobacco control: Windome, R., Samet, J. M., & Hiatt, R. A. (2010). Science, prudence, and politics: The case of smoke-free indoor spaces. *Annals of Epidemiology 20,* 428–435.

Archimedes: Eddy, D. M., & Schlessinger, L. (2003). Validation of the Archimedes diabetes model. *Diabetes Care. 26,* 3102–3110; Eddy, D. M., Schlessinger, L. (2003). Archimedes: a trial-validated model of diabetes. *Diabetes Care 26,* 3093–3101.

Greg Mortenson: Three Cups of Tea: Mortenson, G., & Relin, D. O. (2006). *Three Cups of Tea: One Man's Mission to Promote Peace…One School at a Time.* New York, London: Penguin.

Clinical diagnosis: The New York Times Magazine. Diagnosis; Dizzying symptoms. Accessed October 24, 2011 from http://topics.nytimes.com/topics/news/health/columns/diagnosis/

Anemia in renal failure trial: Besarab, A., Bolton, W. K., Browne, J. K., et al. (1998). The effects of normal as compared with low hematocrit values in patients with cardiac disease who are receiving hemodialysis and epoetin. *New England Journal of Medicine 339,* 584–590.

Gain of 30 years in life expectancy: Centers for Disease Control and Prevention. (1999). Ten great achievements – United States 1900–1999. *Morbidity & Mortality Weekly Report. 48,* 241–243.

Food borne illness: Centers for Disease Control and Prevention. Emerging infectious disease. Foodborne illness and deaths in the United States. Accessed October 24, 2011 from http://www.cdc.gov/ncidod/eid/vol5no5/mead.htm

Hypertension: American Heart Association. Statistical fact sheet – risk factors 2011 update. High blood pressure statistics. Accessed October 24, 2011 from http://www.heart.org/idc/groups/heart-public/@wcm/@sop/@smd/documents/downloadable/ucm_319587.pdf

Car parking: de Bono, E. (1994). *De Bono's Thinking Course: Revised Edition.* New York: Facts on File.

Better Place electric cars: Senor, D., & Singer, S. (2009). *Start-up Nation: The Story of Israel's Economic Miracle.* New York: Hachette Book Group.

Andrea White: White, A. (2005). *Surviving Antarctica: Reality TV 2083.* New York: EOS.

Angela Belcher and engineered virus: Markoff, J. *Team's work uses a virus to convert methane to ethylene.* New York Times. Accessed October 24, 2011 from http://www.nytimes.com/2010/06/29/science/29ethyl.html

Joelle Frechette and German Drazer: Scientific American. Thinking outside the box: 4 children's gizmos that inspired scientific breakthroughs. Accessed October 24, 2011 from http://www.scientificamerican.com/article.cfm?id=toy-box-tech

Functional fixedness:. Psychological Report. Functional fixedness in a technologically sparse culture. German TP, Barrett HC. Accessed October 24, 2011 from http://www.sscnet.ucla.edu/anthro/faculty/barrett/german-barrett-PS.pdf

Research employing ex-cons: Richard Rothenberg, Georgia State University: private correspondence. January 8, 2011.

Large Haldron collider: European Organization for Nuclear Research. The Large Haldron Collider. Our understanding of the universe is about to change. Accessed October 24, 2011 from http://public.web.cern.ch/public/en/LHC/LHC-en.html

A Man Walked into a Bar

Wise Chinese farmer: Hagen, S. (1997) *Buddhism Plain and Simple.* New York: Broadway Books.

Lateral thinking, DeBono: de Bono, E. (1990). *Lateral Thinking: Creativity Step by Step.* New York: Harper Perennial.

Gestault psychology: Gerard, R. W. (1952). The Biological Basis of Imagination. In B. Ghiselin (Ed.). *The Creative Process.* Berkley, CA: U California Press

Brain teasers: Are you crazy? Yahoo answers. Accessed October 24, 2011 from http://answers.yahoo.com/question/index?qid=20080421124644AA5MppU

Jokes from the Onion: The Onion: America's Finest News Source. Accessed February 24, 2011 from http://www.theonion.com.

Demotivators: Despair, Inc. The 2011 Demotivators calendar. Accessed February 24, 2011 from http://www.despair.com.

Johnathan Swift: Swift, J.(1729). *A Modest Proposal for Preventing the Children of Poor People in Ireland from Being a Burden to Their Parents or Country, and for Making Them Beneficial to the Public.* The Project Gutenberg E-book. Accessed October 24, 2011 from http://www.gutenberg.org/files/1080/1080-h/1080-h.htm

PO: cups made of ice and eliminate traffic signals: de Bono, E. (1994). *De Bono's Thinking Course: Revised Edition.* New York: Facts on File.

Eliminate traffic signals: McNichol. Roads gone wild. Wired Magazine. Accessed October 24, 2011 from http://www.wired.com/wired/archive/12.12/traffic.html

Malaria control: Malaria.Fact Sheet No. 94. World Health Organization.Accessed October 24, 2011 from http://www.who.int/mediacentre/factsheets/fs094/en/

Reprogrammed skin cells: Time Specials. Top 10 Everything of 2007. Top 10 scientific discoveries. Stem cell breakthroughs. Accessed October 24, 2011 from http://www.time.com/time/specials/2007/article/0,28804,1686204_1686252_1690920,00.html#ixzz0sO9XkmUi; Wired Science. Top 10 scientific breakthroughs of 2008. 10. Trouble shooting stem cell therapy. Accessed October 24, 2011 from http://www.wired.com/wiredscience/2009/01/top-10-scientif/#ixzz0sOAOS3NJ

HIV resistance: Wired Science. Top 10 scientific breakthroughs of 2008. 4. Curing HIV in Germany. Accessed October 24, 2011 from http://www.wired.com/wiredscience/2009/01/top-10-scientif/#ixzz0sO79c2tg

Love brain scans: Fisher, H., Aron, A., & Brown, L. L. (2006). Romantic Love: A Mammalian Brain System for Mate Choice. In K. Kendrick (Ed), *The Neurobiology of Social Recognition, Attraction and Bonding. Philosophical Transactions of the Royal Society: Biological Sciences. 361,* 2173–2186.

Nelson Mandela: Carlin, J. How Nelson Mandela won the rugby world cup. Telegraph.co.uk. Accessed February 24, 1011 from http://www.telegraph.co.uk/news/features/3634426/How-Nelson-Mandela-won-the-rugby-World-Cup.html

The Power of Group Intelligence

USS Scorpion: Surowiecki, J. (2005). *The Wisdom of Crowds.* New York: Anchor Books; Sontag, S., Drew, C., & Drew, A. L. (1998). *Blind Man's Bluff: The Untold Story of American Submarine Espionage.* New York: Harper Collins;

Estimating jelly beans: Surowiecki, J. (2005). *The Wisdom of Crowds.* New York: Anchor Books.

Encyclopedia Britannica vs. Wikipedia: Nature. Special report Internet encyclopaedias go head to head. Jim Giles. Accessed October 25, 2011 from http://www.nature.com/nature/journal/v438/n7070/full/438900a.html

Open Street: Open StreetMap. The free wiki world map. Accessed October 25, 2011 from http://www.openstreetmap.org

HapMap: International HapMap Project. Accessed October 25, 2011 from http://www.hapmap.org

Group intelligence (c factor): Woolley, A. W., Chabris, C. F., Pentland, A., Hashmi, N., & Malone, T. W. (2010). Evidence for a Collective Intelligence Factor in the Performance of Human Groups. *Science 330*, 686–688.

Intelligence community and Sept 11: CNN Wire Service. *Obama nominates new director of national intelligence..* (2010). Accessed June 5, 2011 from http://articles.cnn.com/2010-06-05/politics/obama.dni.director_1_director-of-national-intelligence-dni-national-geospatial-intelligence-agency?_s=PM:POLITICS; Gertz, B. (2002). *Breakdown: How America's ingelligence failures led to September 11.* Washington, DC. Regnery.

Invention of the internet: Tobin, J. E. (2001). *Great Projects. The Epic Story of the Building of the America, from the Taming of the Mississippi to the Invention of the Internet.* New York: The Free Press.

DARPA: DARPA. The Defense Advanced Research Projects Agency. Accessed October 25, 2011 from http://www.darpa.mil/

DARPA 10 balloon challenge: WSJ Blogs. *Spot 10 balloons; Win $40,000.* Wall Street Journal. December 4, 2009. Accessed February 25, 2011 from http://blogs.wsj.com/digits/2009/12/04/spot-10-balloons-win-40000/

ADNI: Archives Neurology 8/10; New York Times Aug 13, 2010. Page A1

Evolutionary biology meets regenerative medicine: *Two New Paths to the Dream: Regeneration.* New York Times Aug 6, 2010 p. A1; Pajcini, K. V., Corbel, S. Y., Sage, J., Pomerantz, J. H., Blau, H. M. (2010). Transient inactivation of Rb and ARF yields regenerative cells from postmitotic mammalian muscle. *Cell Stem Cell 7*, 198–213; Johansson, F. (2004). *The Medici Effect: Breakthrough Insights at the Intersection of Ideas, Concepts, and Cultures.* Johansson self-published.

Swarm intelligence: Bonabeau, E., Dorigo, M., & Theraulaz, G. (1999) *Swarm Intelligence: From Natural to Artificial Systems (Santa Fe Institute Studies in the Sciences of Complexity Proceedings).* Oxford: Oxford University Press. Deneubourg JL, Goss S, Franks N, Pasteels JM. (1989) The blind leading the blind: Modeling chemically mediated army ant raid patterns. Journal of Insect Behavior 2, 719–25.

Getting the Most from a Group

Chuck Reynolds post-doctoral program: Reynolds, C. F., Martin, C., & Brent, D. (1998). Post-doctoral clinical research training in psychiatry. *Academic Psychiatry. 22*, 190–196.

Doers, dreamers, and incrementalists: Belsky, S. (2010). *Making Ideas Happen: Overcoming the Obstacles between Vision and Reality.* New York: Portfolio.

HOT teams and brainstorming: Kelley and Littman (2001). *The Art of Innovation: Lessons in Creativity from IDEO, America's Leading Design Firm.* New York: Random House.

Incubation

Henri Poincare: Poincare, H. (1952). Mathematical Creation. In B. Ghiselin (Ed). *The Creative Process.* Berkley, CA: U California Press

Life of Buddha and mindfulness: Hagen, S. (1997) *Buddhism Plain and Simple.* New York. Broadway Books.

Stress and the common cold: Cohen, S., Tyrrell, D. A. J., & Smith, A. P. (1991). Psychological stress and susceptibility to the common cold. *New England Journal of Medicine 325,* 606–612.

Meditation and stress: Kabat-Zinn, J., Massion, A. O., & Kristeller, J. (1992). Effectiveness of a meditation-based stress reduction program in the treatment of anxiety disorders. *American Journal of Psychiatry 149,* 936–943; Speca, M., Carlson, L. E., & Goodey, E. (2000). *Psychosomatic Med 62,* 613–622.

Meditation and concentration; brain connections: Budilovsky, J., & Adamson, E. (1999). *The Complete Idiot's Guide to Meditation.* New York: Alpha.

Meditation and creativity: Hock, R. R. (2009). *Forty Studies That Changed Psychology.* Hightstown, New Jersey: Pearson; Travis, F. (1979). The Transcendental Meditation Technique and Creativity. *Journal of Creative Behavior 13,* 169–180.

Practice of mediation: Barbor, C. (2001). The Science of Meditation. *PsychologyToday.com.* Psychology Today, 1 May 2001. Web. 24 March 2009; Budilovsky, J., & Adamson, E. (1999). *The Complete Idiot's Guide to Meditation.* New York: Alpha.

Testing Your Ideas

The Magic Years: Fraiberg SH. (1959). *The Magic Years: Understanding and Handling the Problems of Early Childhood.* New York: Simon and Schuster.

Francis Bacon and David Hume: Rothman, K. J., & Greenland, S. (1998). Causation and causal inference. In K. J. Rothman, & S. Greenland (Eds.) *Modern Epidemiology.* 2nd Edition. Philadelphia: Lippincott Williams &Wilkins.

Bertrand Russell: Russell, B. (1945). *A History of Western Philosophy.* New York: Simon and Schuster.

Karl Popper: Magee, B. (1985). *Philosophy and the Real World: An Introduction to Karl Popper.* La Salle, IL: Open Court.

Hill's tenets: Hill, A. B. (1965). The environment and disease: Association or causation? *Proceedings of the Royal Society of Medicine,* 58, 295–300

Endometriosis blog: Endo-resolved.com: Endometriosis stories blog. Accessed August 23, 2011 from http://www.endo-resolved.com/symptoms.html

Endometriosis and ovarian cancer: Ness, R. B. (2003). Endometriosis and ovarian cancer: Thoughts on shared pathophysiology. *American Journal of Obstetrics and Gynecology 189,* 280–294. Brinton LA, Gridley G, Persson I, Baron J, Bergqvist A. Cancer risk after a hospital discharge diagnosis of endometriosis. *American Journal of Obstetrics and Gynecology.* 176, 572–9.

HT: Writing Group for the Women's Health Initiative Investigators. (2002). Risks and benefits of estrogen plus progestin in Healthy postmenopausal women: Principal results from the Women's Health Initiative randomized clinical trial. *JAMA 288,* 321–333; Wilson, R. A. (1966). *Feminine Forever.* London: WH Allen; Watkins, E. S. (2007). *The Estrogen Elixir: A History of Hormone Replacement Therapy in America.* Baltimore, MD: The Johns Hopkins University Press.

That Right Idea

Prototyping and Interact with the world: Kelley, T. (2001). *The art of innovation: Lessons in creativity from IDEO, America's leading design firm.* New York: Currency Doubleday.

Disney three rooms: Trickey, K. The Walt Disney Strategy. The Walt Disney creative strategy. Accessed October 25, 2011 from http://www.wiredportfolio.com/blog/wp-content/uploads/2008/10/DisneyPaper.pdf

Organizing Your Ideas: Belsky, S. (2010). *Making Ideas Happen: Overcoming the Obstacles between Vision and Reality.* New York: Portfolio.

Action steps; Backburner; References: Belsky, S. (2010). *Making Ideas Happen: Overcoming the Obstacles between Vision and Reality.* New York: Portfolio.

Mind maps: Buzan, T. (1974). *Use Your Head.* Educational Publishers LLP. Part of the Pearson Education Group, Edinburgh Gate, Harlow, Essex, England.

Ocham's Razor: Hutter, M. (2005). *Universal Artificial Intelligence: Sequential Decisions Based on Algorithmic Probability.* New York: Springer.

Edison quote: Think Exit.com. Thomas Alva Edison quotes. Accessed September 1, 2010 from http://thinkexist.com/quotation/i_haven-t_failed-i-ve_found-ways_that_don-t/346094.html.

Time management: Belsky, S. (2010). *Making Ideas Happen: Overcoming the Obstacles between Vision and Reality.* New York: Portfolio.

The Stodginess of Science

Humphry Davy: Knight, D. (1992). *Humphry Davy: Science and Power.* Cambridge, UK: Cambridge University Press.

ALLHAT: The ALLHAT Officers and Coordinators for the ALLHAT Collaborative Research Group. (2002). Major outcomes in high-risk hypertensive patients randomized to angiotensin-converting enzyme inhibitor or calcium channel blocker vs. diuretic. *JAMA 288*, 2981–2997; The New York Times. The minimal impact of a big hypertension study. Accessed October 25, 2011 from http://www.nytimes.com/2008/11/28/business/28govtest.html

Bandwagon effect: Asch, S. E. (1955). Opinions and social pressure. *Scientific American 193*, 31–35; Goidel, R. K., & Shields, T. G. (1994). The vanishing marginals, the bandwagon, and the mass media. *The Journal of Politics 56*, 802–810.

Overimmitation: Balter, M. (2010). Probing Culture's Secrets, from Capuchins to Children. *Science 329*, 266–267.

Thomas Kuhn: Kuhn, T. S. (1962). *The Structure of Scientific Revolutions.* Chicago: The University of Chicago Press.

HT: Watkins, E. S. (2007). *The Estrogen Elixir: A History of Hormone Replacement Therapy in America.* Baltimore, MD: The Johns Hopkins University Press.

Overcoming the Stodginess of Science

Emperor Akbar: Braingle Grain teasers. Accessed July 15, 2010 from http://www.braingle.com/All.html.

Scholarly publications: The Andrew W. Mellon Foundation. Scholarly publishing initiatives. 2007 annual report. Accessed October 25, 2011 from http://www.mellon.org/news_publications/annual-reports-essays/presidents-essays/scholarly-publishing-initiatives

Malcolm Gladwell Tipping Point (Law of Few; Stickiness Factor; Law of Context): Gladwell, M. (2002). *The Tipping Point: How Little Things can make a Big Difference.* New York: Little, Brown.

Milgram experiment and Zimbardo prison experiment: Gladwell, M. (2002). *The Tipping Point: How Little Things can make a Big Difference.* New York: Little, Brown; Plotnik, R., & Kouyoumdjian, H. (2011). *Introduction to Psychology.* Belmont, CA: Wadsworth Cengage Learning.

McNamara and seat belts: Levitt, S. D. & Dubner, S. J. (2009). *Super Freakonomics: Global Cooling, Patriotic Prostitutes, and Why Suicide Bombers should buy Life Insurance.* New York: Harper Collins.

US National Highway Safety statistics: The US Department of Transportation. National Highway Traffic Safety Administration. Lives saved calculations for seat belts and frontal air bags Glassbrenner D, Starnes M. (2009). Accessed October 25, 2011 from www-nrd.nhtsa.dot.gov/pubs/811206.pdf

Folic Acid: Centers for Disease Control and Prevention (CDC). (2004). Spina bifida and anencephaly before and after folic acid mandate--United States, 1995–1996 and 1999–2000. *Morbidity & Mortality Weekly Report 53*, 362–365; De Wals, P., Tairou, F., Van Allen, M. I., et al. (2007). Reduction in neural-tube defects after folic acid fortification in Canada. *New England Journal of Medicine 357*, 135–142; Smithells, R. W., Sheppard, S., Wild, J., Schorah, C. J. (1989) Prevention of neural tube defects in Yorkshore: Final report. *Lancet 2*:498.

Better Place electric cars: Senor, D., & Singer, S. (2009). *Start-up Nation: the Story of Israel's Economic Miracle*. New York: Hachette Book Group.

ADNI Alzheimer's disease collaborative: New York Times Aug 13, 2010. Page A1

Innovation Incubators

Teresa Amabile: Amabile, T., & Gryskiewicz, S. (1987). *Creativity in the R&D laboratory*. Greensboro, NC: Center for Creative Leadership Press.

Experiment in Shakespeare Quarterly: Cohen, P. (2010) Scholars test web alternative to peer review. New York Times. August 23, 2010. Accessed February 24, 2011 from http://www.nytimes.com/2010/08/24/arts/24peer.html.

Extrinsic motivation chills creativity: Amabile, T. M. (1998). How to kill creativity. *Harvard Business Review 76*: 77–87; Amabile, T. M., Hennessey, A., & Grossman, B. S. (1986). Social influences on creativity: the effects of contracted-for reward. *Journal of Personality and Social Psychology 50*, 14–23; Kruglanski, A. W., Friedman, I., & Zeevi, G. (1971). The effects of extrinsic incentive on some qualitative aspects of task performance. *Journal of Personality. 39*, 607–616.

Edison time to light bulb: Israel, P. (2000) *Edison: A Life of Invention*. New York: John Wiley & Sons.

Wright brothers time to air flight: Anderson, J. D. (2004). *Inventing Flight: The Wright Brothers and Their Predecessors*. Baltimore, MD: Johns Hopkins University Press.

Don't Read this Book

Exercises

1. Connect the dots (3 × 3 block)

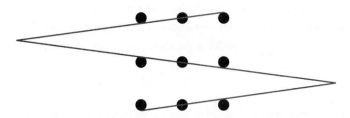

2. How do you correct this equation without changing it?

   Turn "8 + 8 = 91" upside down:

   16   8 + 8

3. Name all of the things you can think of that are associated with a table.

   Table of contents, a water table, a multiplication table, a wooden table, a glass, napkin, vase, tree, woodcutter...

4. Name all the uses for a needle.

   Metaphor for a nagging spouse (a la "quit needling me!"), to pop a balloon, to sew something, jab someone, knit, play a record...

It All Depends on How You Look at It

Exercises

1. To get a sense of how powerful frames are, take a look at these images.

   Don't sign—could be a logo on a shirt; a figure 8 using one straight line and a circle; a poorly made drain grate, a pattern on tiles.

   Hexagon—could be the bottom side of a piece from Trivial Pursuit, an early cave drawing where early humanoids were exploring various shapes, a letter within a distant language.

   Thought bubble—could be a stack of cotton balls glued together and strung on a wire, a cloud, a ruffled pillow.

2. There is something odd about this map:

    This is an economic equivalence map, with the GDP of other countries overlaid on states who share their gross production.

3. Consider the following mismatches between expectations and occurrence:

    In a Classroom—(1) Strange: teacher tells a student to get up and teach the whole class. Makes sense in a Montessori School where peer teaching is the norm. Makes sense in a university were some students are teaching assistants. (2) Strange: university tells students they will get paid to attend. Makes sense if the students are on athletic scholarships. (3) Strange: classroom does not involve a textbook or a curriculum. Makes sense if the classroom is a ballet studio or a karate school.

    At a Scientific Conference—The speaker launches into a full-fledged comedy routine. The speaker talks about his children the whole time. The speaker insults the hosts. The speaker begins to undress. All make sense in other environments but not a scientific conference.

4. Design an experiment looking at the issue of military vaccination from two frames:

    Assuming that you believe military vaccination provides group protection, you might design a study comparing the most effective ways to administer vaccine to the troops. Assuming that you believe military vaccination is an involuntary intrusion, you may assess whether women vaccinated while unknowingly pregnant have children with congenital defects.

Overcoming Frames

Try to find solutions to these brainteasers.

1. A visitor to a mental asylum

    The Director answered, "A normal person would pull the plug."

2. Consistent bullseyes

    The boy shot the arrows and then painted the circles around each.

3. Tom starts losing control over his body and no one comes to his aid.

    Tom and his wife were in a comedy club and he was overcome by laughing.

4. The ransom money gets away

    In the phone booth was a carrier pigeon in a cage with a small bag around its neck. Instructions on the cage were to put the diamond in the bag and release the bird. The police never found the bird nor its owner.

Exercises

1. Continue to work on identifying frames and alternatives.

    • Time

    Frame—Time as a resource.

Implications—(*1*) Time is an absolute feature of reality and not defined by perception and (*2*) time is a limited and quantifiable commodity.

Alternative frame—Time is an endless sea or open sky.

Implications—Time is capacious, unhurried, less easily quantified.

- Labor

Frame—Labor as a resource.

Implications—People are assumed to be separable from the work they do; labor can be monetized and is tradable.

Alternative frame—Labor is central to a person's identity.

Implications—Labor defines the skills and knowledge of a person. Professional identity is everything.

- Social group

Frame—Social group as a container

Implications—There is a clear definition to boundaries (in/out), boundaries are rigidly constructed and give form to the whole.

Alternative frame—Social group as an expansive gas.

Implications—The boundaries of the social group would be imposed from beyond the group rather than define the group. The social group would expand until it filled the boundaries of the whole and would be defined more by internal consistency than by external boundaries

- Discovery

Frame—Discovery is linear.

Implications—Discoveries are portrayed as built on past observations, they represent step-by-step progression of ideas; rarely does the evolution of ideas take a wrong turn.

Alternative frame—Discovery is spontaneous.

Implications—Discovery as spontaneous explains incubation: the process wherein extensive thought cannot solve a problem but because the subconscious continues the work the solution appears "suddenly." Spontaneity implies that invention can come from an epiphany.

- Ideas

Frame—Ideas are valuable possessions

Implications—Ideas are commodities; ideas should be protected until one receives benefit and credit for them; sharing of ideas is dangerous.

Alternative frame—Communal ideas.

Implications—Ideas arise from an assortment of influences, all of which influence the mind that gives them clearest definition. Sharing ideas allows one greater objectivity. Ideas in the public domain allow for greater collaboration and leveraging.

- Theories

  Frame—Theories as buildings

  Implications—Once established, theories can "stand up" or persist independent of any particular individual. Theories must be supported by ideas as buildings are supported by columns or walls.

  Alternative frame—Theories are rivers or oceans.

  Implications—Theories can be useful for moving from one step in discovery to another. Theories are not static but instead take you somewhere.

- Unknown

  Frame—Unknown is a box.

  Implications—What is unknown is like Pandora's box—frightening and dangerous.

  Alternative frame—Unknown is up.

  Implications—The expansive sky has an enormity of unknowns that can appear limitless. The known connects us to certainty just as gravity connects us to the earth.

2. Try to find solutions to these problems that force you to think outside the parameters given or to set aside assumptions.

   - Water lilies double in number every day

     Day 59

   - A boy goes to visit his mother

     The building is a hospice; she was on a respirator and the elevator stopped for several minutes on the way down, indicating the power had gone off. Alternative: She died before he left and he kissed her cold lips.

   - How did he hang?

     He stood on an ice cube and when it melted, he hung.

   - What always runs but never walks; often murmurs but never talks; has a bed but never sleeps; has a mouth but never eats?

     A river

3. Think of different ways to frame an initiative to tax sugared beverages so that even the supermarkets will see it as desirable

   Supermarkets compete for market share. No market could increase the price of sugared beverages on their own, even if they wanted to do so to limit consumption of these obesity-causing products. Consumers would simply go elsewhere for a better price. If externally taxed, the price would rise equally, thereby eliminating individual competitive pricing advantage.

Say it Like You Mean it

Exercises

1. Consider the metaphors "Child-bearing hips…"

   Child-bearing hips is a compliment in cultures where childbearing is highly valued such as in India, but in a country such as the United States, that is trying to prevent obesity, child-bearing hips might be considered unsightly or unhealthy. Dependent on the time and location, fatness has represented either wealth and beauty or over-indulgence and slovenliness.

2. Make a metaphor…

   Death—the last great adventure, a deep sleep, a climax, game over…

   Time—is money, ticks, passes…

   Compliance with rules—a real stickler (as though rules were glue or something that could be "stuck" to), strict taskmaster (as though rules were tasks and not a means to an end)

   Discovery—an awakening, breakthrough…

   Overeating—shoveling food down, devouring, stuffing, porking out…

   Lack of exercise—not tending the garden, living like a pig, couch potato…

Overcoming Metaphors

1. Identify the metaphors for the frame and alternative frame in exercises from the Chapter "Overcoming Frames."

   - Time

     Frame: Time as a resource—Time is running out. I lost those five minutes of my life. How should I most efficiently use my time?

     Alternative frame: Time is an endless sea or open sky—Love is eternal. Here to eternity. Now and forever.

   - Labor

     Frame: Labor as a resource—With parts and labor, that will come to $375. Labor negotiations…Labor force, labor markets.

     Alternative frame: Labor is central to a person's identity—Day laborer, office labor, slave labor

   - Social group

     Frame: Social group as a container—She really wants to fit in; He is concerned that he will be an outcast if he doesn't go to the party.

     Alternative frame: Social group as an expansive gas—We've always been inclusive; our social network is blowing up.

- Discovery

  Frame: Discovery as a straight line—The research is progressing; each discovery builds on the last; nothing is new but what has been forgotten.

  Alternative frame: Discovery as spontaneous—Eureka, I've found it!; the discovery was pure serendipity.

- Ideas

  Frame: Ideas are valuable possessions—Stealing other people's ideas is plagiarism; don't give away your ideas; that idea is worth something.

  Alternative frame: Communal ideas—We came up with that together; group think.

- Theories

  Frame: Theories as buildings—Various constructs were used to support for this theory; the theory will not hold up to scrutiny.

  Alternative frame: Theories are rivers or oceans—Don't be afraid to head off into uncharted waters; the data to support that theory is drying up; you can use that theory to navigate these new data.

- **Unknown**

  Frame: Unknown is a box—Who knows what the future holds; danger lies beyond those walls.

  Alternative frame: Unknown is up—The answer lies over the rainbow; I'm wishing on the stars that I'll get what I want; whatever happens, the sky's the limit.

Observation

Exercises

Find the differences between pictures.

1. *On the image to the right, the claw is shaded on both sides.*
2. *On the image to the right, the leftmost tree isn't shaded.*
3. *The leaf on the upper left corner is facing opposite directions.*
4. *On the image to the right, there is a bird in the upper left corner.*
5. *On the image to the left, the knob connecting the claw is shaded.*
6. *On the image to the right, the rightmost tree is shaded.*
7. *The leaf on the bottom left is facing different directions.*
8. *On the image to the right, the signpost on the bottom right is taller.*
9. *The arrow sign pointing to the right has different numbers on it.*
10. *On the image to the right, there's a third rock in the bottom left corner.*

Becoming a Keener Observer

Exercises

1. Open your eyes…Observe the following tools during use and find the design flaws:

   a. Screwdriver:

   Most screwdrivers require an awkward turning of the hand to continue extracting or furthering the screw. Often screws are placed in ways that are difficult to reach with a lengthy screwdriver. There's not one standard screw head size requiring many different screw bit sizes.

   b. A Vacuum Cleaner:

   Many vacuum cleaners require being emptied which can lead to release of clouds of dust and dirt littering the floor. The exchange of heads for the hose is time consuming and awkward. Most vacuum cleaners do not fit on stairs and the hose is not long enough to get to all steps on a stairwell.

2. Design a better…

   a. Screwdriver:

   Reduce the variations in sizes and shapes of screws; develop a short screw bit that fits on the tip of one's finger and can be set at an angle—the finger would provide torque and the arrangement would provide greater dexterity.

   b. A Vacuum Cleaner:

   A gel can be developed that clumps dust together and creates one connected substance that can be thrown away without the release of dust particulates and maintaining a supply of bags that will be replaced.

3. Pick up an object from somewhere in the room…"

   A plastic storage bin—is it really 2.5 bushels large? How much should "bushel" be used as a common measurement of capacity? The English system shouldn't be used in common culture anymore, especially in a globalized world. How many other countries is that bin sold in? How many other countries understand the English system of measurement? Does the production company have to produce two different sizes of bins, one in the English system and one in the Metric system? Is it really blue? Blue isn't a really good color for that sort of bin, unless it belongs in a children's room. There aren't many interior designs that incorporate that color of blue, so if it's meant for children's areas is it safe to chew on? Are rope handles really appropriate for children's areas? What if a child were to fall on it and get rope burn? How are the dimensions determined? Are there people who study the most beneficial dimensions of cylindrical bins? Is it the optimum shape for carrying water or toys? Would a toy carrying bin be better if it were wider and shallower since toys are oddly shaped oftentimes?

How Biased Are You?

Exercises

1. Can contextual bias be used to advantage to benefit science and society?
   a. The Biggest Loser

      An ideal weight can become the anchor in anchoring bias. If enough individuals in a social network engaged in losing weight, the comparison weight would decline and spread through contextual bias.

   b. Quantity of excess radiation in a mammogram or CT.

      Radiation dose can be compared to some more familiar value, such as the amount of radiation you get every time you go up in a plane or in a high altitude city such as Denver or Mexico City.

2. Consider a recent purchase you made at a swanky shop.

   $300 for a 100% Suri alpaca blanket bought at an upscale import shop in New York. Same item sells for about $100 online and the same at an alpaca shop in Peru.

3. Use anchoring and contextual bias to advantage in increasing medication compliance.

   Anchoring Bias—Free sample medications are ubiquitous in the doctor's office. Drug representatives give these to the physician as a way to get patients anchored to or familiar with a brand. A somewhat more ethically questionable approach might be to post signs about a medication in the office with a price that is higher than offered by most pharmacies and benefits with that are fewer than expected. The patient would then feel that s/he is receiving a great deal and is seeing better efficacy than hoped for.

   Contextual Bias—The use of familiar athletes and entertainment personalities is a common way to market medications. Patients emulate these figures and so take the drugs. Another possibility might be to ask patient volunteers who have used the medication to sit in the office and provide testimonies about their good experiences with consistent use.

4. Invent a medical treatment that capitalizes on the beneficial effects of a placebo.

   According to research by de la Fuente-Fernandez, Schulzer, and Stoessl (2004), Parkinson's disease can be positively affected by the use of placebos that seem to have an effect by activating the reward circuitry through the release of dopamine. It is, of course, unethical to give a placebo when a better active alternative is available. Although placebo medications can work, their use is controversial because generally the prescriber does not divulge to the patient they are inactive. However, recent research showed that even when a patient has been told they are taking a placebo, the patient often experiences a beneficial effect.

Overcoming Bias

Exercises

1. Perseverance bias

   Decision—Should you advise your postmenopausal patients to continue to take Hormone Replacement Therapy (HT)?

   - *Frame*—Perseverance bias leads you to think that what you've been doing is what is best.
   - *Remove Frame*—Although HT was commonly prescribed by physicians, the Women's Health Initiative linked HT to increases in breast cancer, heart attack, deep venous thrombosis, and stroke. Discontinuing the thought that what you've been doing is what is best allows patients to consider in an unbiased way the risks and benefits of HT use.
   - *Consequences*—Patients and physicians must weigh the acute benefits of preventing hot flashes with the longer term risks of possible serious and even life threatening adverse events. Parameters that should figure into this weighing include age of patient, years since menopause, and duration of HT use.

2. Contextual bias

   Decision—Should you ride a motorcycle, drive a car, or bike the four miles to work?

   - *Frame*—Contextual bias in an environment where everyone drives suggests that one should drive, even if exercise and environmental health would be improved by walking or riding a bike. In a context where everyone walks, such as New York City, driving appears less desirable and people often prolong learning to do so.
   - *Remove the frame*—Disregarding the actions of everyone else, allows you to consider and balance your own values with respect to cost, improving personal health and decreasing carbon emissions. This may lead you to deciding to ride your bicycle on safe paths over relatively short distances.
   - *Consequences*—You become healthier and feel better about your contributions to your purse and the environment, although everyone else is driving and considers your behavior a bit wacky.

Joy of Science

Unleash the curious cat within, and ask as many "why" questions as you can think of.

Why don't sheep shrink when it rains? Why do we depart from "the terminal" if planes are so safe? Why does everyone smell the same scent from a rose? Why do you let your investment portfolio be handled by a "broker?" Why does the sun darken our skin but lighten our hair? Why does the word lisp have an "s" in it? Why is "abbreviated" such a long word? Why do we call them buildings when they've already been built?

Asking the Right Question

Exercises

1. For each of the classic questions, identify a Who, What, When, Where, and, if relevant, Why?
   - Semmelweis

     Who—women shortly after childbirth; *What*—death from puerperal fever; *When*—in the mid-1800s; *Where*—a single obstetrical hospital; *Why*—why did some women die whereas others did not?
   - Women's Health Initiative

     Who—early postmenopausal women; *What*—post-menopausal Hormone Therapy reduces coronary heart disease; *When*—1990s; *Where*—United States; *Why*—not relevant.
   - Archimedes

     Who—king; *What*—know that a crown said to be made of pure gold is really made of pure gold; *When*—third century B.C.; *Why*—not relevant
   - Gladwell

     Who—teenagers; *What*—smoking prevention; *When*—modern; *Where*—United States; *Why*—not relevant.
   - Goodall

     Who—chimpanzees; *What*—behaviors while living in natural conditions; *Where*—Gombe National Park; *When*—1960s through present; *Why*—not relevant.
   - Goldberger

     Who—patients in mental asylums and orphanages; *What*—pellagra; *When*—turn of the twentieth century to die; *Where*—southern United States; *Why*—why did some die?
2. From the newspaper, find a science story and identify a carefully worded question. Re-pose the question in ways that would not have lead to the solution.

   Brody, J. E. Weight problems may begin in the womb. New York Times. Tues, September 7, 2010. (p D7). A new study by Currie et al. found a consistent relationship between the amount of weight a mother gained and her baby's birth weight. Large babies, in turn, are more likely to become overweight children. Question: Among babies born in the United States in 2010, to what extent did a mother's weight gain during pregnancy correlate with her baby's birth weight? Re-posing the question so it would not have led to the same solution: Among babies born in India…; Among babies born in the 1800s; How does a mother's prepregnancy weight relate to the baby's weight? How does pregnancy weight gain relate to baby's height?

3. Identify the Who, What, When, and Where of a current scientific or medicinal problem in the world. Ask the question as a frame-free question.

"Why do modern American children get fat?" Who: American children; What: get fat; When: modern; Where: America; Why: why is this happening? Data: over-weight and obesity occurs in about one-third of American children in the year 2010. Higher income children are far less likely to be obese than lower income children. Minority groups such as African-Americans and Hispanics are more likely to be obese than Whites. Weight gain is a simple equation of calories in (from food) exceeding calories out (from exercise). Solutions in the form of public health experi-ments: (1) Re-price the marketplace by making lower calorie nutritious foods (e.g., fruits and vegetables) less expensive and higher calorie less nutritious foods (e.g., chips, sugared beverages) more expensive to see if this changes the number of chil-dren developing obesity. (2) Implement aggressive school-based mandatory exercise programs and see if this reduces the number of children getting fat.

How is a Marriage like a Matchbox?

Exercises

1. Complete the following sentences and explain the concept that linked the two analogies:

   - Wolf is to Mammal as Frog is to _____   *Amphibian*
   - Allow is to Permit as Find is to _____   *Locate*
   - Warm is to Hot as _____ is to Cold   *Cool*
   - Glove is to Hand as _____ is to Computer   *Monitor*
   - Furs are to Eskimos as Credit is to _____   *Shopper*

2. Similarities between these things.

   - How is history like a mango?
     Peel them and you see something different; impenetrable on the outside and juicy on the inside; grow over time to become ripe.
   - What makes temperature like a yo-yo?
     Moves up and down; always goes back to a fixed point; affected by outside influ-ences; can get tangled up.
   - How is photosynthesis like a symphony?
     Lots of elements; interactions; sequential steps; need care and feeding (photosyn-thesis: water and light; symphony: patrons and funds).

- How is a dream like a painting?

Similarities—*Come from imagination; can be colorful; can be fanciful and intriguing.* Differences—*in head versus on canvas; personal versus communal; fleeting versus permanent.*

3. Find examples of scientists using analogies:

Einstein used thought experiments in which concepts were considered in tangible form to solve problems in physics. Here is one that demonstrates relativity. A man loses his bottle of whiskey in a moving stream and only realizes after 20 minutes of going upstream. He then turns the boat and goes downstream with the same velocity for a mile and picks up the bottle. What is the velocity of the river? This problem stumped mathematicians. It can be easily solved if, rather than thinking in relation to the shoreline, one thinks in relation to the moving river. When we look from the river, it appears to be at rest but the shore is moving. The bottle in the stream is then not moving. The boat goes upstream 20 minutes and then downstream the same speed (so same time—20 minutes). The bottle is in the river 40 minutes. During that time, the shoreline moved 1 mile. So, the velocity of the shore (or the water in relation to the shore) is simply 1 mile in 40 minutes or 1.5 miles/hour. So, the solution to the problem is to think of the movement of the bottle as relative to the moving water.

Flip it!

Exercises

1. How to get kids to eat better?

An expanded question might be: How can we improve the nutritional quality of foods children eat? Widening this question further might entail: Why are foods of low nutritional value generally less expensive than those of high nutritional value?; What effect do agricultural subsidies have on obesity?

2. Design a convenient and low-cost rain jacket: novel materials; convenience; fashion.

Manufacture a rain jacket out of recyclable plastic. Roll up the jacket into an open cylinder that would slide over an umbrella. Embellish the plastic with crazy patterns (leopard skin; paisley; zig zags) or wild colors so cars can readily see the wearer when crossing the street. The rain jacket would be not much more expensive than a heavy duty trash bag so a consumer could buy several patterns and colors to match their wardrobe.

3. Design a convenient and eco-friendly trash container. Break down the problem.

- What novel materials might work?
- How could it be designed to be low cost and convenient?

- Recycle it—how?

Make it fit into the house (i.e., interior design-friendly).

A trash container might be made of heavy-duty paper coated in wax. This is a recyclable material, is quite sturdy, costs only a few cents to manufacture, and could be made in any color or pattern. Although not as long-lasting as plastic or metal, the low cost and recyclability mean it could be replaced more often and still be eco-friendly.

4. Find or imagine a science toy that narrows the perspective to demonstrate some specific aspect of science or technology. Write an advertisement.

"Star Rocket" demonstrates two aspects of airplane engineering: fuel chemistry and fin and fuselage aerodynamics. Its advertisement reads: "The New Scientific Explorer Star Rocket streaks up to 200 feet in the sky! It's the latest advancement in their patented baking soda and vinegar rocket technology… You'll find out whether balsamic vinegar makes better fuel than regular vinegar, and you can test different fin and fuselage configurations for optimum aerodynamics. It's an unforgettable flying experience."

5. Brands can also succeed by total reversal: Rather than assuaging the customer's fears about the product, or trying to fix the negative aspects, they exacerbate them. Apply reversal to enhancing compliance with taking medications.

The Mini-Cooper's small size was showcased in advertisements—for example, by being placed on top of an SUV. Red Bull's bad taste became legendary and developed a cult following. To encourage patient compliance with medication-taking, maybe we should consider manufacturing medications that are LESS appealing. For example, experiments show that expectation bias applies to medications—those that are more expensive are more valued and thus more likely to actually be taken. Also, if a medication has a bad taste, it will be more memorable and, if set in the correct context (e.g., in a pill minder left next to the toothbrush where it is readily seen each morning) may more likely be remembered.

6. Brands like IKEA reverse the status quo. Science can do the same—reverse the prospect of having to exercise to being allowed to exercise.

Employers could organize workplace health programs to include competitive teams. The team with the highest average monthly pedometer score would win a prize. To be accepted on the team, each member would have to commit to a minimum exercise regimen, and of course, the greater the individual contribution, the better the team outcome. Insurance programs could include stepped rebates for increasing levels of exercise. Once a person has shown a commitment to a higher level, he/she could be awarded with membership to an exercise club. In other words, the greater the commitment, the larger the allowance to exercise.

A Man Walked into a Bar

1. Imagine you see a glass full of water sitting on a table. How to get water out?
   Siphon it out; put rocks at the bottom so it spills out; boil the water away; use an absorbent material such as a sponge to sop it out. (from de Bono De Bono's Thinking Course)
2. All the ways to use (a few examples provided):
   Brick
   Construct a barrier for a garden; paint as piece of avant garde deco; door stop; excess weight to hold something down; crush into dust, add to clay to make a pot.
   Wheelbarrow
   Transport stuff; use as planter; take joy rides; establish a manmade coral reef; turn upside down and protect vulnerable creatures from outside predators or elements
   Comb
   Comb hair; apply texture to a painting; use as an analogy for close examination; sift through material of different thicknesses; rake sand back in an ant farm.
   Pipette
   Mix chemicals at a known and controlled rate; as a way to think about hydrodynamic properties of tunnels on a small scale; to punch holes in soft things; heat and bend to make a sculpture.
   Incubator
   Hatch chickens; as a metaphor for the creative process; grow microorganism cultures; keep food warm
3. In a movie called *Rock Round the Clock*, how might Gave snag the contract and her man?
   Marry before the contract begins. Thus does not marry during the period of the contract and does not violate the terms.
4. Young man pouring beer into the gas tank of a car.
   Consider alternative explanations. Obviously, he may be drunk and confused. He also may be trying to sabotage the car; the beer can may be the only container he has to pour gasoline into the tank; it may be a stunt for a beer commercial. (from de Bono, De Bono's Thinking Course)

Exercises

1. Defend the following counterfactuals:
   - Women should get paid more
     They have been paid less for a long time so paying them more would be an equity adjustment. They can be highly productive; sometimes take jobs men don't want;

have less physical fights; are team players; worth keeping happy or they'll stop bearing the next generation.

- All dogs should be taxed
  They sometimes pollute the environment with poop; they can cause noise pollution from barking; it would promote dog birth control.
- Corn products should be taxed
  Corn has remained inexpensive while fruits and vegetables have skyrocketed in price so this would bring them more into parity; corn products are often used to make high-fat/sugar/salt foods, which should be consumed less to limit weight gain.
- Corn products should be free
  Corn is ubiquitous in the food chain, used also for feeding livestock. This would dramatically bring down the price of foods for the poor and undernourished. Access to food, just like democracy, free speech, and health, should be guaranteed in a free society.
- Tenure should not exist
  Once position and salary are guaranteed, there is sometimes less incentive to be highly productive. In a society where federal rules preclude mandated retirement, top-heavy faculties limit the number of positions available to young people. The days tenure was required for freedom of speech are over, making tenure unnecessary.
- All academic positions should be tenured upon hire
  Tenured positions would attract the best and brightest. More innovation could be done at a young age if position and salary were guaranteed.
- Universities should have no physical campuses.
  The Internet now allows most teaching to occur virtually. Some universities (e.g., University of Phoenix) are entirely virtual. Physical campuses are expensive; discarding these expenses would free resources for better teaching and lower tuition.
- Web-based courses should be outlawed.
  Face-to-face interactions are different from Web-based and perhaps important. Personal face-to-face friendships among students can be an important part of the instructional process. Internet-based universities can potentially out-compete physical ones and may make the latter obsolete.

2. Work through these problems using the APC method:
  - What alternative approaches might there be for reducing consistent smoking among young people?
    Of teenagers who experiment with smoking, only about one-third go on to become regular smokers. Moreover, it takes about 5 years, on average, to establish a commitment to everyday smoking. In The Tipping Point, *Gladwell suggests*

two strategies to limit the stickiness of cigarettes. One is the use of Bupropion (Zyban), an anti-depression medication that increases dopamine and replaces norepinephrine, thereby making up for the neurotransmitter effects of smoking. The other is to reduce nicotine in cigarettes such that even a pack a day would not deliver enough to be addictive. With this latter strategy, teens could experiment with smoking and not develop a physical dependence.

- What alternative explanation might you give for a rise in the rates of homicide in a large American city?

  In the book Freakonomics, *Dubner and Levitt argue that when abortion became legal, thousands of children who would have been born to mothers unprepared or unable to have them (the living situation in which crime rates are highest) were never born, and so the 1990s drop in crime rates resulted from all of those unborn children not coming of age. Using this argument, making abortion less available would increase homicide.*

- Find alternatives to the increasingly difficult American commute.

  Provide more public transportation in lieu of car-based commuting; give tax incentives to live close to work; increase the tax on gas and implement commuter taxes (i.e., negative incentive to live far away); provide more green spaces, better schools, better public transportation to cities to lure people closer to workplaces. Note that moving people closer to work will reduce traffic for those who continue to choose to commute.

3. Use PMI to think through these innovative suggestions:

- Everyone should wear a badge showing his or her mood.

  Plus: communicates mood. Minus: may not want this known. Interesting: new modes of communication; new insights into how much people want known.

- Every child should adopt a senior citizen to look after.

  Plus: children learn respect for elders and seniors have helpmates. Minus: limits the time children have to spend on other things and mandates are onerous. Interesting: a new way to provide eldercare as the elderly become an increasing large component of the population. May be some way to incent youngsters to enlarge the pool of caregivers.

- Everyone should be required to work on a farm for a summer during college.

  Plus: would teach young people where food comes from and the economics of farming; Minus: limits the time children have to spend on other things and mandates are onerous. Interesting: might increase the amount of labor intensive sustainable farming. Might increase knowledge of and change attitudes toward farm legislation.

- Military service should be mandatory in the United States.

  Plus: expands capacity and reduces cost of maintaining armed forces. Minus: puts more Americans in harm's way and is politically untenable. Interesting:

provides discipline, training, camaraderie, and national loyalty for young people.

4. Consider the problem from two different points of view: scientists and non-scientists

   - Design a better method of testing environmental toxicants from the point of view of a microbiologist.

     The Ames test currently used to test cell killing in bacteria; future tests might use various markers for direct DNA damage. A toxicologist—mice used to test both toxicity and mutagenesis (cancer causing); future use of computer models extrapolated from known toxic chemical structures. An engineer—consider the flow of chemicals from a plant based on novel markers in water and computer models of water flow using swarm intelligence (see Chapter on "The Power of Groups"). An epidemiologist—does studies in human populations. Start with prototype studies—carefully monitor sentinel groups with high occupational exposure, which may not be large or unselected but would give a sense of any worrisome toxicity.

   - Design a better method of testing environmental toxicants from the point of view of

     A mayor—Focus on constituent groups responsible and affected. Use GPS to get a sense of where the chemicals are coming from and where they are going to. *A policeman*—concern about neurotoxicity that may influence criminal behavior. Consider long-term effects (such as Needleman has hypothesized for lead). *A professional athlete*—concern about climate change causing extreme weather that cancels games and on air quality. Consider effects on the larger environment as part of the definition of toxicity. *A school child*—weight current financial interests as far less meaningful than future environmental influences. Concern about persistence of chemicals and effects in the environment so design long-term health and environmental outcomes studies in large cohorts starting at birth.

Testing your Ideas

1. How might you approach the question of whether fertility rates have been dropping over the last decades with only a $1 million study?

   A highly efficient way to design studies is to leverage from already collected data. National surveys conducted every few years collect self-reports of how long it takes couples to get pregnant and comparing these over time should be a starting point. However, self-reports can be biased, so it would be great to get a biological marker. Sperm banks have also been in the business of collecting specimens, and using these, sperm counts could be compared over time. Finally, sophisticated studies of fertility were conducted in the 1980s (by Wilcox and others). Women trying to get pregnant took daily pregnancy tests so it was clear exactly how long they took to get pregnant. This exact same study design could be repeated so as to compare time to pregnancy then and now.

2. Read the review about the relationship between salt and hypertension, and using Hill's criteria, decide whether you think the relationship is causal.

   Using a ranking of strong, moderate, and none, I would rank Hill's tenets as follows: Strength of association: moderate; Consistency: strong; Temporality: strong; Biological gradient: strong; Biological plausibility: strong; Experimental studies: strong.

That Right Idea

The exercises in this chapter don't have answers *per se*. They consist of personal insights and plan. Hopefully you will find these useful.

Overcoming the Stodginess of Science

Exercises:

1. Think of modifications of products either by finding a right environment or by modifying the product to make it the right idea.

   Make pills more glamorous by changing the shape of the bottle they come in; market TOMs (essentially a type of slipper) as an outdoor shoe; diapers that show when a baby has peed without having to look in—uses a pH-treated diaper material that changes color on the outside of the diaper; a T-shirt that says, "I am an embarrassment to my children" (a must-have for parents of adolescents).

2. What might the current U.S. president do to become a champion for innovative solutions to some of our most pressing problems?

   Global warming: Create climate clubs in schools to engage students in hands-on learning and discussions around the effects of global warming. Put up funds for Internet-based grand challenges to create new eco-friendly sources of energy, transportation, and farming; a youth version could target school-age children and an adult (much larger prize) version could target industry. Create financial (e.g., tax) incentives for living closer to work. Provide financial incentives or low-cost loans to build the infrastructure around new modalities such as electric cars, nuclear power plants, and solar plants.

3M, office supply division, 125

Academia
environment, 211–212
funding, 211–214
limitations, 213–215
possible wanderings, 211, 212, 214, 216
Accidents
frontal lobe syndrome, 82–83
Phineas Gage, 81–82
Action steps, ideas, 184–185
Adenovirus, common cold, 164
ADNI, consortium between NIH,
industry and academia, 153–155, 215
Advanced directives, living wills, 36–37
Afghanistan, 13th Marine Expeditionary Unit,
14–15
Agassi, Shai, Better Place, 124–125
Alcoholics Anonymous, recovery, 36
Alice in Wonderland, ideas, 184
ALLHAT clinical trial, hypertension, 192
Alternatives, possibilities, and choices (APC),
de Bono tool, 136–138
Alzheimer's disease
brain imaging technique, 153–154
collaboration, 215
treatment, 3
Amabile, creative business environments,
208–209
America
creativity crisis, 3
losing dominance in science, 4
American West, explorers, 107
Amundsen, Roald, 126
Amygdala, prefrontal cortex and, 85–86
Amyloid-beta, Alzheimer's disease, 153
Analogy
adaptable tool, 109, 115
extending concept of metaphor, 109
Hofstadter, 110–111
horizontal integration, 113–114
logic, 109
scientific discovery, 108
scientific innovation, 111–113
vertical integration, 113–114
Anchoring bias
example, 72–73

framing thinking, 69
wine purchase, 65–66
Anchoring effect, Better Place, 124–125
Anesthetic, Davy's discovery, 191–192
Ant self-organization, computer science and
ecology, 151–152
Apple Mouse, IDEO design firm, 56
Archimedes, 102, 108
ARCHIMEDES, systems modeling, 120
Ariely, Dan, *Predictably Irrational: The Hidden
Forces that Shape Our Decisions*, 63
ARPANET system, implementation, 148–149
The Art of Innovation, Kelley, 56
Atomic bomb project, World War II, 94–95
Attitude for end of life, frame
shifting, 27
Australia, kangaroo gastrointestinal flora,
137–138
Autonomic nervous system
decision making, 85–86
emotional arousal, 83
skin conductance testing, 83–84

Babe Ruth, 144
Backburner, future projects, 185
Bacon, Francis, *Novum Organum*, 169
Bacteria
Fleming and penicillin, 49–50
puerperal fever, 104
scientific observations, 48–49
Bandwagon effect
hormone therapy, 195
science, 215
social beliefs, 192–193
Barran, Paul, communications
framework, 148, 149
Batman Returns, movie, 152
Batteries, Better Place, 125
Belcher, Angela, bacteriophage virus, 127
Bell, Alexander Graham, telephone, 113
Bell, Joshua, expectation bias, 66–67
Belsky, Scott
Making Ideas Happen, 157, 184
time-management strategies, 188–189
Benzene, Kekulè and, structure, 113
Bernoulli, Daniel, expected utility theory, 62
Better Place

electric cars, 204–205
Israeli start-up company, 124–125
Betting behavior, expected utility
  theory, 62
Bias
  anchoring, 65–66, 72–73
  contextual, 63–65, 71–72
  expectation, 66–68
  framing thinking, 69
  hindsight, 68–69, 73–74
  overcoming, 71–74
  perseverance, 66
Biological sciences, Hill's tenets, 172–173
Birth control, social marketing, 201
Birth weight
  Canada, 98, 99
  United States, 98
Black holes, 24
Blau, Helen, 150
Blind Man's Bluff, Sontag and
  Drew, 145
Blink: The Power of Thinking Without Thinking,
  Gladwell, 45
Blood flow, cerebral, 77–78
Boston, environmental lead, 25
Brain
  autonomic nervous system, 83, 85
  creativity, 79–80
  hemisphere dominance, 77–79
  left, 77
  right, 76–77
  seat of creativity, 75, 79
  split-brain research, 76–77
Brain injury, Phineas Gage, 81–82
Brain research, Innovation-Frame Hypothesis,
  89–90
Brainstorming
  "brainstorm killers" to avoid, 160–161
  HOT teams at IDEO, 158–160
  Mind Map, 185–186, 187f
  secrets, 159
Brainteasers
  examples, 23–24, 197–198
  frames, 22
Brain tumor, frontal lobe syndrome, 82–83
Breast cancer
  hormone replacement therapy, 176–177,
    177–178
  screening and prevention, 38
Brinton, Louise, endometriosis and ovarian
  cancer, 174, 175
Brooks, David, *Innovation Stagnation is Slowing
  U.S. Progress*, 4
Brownell, Kelly, taxation of sugared beverages,
  21–22
Buckholtz, Neil, National Institutes on Aging, 154
Buddha, term, 163
Buddhism, mindfulness, 164

Business Week, innovation
  slow-down, 3
Buzan, Tony, *Use Your Head*, 186

Caenorhabditis elegans, roundworm, 43
California Institute of Technology, Sperry, 76
Canada
  infant mortality, 98
  low-birth-weight babies, 98–99
Canadian Centre for Disease Control,
  babies, 98
Cancer
  endometriosis and ovarian, 173–175
  stem cell research, 139
  war on, 3, 37–39
Cardiovascular disease, pregnancy, 115
Cardiovascular research, Kuller, 21
Carnegie Mellon University, stress and illness,
  164–165
Carrel, Alexis, 53
Cell phones
  communication, 195–196
  invention, 3
Cell Stem Cell, 150
Centers for Disease Control and Prevention
  (CDC)
  cigarettes, 120
  folic acid and spina bifida, 204
  life expectancy, 123
Challenger, Space Shuttle explosion, 95
Change blindness, phenomenon, 47
Chelating agents, lead poisoning, 24–26
Chemotherapy, cancer, 38
Childbirth, puerperal fever, 104–105
Childhood, creativity test scores, 6
Children
  environmental lead, 24–26
  inventiveness, 4–5
Chimpanzees, Goodall, 16–17, 103
China
  President Nixon and, 68
  venture capital investments, 96–97
Chinese proverb, 42
Christmas Carol, 97
Cigarettes, shifting frame, 119–120
City planning, paradigm, 15
Clinical trial, ALLHAT, 192
Clothes dryer, dreams, 110
Cocaine addicts, drugs and infection, 113
Cochlear implants, invention, 3
Cognitive bias, decision making and, 62–63
Cognitive frames
  expectations or assumptions, 11
  logic and passion, 15–16
Cohen, Sheldon, stress and illness, 164–165
Collaboration, ADNI consortium
  between NIH, industry and
  academia, 153–155, 215

Communication, cell phones, 195–196
Companies, high-tech start-ups, 96–97
Computer science, fusion with ecology, 151–152
Constraint, frames, 16
Container technology, shipping, 118–119
Contextual bias
  decision making, 63–65
  example, 71–72
  framing thinking, 69
Contour drawing, observation, 54
Cooking, metaphors, 32–33
Cotes du Rhone wine, anchoring effect, 65
Counterfactuals, jokes, 133
Cowen, Tyler, *The Great Stagnation*, 4
Craven, Dr. John, group intelligence, 145–146
Creativity
  brain, 79–80
  business environments, 208–209
  crisis in America, 3
  decision making, 87–88
  Feynman, 94–95
  front vs. back of brain, 81
  innovation, 2–3
  Montessori method, 209–211
  practice, 7
  scientist role models, 7
  test scores, 6
  training programs, 5–6
Damasio, Antonio
  Descartes' Error, 82–83
  Somatic Marker Hypothesis, 84–86
Darwin, Charles, evolution, 16, 119
Davies, Donald, National Physical
  Laboratory, 149
da Vinci, Leonardo, drawing, 54
Davy, Sir Humphrey, discovery of nitrous oxide,
  191–192
Death
  framing, 27, 37
  metaphor, 37
  toll of 1918 flu, 1
de Bono, Edward
  alternatives, possibilities, and choices (APC),
    136–138
  Lateral Thinking, 71, 124, 131
  plus, minus, interesting (PMI), 138–139
  provocative orientation, 135–136
Decision making
  Bernoulli, 62
  context bias, 63–65
  creativity and innovation, 87–88
  emotional arousal, 83–84
  expected utility theory, 62
  frames, 62–63
  Innovation-Frame Hypothesis, 86–87
  prefrontal cortex and autonomic
    nervous system, 85–86
  Somatic Marker Hypothesis, 84–86

Defense Advanced Research Projects Agency
  (DARPA)
  creation of Internet, 149
  helium balloons, 150
  packet–switching network, 148–149
Delivery rooms, puerperal fever, 104–105
Demotivators, jokes, 133–134
de Saint-Exupery, Antoine, 93
Descartes' Error, Damasio, 82–83
Design firm, IDEO, 56, 214
Detre, Katherine, 93
Diabetes, ARCHIMEDES systems
  modeling, 120
Diagnosis, ovarian cancer, 59–60
Directions, map, 47
Discovery, frame shifts, 40
Disease, war on, 37–39
Disney, Walt, creative thinker, 183–184
DNA sequencing, invention, 3
Doers, groups, 157–158
Dog experiments, Pavlov, 84, 85
Drawing. *See also* Observation
  contour, 55
  enhancing observation, 54
  Leonardo da Vinci, 54
  negative shapes, 55–56
  regrouping, 57
  upside-down, 54
Drawing on the Right Side of the Brain,
  Edwards, 54
Dreamers, groups, 157–158
Dreams, clothes dryer, 110
Drew, Christopher, *Blind Man's Bluff*, 145
Driving, traffic planning, 15
Drucker, Peter F., 191
Drugs
  observing neighborhood, 44–46
  rapid prototyping, 182
Duncker, Karl, functional fixedness, 127–128

Ecology, fusion of computer science with,
  151–152
Economic refugees, term, 33
Ecosystems, Earth's, 3
Edison, Thomas, light bulb, 96, 212
Education
  female, 121–122
  frame shifting, 27–28
Edwards, Betty, *Drawing on the Right Side of the
  Brain*, 54
Einstein, Albert, 11, 131
  quantum mechanics, 111
  scientific world, 20
  theory of relativity, 24
Electric cars, Better Place, 204–205
Electromagnetism, telephone, 113
Emerson, Ralph Waldo,
  perceptions, 43

Emotion
    decision making, 83–84
    metaphors, 33
Endless Knot, structure of benzene, 113
End of life
    advanced directives, 36–37
    frame shifting, 27
Endometriosis, ovarian cancer, 173–175
Environment
    academia, 211–212
    creative business, 208–209
    funding agencies, 211–212
    influence of right, 201–202, 206–207
    Montessori method, 209–211
Environmental lead, Needleman, 24–26
Epidemics, smallpox, 114
Etch a Sketch®, design for
        semi-conductors, 112
Evolution, Darwin, 119
Evolutionary biology
    newts, 150
    regenerative genes, 151
Evolutionary theory
    Darwin, 16
    frames, 12
Expectation bias
    framing thinking, 69
    Joshua Bell, 66–67
    placebos, 67–68
    science, 67–68
Expectations, observations and
        testing, 171
Expected utility theory, Bernoulli, 62
Experience, posing questions, 101–102
Explorers, American West, 107
Eyewitness testimony, hindsight bias, 69

Failure, funding, 212
Fausey, Caitlin, Stanford University, 30–31
Female education, World Health Organization,
        121–122
Feminine Forever, Wilson, 178
Feynman, Richard
    creativity, 94–95
    joy of learning, 96
    Nobel Prize in physics, 93–94, 95
    The Pleasure of Finding
        Things Out, 94
    quantum electrodynamics, 94
Fleming, Alexander, penicillin, 49–50
Flying, frames, 13–14
Folic acid, innovation, 203–204
Food and Drug Administration (FDA)
    brain imaging for Alzheimer's, 153–154
    folic acid, 204
    Hill's tenets, 172–173
Ford Motor Company, seatbelts, 202–203
Fraiberg, Selma, The Magic Years, 168

Frames
    approach for shifting, 26–28
    attitudes toward end of life, 27
    biases and thinking, 69
    brainteaser examples, 23–24
    brainteasers, 22
    changing, 20
    cognitive, 11
    constraint, 16
    decision making, 62–63
    education, 27–28
    identifying and overcoming, 71
    impacting innovation, 13–14
    language reinforcing, 30–31
    logic and passion, 15–16
    metaphors, 31–35
    observations, 44
    reframing, 24, 28
    restaurant, 11–12
    science, 16–17, 193–194
    scientific questions, 103
    sensory information, 46–47
Frame-shift
    ADNI consortium between NIH, industry
        and academia, 154–155
    approach for shifting, 26–28
    seatbelts, 202–203
Free Willy whale, IDEO design firm, 56
Friendships, behaviors, 64
From the Earth to the Moon, Verne, 101
Frontal lobe syndrome, Gage, 82
Frost, Robert, good neighbors, 39
Fry, Art, Post-Its, 125
Functional fixedness, term, 127–128
Funding agencies
    academia, 211–214
    environment, 211–212
    failures, 212
    limitations, 213–215

Gage, Phineas, railroad rod accident, 81–82
Gambling game, life as, 39–40
Gasoline, lead content, 25
Gassett, Ortega Y., 30
Gastrointestinal flora, kangaroos, 137–138
The Gathering Storm, scientific innovation, 4
Gazzaniga, Michael, brain work, 75–76
Genes, regenerative, 150–151
Germ theory
    expectations, 14
    frames, 12
Gladwell, Malcolm
    Blink: The Power of Thinking Without
        Thinking, 45
    "Law of the Few," 200
    right environment, 201–202
    right idea, 201
    smoking, 103

The Tipping Point: How Little Things Can Make A Big Difference, 200
Global positioning systems (GPS), 24
Global warming, alternative solution, 137–138
Goedel Escher Bach, Hofstadter, 34
Goethe, 53
Goldberger, Joseph, pellagra research, 87–88, 103, 122, 169
Goodall, Jane
    chimpanzee behavior, 16–17, 103
    The Chimpanzees of the Gombee: Patterns of Behavior, 17
    paradigm shift, 87
    scientist role model, 7
Google Maps, navigation, 147
Grady, Deborah, women's health, 176
The Great Stagnation, Cowen, 4
Greenhouses gases, agriculture, 137–138
Gross, David, Nobel Laureate in physics, 98
Group expertise
    Nature, 146–147
    online encyclopedia *Wikipedia*, 146–147
Group intelligence
    ADNI consortium between NIH, industry and academia, 153–155
    brainstorming, 48, 158–161
    computer science and ecology, 151–152
    Defense Advanced Research Projects Agency (DARPA), 148–149
    Doers, Dreamers, and Incrementalists, 157–158
    evolutionary biology, 150–151
    innovation, 144–145
    Navy and oceanographic research, 145–146
    social sensitivity, 147–148
Guns, drug-infested neighborhood, 44–46
Gyorgi, Albert Szent, 117

H1N1, viral epidemic, 2
Hadron Collider, high energy particle accelerator, 129
Hamilton, Gordon, hydroacoustics, 145
Hand-washing, puerperal fever, 104–105
HapMap, genetics open source website, 147, 215
Heart disease, similarity to preeclampsia, 115
Heliobacter pylori, scientific observations, 49
Hemisphere dominance, brain, 77–79
Higgs boson, scalar elementary particle, 129
Higher education, frame shifting, 27–28
Hill, Sir Bradford, criteria for confidence, 172–173
Hilton, Conrad, 162
Hindsight bias
    example, 73–74
    memory recollection, 68–69
The Hitchhiker's Guide to the Galaxy, 106
HIV resistance, Huetter's discovery, 139–140
Hofstadter, Douglas, 107

Goedel Escher Bach, 34
    metaphor and analogy, 110–111
Horizontal integration, analogies, 113–114
Hormone replacement therapy,
    Women's Health Initiative, 102, 176–177, 178, 195
Hormones, ovarian cancer, 59–60
Huetter, Gero, HIV resistance, 139–140
Humor. *See also* Jokes
    evolution, 134
Hutter, Marcus, 186
Hypertension, ALLHAT clinical trial, 192
Hypothesis, observations and testing, 170–172

Idea generation
    action steps, 184–185
    Backburner, 185
    bucking societal norms, 198–199
    Mind Maps, 185–186, 187f
    Nike's "Just Do It," 186, 188
    primary rules, 180–181
    prioritizing ideas, 182–183
    safely excluding ideas, 181–182
    time management, 188–189
    Walt Disney, 183–184
Idea promotion
    audience, 199
    folic acid, 203–204
    persuasion, 199–200
    right environment, 201–202, 206–207
    right idea, 201, 206, 207
    right person, 202–203, 205–206, 207
    seatbelts, 202–203
    social epidemics, 200–201
IDEO design firm
    ABC Nightline, 56, 182
    brainstorming, 158–161
    HOT Teams, 157, 158
    interactions between clients and products, 58
    key to success, 57
    paying attention to problems, 58–59
    product innovation, 57–58
    real world observation, 56
Illegal aliens, term, 33
Illness, stress and, 164–165
Imagination, meditation, 165
Imaginative rationality, 33
Incrementalists, groups, 157–158
Incubation
    creativity, 89, 166
    describing, 163
    innovation, 162–163, 166
Induction, theory of scientific thinking, 169–170
Inductive reasoning, fallacies, 169–170
Infant mortality, Canada and United States, 98
Infections, cocaine vaccine, 113
Inferences, observations and testing, 171

Influenza
    pandemic, of 1918, 1
    spring of 2009, 2
Innovation
    brainstorming, 158–161
    broadening perspective, 118
    changing point of view, 140–142
    creativity with purpose, 2–3
    DARPA's creation of Internet, 149
    folic acid, 203–204
    frames impacting, 13–14
    functional fixedness, 127–128
    human thinking, 215–216
    IDEO's steps to product, 57–58
    incubation, 162–163, 166
    Innovation (continued)
    jokes, 132–133
    narrowing perspective, 121–123
    prefrontal cortex, 86–87
    recombination and rearrangement, 126–127
    reversal, 123–126
    seatbelts for cars, 202–203
    teaching, 6
    testing ideas, 178
Innovation-Frame Hypothesis
    brain research, 89–90
    decision making, 86–87
    innovative thinking stages, 89
Innovation Stagnation is Slowing U.S. Progress,
    Brooks, 4
Innovative thinking
    cognitive frames, 11
    testing an idea, 171–172
Inspiration, semi-conductors, 112
Intelligence
    children and lead poisoning, 25–26
    power of group, 147–148
    September 11, 2001 tragedy, 152–153
Intelligence Reform and Terrorist Prevention
    Act of 2004, 153
International Hapmap, open-source project,
    147, 215
Internet, invention, 3
Interpretation, visual system, 46–47
Ireland, starving poor, 134–135
Israel
    high-tech start-up companies, 96–97,
        204–205
    military, 97

Jenner, Edward, smallpox, 114
Johansson, Frans, The Medici Effect, 151
Jokes
    brainteasers, 23–24, 197–198
    counterfactuals, 133
    Demotivators, 133–134
    evolution and humor, 134

innovation, 132
    one-liners, 132–133
    provocative orientation, 135–136
Jones, Franklin P., 156
Jones, Tommy Lee, Men in Black, 127
A Journey to the Centre of the Earth, Verne, 101

Kangaroos, gastrointestinal flora, 137–138
Kekulè, Fredrich August, structure of benzene,
    113
Kelley, Tom, The Art of Innovation, 56, 157, 159
Kerkstra, Koop, traffic planner, 15
Khine, Michelle, microfluidics chips, 112
Koch, Robert, germ theory, 14
Kolletschlea, Jacob, puerperal fever, 104
Koppel, Ted, ABC Nightline, 56, 182
Kosten, Thomas, cocaine vaccine, 113
Kuhn, Thomas
    normal science, 194
    The Structure of Scientific
        Revolutions, 87, 177, 180, 194
Kuller, Lewis, 93
    reading, 102
    University of Pittsburgh, 21
Kyoto University, stem cell research, 138–139

Lakoff, George, Metaphors We Live By, 33
Language, reinforcing frames, 30–31
Laser surgery, invention, 3
Lateral Thinking, de Bono, 71, 124, 131
Laughing gas, Davy's discovery, 191–192
Lead poisoning, Needleman, 24–26
Learning
    Montessori method, 209–211
    posing questions, 101–102
Legislation, smoking, 120
LEGOs®
    microparticles, 127
    prototypes, 57
Levy, Jeremy, semi-conductors, 112
Life
    advanced directives, 36–37
    frame shifting, 27, 39–40
Lifeguard, seatbelt and dished steering wheel,
    202
Light bulb, Edison, 96, 212
Linguistics
    frames, 30–31
    metaphors, 31–35
Living wills, advanced directives, 36–37
Logic, cognitive frames, 15–16
Logue, Christopher, 1
Love, MRI scan of brain, 140–141
Lung cancer, smoking, 120

McArthur genius awards, 214
McNamara, Robert, seatbelts, 202–203

The Magic Years, Fraiberg, 168
Magnetic resonance imaging (MRI)
    blood flow, 77
    love and brain scans, 140–141
Magnetron, microwaves, 50–51
Making Ideas Happen, Belsky, 157, 184
Malaria, global problem, 138
Mandela, Nelson, sports in South Africa, 141
Marine Expeditionary Unit (13th)
    expectations, 13–14
    strong emotions, 14–15
Marriage, matchbox, 109–110
Marshall, Barry
    bacteria, 48–49
    paradigm shift, 87
Maslow, Abraham, 117
Massachusetts Institute of Technology (MIT),
    engineered virus, 127
Matchbox, marriage, 109–110
Mathematics, Archimedes, 108
Medical care, public health, 123–124
Medical illnesses, physicians diagnosing,
    122–123
Medicare dollars, end of life, 36–37
The Medici Effect, Johansson, 151
Medicine, new surgical techniques, 196
Meditation
    brain and imaginative thinking, 165
    decreasing stress, 164, 165
    exercise, 167
    incubation stage of creativity, 166
    Vipassana, 166
Men in Black, Will Smith and Tommy Lee
    Jones, 127
Metaphors
    analogy extending concept of, 109
    cancer as war, 37–39
    changing meaning, 35
    cooking, 32–33
    creation of, 34
    death and taxes, 37
    Hofstadter, 110–111
    linguistics, 31–35
    ontological, 32
    orientational, 32
    shifting frames, 35
    structural, 31–32
Metaphors We Live By, Lakoff, 33
Microfluidics chips, Shrinky Dinks, 112
Microscopy, germ theory, 14
Microwaves, discovery, 50–51
Milgram, Stanley, six degrees of freedom, 200
Military, Israel, 97
Mindfulness, Buddhism, 164
Mind Maps, organizing ideas, 185–186, 187f
Mobile phones, communication, 195–196
Monderman, Hans, personal responsibility, 15

Montessori, Maria, 42, 208
Montessori Method, 209–211
Morris, Jeremy, 93
Mortenson, Greg, *Three Cups of Tea*, 121
Music Academy of West Berlin, violin students,
    7–8
Mutagenesis, ovarian cancer, 59–60

National Institutes of Health (NIH), ADNI
    consortium between NIH, industry and
    academia, 153–155
National Institutes on Aging, Alzheimer's, 154
National Review, innovation slow-down, 3
Natural selection, Darwin, 119
Nature, group expertise, 146–147
Needleman, Herb, 93
    lead poisoning, 24–26
    paradigm shift, 87
    scientist role model, 7
Negative shapes, drawing, 55–56
Neighborhood, drugs and guns, 44–46
Neighbors, Frost's notion, 39
New England Journal of Medicine
    obesity, 64
    stress and illness, 165
Newton, Isaac, forces, 111–112
Newts, evolutionary biology, 150
New York Police Department (NYPD),
    observation, 53
Nike, "Just Do It," 186
Nitrous oxide, discovery, 191–192
Nixon, President Richard, hindsight bias, 68
Nobel Peace Prize, Mandela, 141
Nobel Prize in physics, Feynman, 93–94, 95
Nuclear submarines, Navy, 145

Oakley, Godfrey, folic acid, 204
Obesity
    consequences, 3
    epidemic conference, 21
    social networks, 64
    water, 21–22
Observation. *See also* Drawing
    drugs and guns in neighborhood, 44–46
    enhancing keen, 60–61
    exercises, 42, 59
    Fleming and penicillin, 49–50
    frames, 44
    IDEO design firm, 56
    map and directions, 47
    microwaves, 50–51
    New York detectives, 53
    normal, 42
    paying attention, 43–44
    sensory input, 43–44
    tools for keen observer, 53
    visual inputs, 46–48

Occam's Razor, 186
Office supply, 3M, 125
Olmert, Ehud, backing Better Place,205
The Onion, one-liners, 132–133
Ontario, infant mortality, 98, 99
On the Origin of Species by Means of Natural Selection, Darwin, 119
Ontological metaphors, 32
Open Street, Google Maps, 147
Organ donation, advanced directives, 37
Orientational metaphors, 32
Osborn, Alex, HOT Teams, 158
Outside of the box
    science, 194
    thinking, 6–7
Ovarian cancer
    diagnosis, 59–60
    endometriosis, 173–175

Painkillers, expectation bias, 67–68
Paint, lead content, 25–26
Pajcini, Kostandin, 150
Palm handheld, IDEO design firm, 56
Pan troglodytes, Goodall, 16–17
Paradigms
    Goodall, 17
    science, 16–17, 194–195
    science of city planning, 15
    term, 12
Parkinson's disease, 68, 155
Particle accelerator, high-energy, Hadron Collider, 129
Passion, cognitive frames, 15–16
Pasteur, Louis, germ theory, 14
Patent medications, expectation bias, 68
Pavlov, dog experiments, 84, 85
Pellagra, Goldberger, 87–88. 122, 103, 169
Pelvic inflammatory disease (PID), treatment, 205–206
Penicillin, Fleming and observation, 49–50
Perpetual Sunshine, 68
Perseverance bias
    framing thinking, 69
    unwillingness to change, 66
Persistence, Goldberger, 87–88
Persuasion, idea promotion, 199–200
Pharmaceutical industry, rapid prototyping, 182
Physics
    Archimedes, 108
    Feynman, 93–94
Pickett, Kate, *The Spirit Level: Why More Equal Societies Almost Always Do Better*, 63–64
PIG In MuD
    acronym for questions, 99–101, 168
    D (disseminate idea), 191
    G (generative) step, 108, 144
    I (incubation) stage, 162–163

reorganization and rearrangement, 117
Planck, Max, quantum mechanics, 111
Plasmodium falciparum, malaria, 138
The Pleasure of Finding Things Out, Feynman, 94
Plus, minus, interesting (PMI), de Bono tool, 138–139
Poincare, Henri, describing incubation, 163
Point of view, changing, 140–142
Pollutants, environmental lead, 25–26
Pomerantz, Jason, 150
Ponge, Francis, 36
Popper, Karl
    hypothesis and observations, 170–171
    testing an idea, 171–172
    thinking like, 181
Populations, cigarette smoking, 119–120
Post-doctoral training program, Western Psychiatric Institute and Clinic, 156
Practice, music students, 7–8
Predictably Irrational: The Hidden Forces that Shape Our Decisions, Ariely, 63
Preeclampsia
    heart disease, 115
    pregnancy, 114
Prefrontal cortex
    decision making, 85–86
    innovation, 86–87
    Innovation-Frame Hypothesis, 89
Pregnancy care
    Canada, 98–99
    folic acid, 204
    preeclampsia, 114–115
Product innovation, IDEO, 57–58
Prototyping. *See* Rapid prototyping
Provider enthusiasm, phenomenon, 64
Provocative Orientation (PO)
    counterfactuals, 135–136
    de Bono tool, 135
Public health, reversal, 123–124
Puerperal fever, hand-washing, 104–105

Quantum electrodynamics, Feynman, 94
Quantum mechanics, light analogies, 111
Questions
    actionable, 100
    characteristics, 100–101, 105–106
    PIG In MuD acronym, 99–101
    plausible, 100
    steps for asking the right, 99–100
    useful, 101

Radiation, cancer, 38
Radio, Feynman, 94
Rapid prototyping
    drug discovery, 182

screening, 214–215
Reading, mind-expanding, 102
Recombination and rearrangement,
    innovation, 126–127
Reframing
    advance directives, 37
    science and prosperity, 24
Regenerative genes, evolutionary
    biology, 150–151
Relativity, Einstein theory, 24
Research
    creativity in, 88–89
    pellagra by Goldberger, 87–88
    stem cell research, 138–139
Reversal
    innovation, 124–126
    public health, 123–124
Reynolds, Charles, Western Psychiatric
    Institute and Clinic, 156
Riddles, brainteasers, 23–24, 197–198
Rising Above the Gathering Storm Revised:
    Rapidly Approaching Category V, science in
    America, 4
Roberts, Lawrence, Defense Advanced Research
    Projects Agency (DARPA), 148–149
Robinson, Sir Ken, United Kingdom, 5
Rock Round the Clock, movie, 137
Roman Empire, lead intoxication, 25–26
Romantic love, MRI scan of brain, 140–141
Rugby World Cup, Springboks, 141
Russell, Bertrand, inductive reasoning, 169–170

Sapir-Whorf hypothesis, frames and
    linguistics, 30
Science
    creativity and breakthroughs, 215–216
    expectation bias, 67–68
    frames, 16–17, 193–194
    Hill's tenets, 172–173
    important questions, 102–103
    inductive reasoning, 169–170
    normal, 194
    paradigm shifts, 194–195
    provocative orientation, 136
    right and wrong answers, 132
Science, America losing international
    dominance, 4
Scientific innovation, analogy, 111–113
Scientific method
    creativity training, 5
    paradigms, 12
Scientific observation, bacteria, 48–49
Scientists
    age and innovations, 93
    freedom of choice, 212
    identifying audience for idea, 199
    possible wanderings, 211, 212, 214, 216

Scott, Robert F., South Pole expedition, 126
Seatbelts, McNamara, 202–203
Semi-conductors, Etch A Sketch® concept, 112
Semmelweis, Ignaz
    puerperal fever, 104–105
    question, 102, 104
    scientist role model, 7
Sensory input, observation, 43–44
September 11, 2001, intelligence
    community, 152–153
Sexually transmitted infections (STIs), study, 128
Shakespeare Quarterly, 215
Shelby, Senator Richard, agency centralization,
    152–153
Shipping industry, cargo and costs, 118–119
Shrinky Dinks, microfluidics chips, 112
Silver, Spencer, 3M, 125
"Six degrees of freedom," Milgram, 200
Slinky®, changing frame, 117
Smallpox, vaccine, 114
Smith, Will, *Men in Black*, 127
Smoking cigarettes
    second-hand smoke, 120
    shifting frame, 119–120
Social beliefs, bandwagon effect, 192–193
Social marketing, birth control, 201
Social networks, obesity, 64
Societal norms, going against, 198–199
Somatic Marker Hypothesis, Damasio, 84–86
Sontag, Sherry, *Blind Man's Bluff*, 145
Sontag, Susan, 20
The Sorcerer's Apprentice, idea generation, 180
South Dakota, living wills, 36
Space Shuttle Challenger, explosion, 95
Space Station, invention, 3
Spencer, Percy LeBaron, microwaves, 50–51
Sperry, Roger, brain work, 76
Spina bifida, folic acid, 204
*The Spirit Level: Why More Equal Societies
    Almost Always Do Better*, Wilkinson and
    Pickett, 63–64
Sports, South Africa, 141
Springboks, South African rugby team, 141
Stanford University
    language reinforcing frames, 30–31
    Zimbardo, 201
Staphylococcus aureus, puerperal fever, 104
Staple, Jeff, Staple Design, 158
Statistics Canada, birth weight records, 99
Stem cell research, Kyoto University,
    138–139
Stress, meditation decreasing, 164
Structural metaphors, frames, 31–32
The Structure of Scientific Revolutions, Kuhn, 87,
    177, 180, 194
Submarines, Navy's oceanographic research,
    145–146

Sugared beverages, obesity and taxation of, 21–22
Super Freakonomics: Global cooling, patriotic prostitutes, and why suicide bombers should buy life insurance, Levitt and Dubner, 202
Surgeon General's Report, second-hand smoke, 120
Surgery, new techniques, 196
Surowiecki, James, *The Wisdom of Crowds*, 146
Surviving Antarctica: Reality TV 2083, White, 126
Swarm intelligence, ant self-organization, 151–152
Swift, Jonathan, poor in Ireland, 134–135
Systems modeling, ARCHIMEDES, 120

Taxation, sugared beverages, 21–22
Taxes, metaphor, 37
Taylor, Bob, Defense Advanced Research Projects Agency (DARPA), 148–149
Telephone, Bell, 113
Testing ideas
    continuous loop, 178
    endometriosis and ovarian cancer, 173–175
    Hill's tenets, 172–173
    hormone replacement therapy, 176–177
    hypotheses and observations, 170–172
Thinking, outside of the box, 6–7
Thompson, Charles, 168
Thoreau, Henry, perceptions, 43
Three Cups of Tea, Mortenson, 121
Time management, strategies, 188–189
The Tipping Point: How Little Things Can Make a Big Difference, Gladwell, 200
Training programs, creativity, 5–6
Transportation, shipping industry, 118–119
Twenty Thousand Leagues Under the Sea, Verne, 101

United Kingdom, creativity, education and economy, 5
United States
    infant mortality, 98
    public health, 123–124
    venture capital investments, 96–97
University of Pittsburgh, Kuller, 21
University of Texas, innovation training, 6
Use Your Head, Buzan, 186
U.S. National Highway Traffic Safety Administration, seatbelts, 203
U.S. Navy, oceanographic research, 145–146
U.S. Preventative Services Task Force, cancer, 38
U.S.S. Scorpion, nuclear submarine, 145

Vaccines
    cocaine, 113
    malaria, 138
    smallpox, 114
Van Leeuwenhoek, Anton, plants and cells, 14
Venture capital investments, 96–97
Verne, Jules, science fiction writer, 101
Vertical integration, analogies, 113–114
Vienna General Hospital, puerperal fever, 104
Violin students, practice, 7–8
Vipassana, meditation, 166
Viruses, bacteriophage virus, 127
Visual system
    hierarchy, 47–48
    sensory information, 46–47
Vitamin B6, pellagra, 88, 122, 123
Vitruvius, sound and waves, 111

War, disease, 37–39
Warner Bros., 62
Warren, Robin
    bacteria, 48–49
    paradigm shift, 87
Water, Kuller, 22
Western Psychiatric Institute and Clinic, post-doctoral training, 156
Western Union, 71
White, Andrea, *Surviving Antarctica: Reality TV 2083*, 126
Whitehead, Alfred North, 131
Wikipedia, group expertise, 146–147
Wilkinson, Richard, *The Spirit Level: Why More Equal Societies Almost Always Do Better*, 63–64
Wilson, R. A., *Feminine Forever*, 178
Wine purchase, anchoring effect, 65–66
The Wisdom of Crowds, Surowiecki, 146
Women, endometriosis and ovarian cancer, 173–175
Women's Health Initiative
    hormone replacement therapy, 102, 176–177, 178
    skepticism, 195
World Health Organization (WHO)
    female education, 121–122
    malaria, 138
    smallpox vaccine, 114
World War II, atomic bomb project, 94–95
Wright Brothers, human flight, 212
Zen Buddhism, 118
Zimbardo, Philip, influence of environment, 201–202